Permissions for Quotations

All quotations have been cited in the text and are identified in notes and bibliography. Permission to reprint has been obtained* from the following:

Golf Magazine

Sports Illustrated

U.S. News and World Report

University of Illinois Press

Taylor Publishing*

Group Fore*

Women's Sports

People Weekly

Cornerstone Library
  (A Division of Simon and Schuster)

Longmeadow Press

Saturday Evening Post

Alfred A. Knopf, Inc.

Women's Sports and Fitness

Doubleday & Co.
  (A Division of Random House)

Dell Publishing Co.

Bantam Books
  (A Division of Random House)

St. Martin's Press*

* We were unable to obtain a response to our permission request from this source. We used single quotation or very limited material and have given adequate credit to the source.

Photographic Credit

Credit is given to the LPGA Communications department for permission to use photographs on the chapter title pages. Credit Jeff Hornback, Chapter 13; Pete Fontaine, Chapter 14 and 15.

Color photographs which are courtesy of LPGA, Patty Berg, Bob Ewell, Jack Stohlman, and Pete Fontaine are identified with the respected photograph.

All photographs of Babe Didrikson Zaharias (except Chapter 1) are courtesy of Joe D. Shamburger, Babe Didrikson Zaharias Foundation, Inc.

All other photography was taken by the author, Jackie Williams.

Author Acknowledgments

The events that led to the writing of this book began 40 years ago in 1959 when I was thirteen years old. My mother – one of the people to whom the book is dedicated–was totally comfortable with the fact that her daughter was interested in athletics and not "normal girl stuff." For an English class book report, she suggested I read Babe Didrikson Zaharias' autobiography, *This Life I've Led*. She wanted me to know that even in the "women as homemaker" world of the 1950's, there were women to whom I could relate. I thank her for introducing me to Zaharias and the by-product of that introduction – golf. I also thank her for her sensitivity to a young woman whose interests were different, and for always honoring and supporting those interests – even though that support resulted in more than a few gray hairs.

My father – another person to whom the book is dedicated – took the time to play catch, shoot baskets, sail and play golf with a daughter. In the 1950's that kind of support for young girl athletes was rare. I thank him for all the experiences we shared. I even thank him for the "extra" support showed – which at the time was one of my most embarrassing moments – when he told the captain of the high school football team that his daughter could play quarterback right along with the rest of the guys.

The book could have been written without the help of Lillian Heyduk – the third person to whom the book is dedicated – but it would not have had the commas in the right place or the words spelled correctly. She read every word, and then had to listen to arguments about her corrections. I thank her for her dedication to the project and her loyal friendship to me.

The most recent catalyst for the book occurred in 1994 when I researched and wrote a two-part story about Mickey Wright. It was through my interviews with Mickey Wright that I came to understand just how much the women who play the game of golf at her level deserve acknowledgment. I deeply appreciate the time she shared with me, and want her to know that I now understand "a few questions" does not mean 15.

Patty Berg may be a legend, but she is also a kind human being. I am especially grateful to have had breakfast with her on the morning of the dedication of the World Golf Hall of Fame in 1998. She did not have to spend that time with me, but she did and she was gracious and fun. She deserves the thanks of all women athletes.

All the people at Women of Diversity Productions, Inc. were brave and patient in their support of a first time author, and I am indebted to them for that.

I also thank several members of Cousins, Inc. – Kathy and Bill, Darlene and Conrad, Jimmy and Jean, and Bonnie. They lent every kind of support, and never failed to ask, with sincere interest, how the project was going. I am proud and grateful to have them as both family and friends. I also thank, Jenny Walker a member of the "parent company." Her interest and prayers were much appreciated, and demonstrated the real meaning of "loving family."

Finally, I would be remiss if I did not thank the two people who were fellow residents so long ago, when we were all much younger, at the "Golden Gate Hotel." First, JoAnne whose encouragement and friendship was unfaltering and who offered "story" after "story." None could be used, they would require another book, but all were great. Second, Lynn, who knew early on that I could be a writer and gave me what she thought I would need most – "White Out."

This book is dedicated to

my mother and father, Fran and Chuck,

and to my friend, Lillian.

Foreword

By Susie Maxwell Berning

Mickey Wright, Marlene Hagge, Marilyn Smith, Patty Berg, Kathy Whitworth, Betsy Rawls, Louise Suggs and Babe Zaharias were names of the greats when I joined the tour in 1964. Also joining the tour during the 60's were the likes of Sandra Haynie, Sandra Palmer, Carol Mann and Judy Rankin. In the middle of my career, new players joined the tour, such as, Pat Bradley, Patty Sheehan, Beth Daniel, Betsy King, Amy Alcott, Joanne Carner, Nancy Lopez and Laura Davies. Arriving on tour when I was finishing my playing career were Annika Sorenstam, Kelly Robbins and Karrie Webb.

I am not in the Hall of Fame. Only sixteen of the above players are. Perhaps all of the above players should be for they love the game as much as those in the Hall of Fame. Each of the above players worked hard, played to win and placed the prize money secondary to being the best they could be. These players have given or are giving their lives to golf and the LPGA. The desire to be the very best breeds the outstanding competition that characterizes the LPGA Tour.

The early founders of the LPGA were survivors. They were totally unique characters. They had no fear, and were driven to have the world accept ladies golf.

I reflect back on my life and can honestly say it was my meeting Patty Berg that started my life in golf. Call it the luck of timing.

My introduction to golf came by way of riding a horse over several golf greens at the Lincoln Park Golf Club in Oklahoma City. As a result, I met the club's head golf professional U.C. Ferguson. My punishment from him was that I teach his two children to ride and he would teach me golf.

He told me to report to him the next day (without my horse.) Thinking I was to get my first golf lesson, I was surprised to be introduced to Patty Berg. I watched her give one of her famous clinics, and I was so inspired by Patty – and she seemed to be having so much fun doing the clinic - that I knew at that moment I wanted to be just like her and play golf. Eight years later I was on the tour playing among all the early greats. The only Hall of Fame member I did not play against in my career was Babe Zaharias.

It is human nature for us to have heroes – to pick a famous person to idealize. I guarantee you as a reader of this book you will be inspired by these ladies and wished to have known them personally. You will also wish that you could have played golf with them.

Hopefully, our future Hall of Famers will continue to inspire youngsters, and leave them with a dream or vision of golf, if not golf, just a vision to always be the best they can be. That is what this book is about.

As Patty Berg says, "If you have a will and desire – you will find a way." *Playing From the Rough* tells how each Hall of Famer developed the desire and found the way.

Golf instructor at Walters Golf Properties (Desert Pines, Royal Links, and Stallion Mountain) Las Vegas, Nevada.
Three-time winner of U.S. Open.
Guest Instructor at the Nicholaus-Flick Golf for Women Magazine Golf School.
Conducts corporate clinic for American Airlines.

Foreword

By Ed Oldfield

The LPGA Tour has been an important part of my life for more than 35 years. The Tour's players have remained a focus in my teaching career because I so respect the talent and dedication that characterizes each of the player's with whom I have worked.

I did not set out to be a teacher of golf. As my career began, like other young men, I wanted to be a tour player. I did all the things necessary to succeed on tour. It was where I thought I wanted to go with my life. Then, as a very young head professional at age 20 a turning point in my career occurred and I found myself on a path that I had not expected.

The catalyst for that turning point was a 13-year-old named Carole Jo Kabler. I introduced Carole to golf. She became my pupil at age thirteen and in 1955, when she was sixteen, she won the National Junior Championship by beating, then JoAnne Gunderson, now Hall of Famer JoAnne Carner.

When Carole returned home and walked off the plane, her face full of joy, my heart couldn't stay in my body. It was at that moment, looking at that face, that I knew I wanted to spend my life teaching. I experienced an unbelievable sense of satisfaction at accomplishing something with and for somebody else.

Carole continued to play golf, but she also married and became the mother of three children. More than ten years after her National Open win, she decided to commit herself to a professional career, and we began working again. Her success on tour in the 1960's and 1970's encouraged other players to find out what this "Oldfield guy" was about. Before long I found myself working with several tour players. As I got to know them personally and as we worked together on their golf games, my respect for these women as athletes began to grow.

It has been a unique privilege for me to have worked with or known all but two of the women profiled in this book. They are the "best and the brightest" of not just golfers and athletes, but also people. Working with and knowing them has enriched my life. They are women who devote themselves to their craft and have an overwhelming drive to succeed.

Playing From the Rough will give all golfers an opportunity to know just how special and talented these women are. As a life-long supporter of women's golf and the LPGA, I am excited that this book will give these players the acknowledgment they so richly deserve.

As readers, you are in for a treat. You are about to get an inside look at some of the finest athletes in the world, and when you have finished reading I think you will join me in appreciating their success. I also believe you will join me in understanding why these Hall of Famers are women of whom we can all be proud.

PGA Teaching Professional based in Chicago and Phoenix. His students include several LPGA Tour players - among them they have accumulated 60 victories, eight of them majors. During his career, Mr. Oldfield has also taught four Curtis Cup players, two World Cup players, a former Junior Girls' Champion, and a former Senior Women's Champion.

Designer and current President of The Merit Club in Libertyville, Illinois. The Merit Club is the site of the 2000 U.S. Women's Open.

CONTENTS

Introduction … … … … … … … … … … … … … … … … … …x

PART I

FIRSTS…the 1950's … … … … … … … … … … … … … … 1
1. The Ultimate Contradictions: **Babe Didrikson Zaharias** … … …5
2. Golf's First "Glamour Girl": **Betty Jameson** … … … … … …39
3. The Consummate Performer: **Patty Berg** … … … … … 45
4. Quiet Hero: **Louise Suggs** … … … … 59

PART II

COMING OF AGE…the 1960's - 1970's … … … … … 69
5. The Academic: **Betsy Rawls** … … … … … 71
6. The Innocent Challenger: **Mickey Wright** … … … … …81
7. One Determined Lady: **Kathy Whitworth** … … … …97
8. The Comeback Kid: **Sandra Haynie** … … … … 113
9. Activist and Advocate: **Carol Mann** … … … … 125

PART III

TRANSITIONS…the 1980's - 1990's … … … … … … 141
10. Lover of the Game: **JoAnne Carner** … … … … … 143
11. The Perfect Star: **Nancy Lopez** … … … … 155
12. Woman on a Mission: **Pat Bradley** … … … … 170
13. Born to Win: **Patty Sheehan** … … … … 185
14. Ice: **Betsy King** … … … … 201
15 A New Breed: **Amy Alcott** … … … … 211
16. Fire: **Beth Daniel** … … … … … 227

PART IV

PERSPECTIVE: Ties to the past… paths ahead … … … … 245

Notes and Bibliography … … … … … 261

Introduction

Mary, Queen of Scots knew what the rest of civilization took over four centuries to understand – women pay a high price for success. Mary, who ruled Scotland from 1559-1567, was a successful sixteenth century "high-powered woman" in a male-dominated world. A masterful politician, Mary was also an avid golfer. In fact, Mary is the first woman recorded as playing the game.

As a golfer, Mary is also one of the first to experience what generations upon generations of females athletes have struggled with – the price women pay for athletic success. In 1567, charged with treason against Elizabeth the First, Mary's interest in golf was presented as "evidence" of her cold, ruthless character. Trial records include a description of the three rounds of golf she played immediately after the suspicious death of her second husband, Lord Darnley. The implication was that Mary's behavior demonstrated a "male-like" cold-heartedness. She was perceived as "unwomanly." Mary was convicted, and eventually beheaded.

Four hundred years later, successful women athletes no longer pay for success "with their heads". For twentieth century women athletes, "paying the price" takes far more subtle forms.

This is the story of modern-day inheritors of Mary, Queen of Scots' athletic tradition as told through the lives of the sixteen women who are members of the Ladies Professional Golf Association (LPGA) Hall of Fame. It is the story of how, like Mary, these women – as part of the larger group of "women athletes" – are often seen as "unwomanly and find their "femaleness" called into question.

It is the story of the very subtle "price" paid by each of these – and all – women athletes. It is the story of the silent struggle that faces all women athletes. The challenge of coping with a life lived as a contradiction – woman and athlete. And it is the story of how these remarkable sixteen women faced that challenge and won.

In the United States, over twenty-four million people play golf. Of these, five million are women. From that group, approximately 250 play as professionals on the LPGA Professional Golf Tour. In the entire history of the LPGA Tour, only sixteen women have been inducted into the LPGA Hall of Fame. To be part of this talented and elite company is to be the best in your field, and among the most successful women in the world. Each of these women managed to succeed in the male-dominated world of golf. Each of these sixteen women inducted into the LPGA Hall of Fame smashed golf's "glass ceiling" using only a 5-iron and the force of her own will.

In 1944, Hope Seignious, Betty Hicks and Ellen Griffin founded and incorporated the Women's Professional Golf Association (WPGA). Operated by Seignious, the organization was the first attempt to provide a vehicle for women golfers to play professionally. Seignious and her co-founders were visionaries. They saw the future and tried to make it a reality. For four years the tour struggled to survive. By 1948, finances were low, tournaments had not increased, and the tour had not really grown in terms of numbers of players. In addition, in 1949 Seignious and the WPGA faced formidable opposition. Wilson Sporting Goods, through an arrangement with Babe Zaharias, agreed to finance a women's golf tour. Wilson would supply the "start-up capital" and the management personnel – in the form of one person, Fred Corcoran – while Zaharias would provide the "star quality" to attract fans.

In 1950 Corcoran, Zaharias and eleven other young, talented – and, depending on your point of view, brave or crazy – women founded the Ladies Professional Golf Association. It was almost impossible for Seignious to compete with the combination of Wilson money and management, and Zaharias' spectator appeal. Seignious, the visionary knew it was time to withdraw, but what she had dreamed would in fact become a reality.

In 1951 the LPGA was incorporated. In its first season (1950), it conducted 11 tournaments with total prize money well under $50,000. Just one year prior to its fiftieth anniversary in 1999, the LPGA tour included 43 tournaments for prize money totaling more than $36 million.

The LPGA Hall of Fame is considered one of the most difficult achievements in the world of sports. It is one of the few Halls of Fame in which qualification criteria are based only on performance standards. Since 1950, the criteria for the LPGA Hall of Fame have been changed three times. Until 1999, the criteria for induction were: an LPGA member in good standing for at least ten years; thirty official wins including two majors or thirty-five official wins with one major or forty official wins with no majors. In 1999 the LPGA membership voted to change the criteria. The current criteria are: active LPGA membership for ten years; won or been awarded at least one of the following – an LPGA major championship, the Vare Trophy, or Rolex Player of the Year honors; accumulated a total of twenty-seven Hall of Fame points awarded according to the following system – one point for each LPGA official tournament win, two points for each LPGA major tournament win, one point for each Vare Trophy earned, and one point for each Player of the Year honor earned.

The story of the sixteen women who are members of the LPGA Hall of Fame represents the entire 50-year history of the LPGA. But it is more than that. It is also the personal history of sixteen remarkable women.

This is their story. It is not about how they won golf tournaments. It is about why they wanted to win. It is about the character traits that allowed these Hall of Famers, who represent several generations of women, to actively search for success in a field that was, and in certain minds still is, considered "unwomanly." It is about why these woman chose to live "outside" what many consider normalcy; what the cost was to each; and, how the risk balanced with the reward.

These sixteen women found what they were seeking – success and fame. They also found a challenge which none expected as part of the bargain. As a woman and an athlete, each personally confronted the explosive issue of gender identity. It is for this that each paid a price, and that each has an intimate and personal story to tell.

Part I

FIRSTS

1950's

Setting the Scene

To be a "first" at anything requires a special talent, a keen desire or perhaps just a bit of luck combined with a lot of reckless ambition. The first members of the LPGA Hall of Fame were inducted in 1951 and possessed all three "first" qualities. Babe Didrikson Zaharias, Patty Berg, Betty Jameson and Louise Suggs were the pioneers of woman's golf.

All four were founding members of the LPGA. They did not just impact the game and the organization, they literally created it "in their own image." Women's golf before these four women was genteel. It could be described as an acceptable activity in which relatively wealthy women participated before they engaged in the real purpose for the day – going to lunch.

That is not to say that there were no talented players – there were. Glenna Collett Vare dominated the game in the early part of the 20th century, winning six U.S. Women's Amateur Championships between 1922 and 1935. Her skill level and competitiveness were beyond question. The competition was fierce when Mrs. C. S. Brown (who shot 132) beat Nellie Sargent (134) in 1895 to win the first U.S. Women's Amateur Championship.

Women golfers of the early 20th century were talented and they took the game seriously – when they were on the course. But golf was not the focus of their lives. It was an "extracurricular" activity that ranked after wife, charity worker and socialite in the hierarchy of their lifestyle.

The story of Mrs. Brown, the first Amateur Champion, points out the difference between women's golf before Zaharias, Berg, Jameson, Suggs and the LPGA, and women's golf after the organization's inception. Mrs. Brown competed in, and won, the very first national championship for women in golf in the United States on a November day in 1895 – certainly a feat worthy of recognition and perhaps a place in history. Yet here, in its entirety, is the article that appeared in the *New York Times* shortly after the event occurred:

> "Thirteen ladies played 18 holes of golf at the Meadow Brook Club, in Hempstead, recently.
> Mrs. Charles S. Brown, whose husband plays at the Shinnecock Hills Club, in Southampton,
> L.I., made the best score and thus won the United States championship for lady golfers."

The writer of this article states that Mrs. Brown won, but there is actually more information about her husband than there is about the new, and first, national champion. As was the custom at the time, Mrs. Brown is referred to by her married name. To this day, her first name remains unknown. In the official records of the United States Golf Association, the first national champion is still listed as Mrs. C.S. Brown.

It was "Babe," "Patty," "Betty," and "Louise" who changed all that. It was Zaharias, Berg, Jameson and Suggs who imprinted women's golf with the context of their lifestyle – competitive, aggressive, and meaningful in itself. Golf existed before they came on the scene, but women golfers had never played with the same intensity these four players brought to the game. Golf the way Zaharias, Berg, Jameson and Suggs played the game to a new level.

The four original Hall of Fame members were all born before 1925. At least three of the four would spend part of their childhood in the rough and tumble atmosphere of the "roaring 20's." All were born into an innocent, naive, lighthearted world. All four would know at least a few years of that innocence. As the four grew into adolescents, the world, like them, began stretching and testing its muscle. That testing would lead to the Great Depression and World War II. The experiences would force the young Zaharias, Berg, Jameson and Suggs into the responsibility of adulthood and the opportunity to shape their own world.

The era in which Zaharias, Berg, Jameson and Suggs matured into adulthood was one in which women were beginning to play a more active role. The four young golfers saw women take their first steps toward acceptance and equality. Although, as adults, all four were enfranchised citizens, Zaharias was born several years before women were given the right to vote. Jameson's birth and the political fruition of the suffrage movement coincided. The House of Representatives and the Senate passed the 19th Amendment on May 21, 1919, just two days after Jameson was born.

Young adults in the early years of the depression, Zaharias, Berg, Jameson and Suggs lived at a time when women became essential to the economic survival of families. The four future Hall of Famers had not only lived through the "tough times," but had seen, or been, the women who helped end those "tough times."

The personality, character and lives of these four women were formed by the times in which they lived. In a sense, the four were almost destined to create the LPGA and become its first Hall of Famers. Zaharias, Berg, Jameson and Suggs were part of a generation of women who were "firsts."

Chapter 1

The Ultimate Contradiction...
Babe Didrikson Zaharias

Before I was even in my teens I knew exactly what I wanted to be when I grew up. My goal was to be the greatest athlete who ever lived." Babe Zaharias wrote those words in 1955 in her autobiography, *This Life I've Led*. She was undergoing radiation treatment for cancer in her lower back. She would die less than a year later. It is difficult to say if the statement reflects the conscious thoughts of Zaharias as a child, or, the perspective of the adult Zaharias – with the benefit of hindsight – imposing the reality of a life lived on the remembrances of her childhood. Whatever the case, it does reflect what happened. Zaharias was the greatest athlete – certainly female, and an argument could easily be made establishing her as the greatest male or female athlete – of the first half of the twentieth century.

Zaharias was not only a great athlete, but also a "great showman." She understood the symbiotic relationship between athletes and the press, and she knew the monetary reward that could be reaped from promoting – perhaps some would argue that it is more accurately described as exploiting – her "greatness."

Zaharias' understanding of the "value" of her greatness, and her life-long ability to "make herself over" into what the public wanted might imply that the goal of greatness expressed in the quote from *This Life I've Led* is more Zaharias writing what would "sound" best. As a young Olympian in 1932, Zaharias listed her age as four years younger than she actually was because she thought her success would be more dramatic as a seventeen year old than a twenty-one year old. For author Zaharias in *This Life I've Led*, it would certainly be better to say, "I planned it this way," than to imply success was a matter of happenstance.

More importantly, the quote is significant because it may be Zaharias' final attempt to resolve the contradiction that was her life. Zaharias is the epitome of the contradiction between the terms "athlete" and "woman." Writing in 1990, David Roberts aptly points out the contradiction when he describes Zaharias as "graceful but crude, extroverted but solitary, an instinctive feminist who yearned to be a housewife." [1]

Like other women who lived in her era, she had to deal with a time and a reality in which women did not gain approval through athletic success. Zaharias was the "greatest" at a time when "greatness" for a woman was underappreciated. The press seemed not quite comfortable with Zaharias. She was great copy, but she simply did not fit their image of a woman. Although her biggest supporter, sportswriter Grantland Rice, called her the "athletic phenomenon of all time – man or woman," more often the press found it necessary to footnote her accomplishments by explaining them and her. In the 1930's her success in track and field, particularly in the 1932 Olympics, led several sportswriters to openly question her gender. Sportswriters often described her as "button-breasted" and "born halfway between masculine flats and angles and the rubbery curves of femininity." A writer in a 1947 article in *The Saturday Evening Post* reiterates some of the controversy surrounding her 1932 Olympic success. "A number of people think that she was really a boy, masquerading in girl's clothing, in spite of the fact that doctors who supervised the women athletes at the Los Angeles Olympic Games would have disqualified her if it had happened to be true."[2]   Later, when she was successful as a golfer, writers often labeled that success as a psychological "compensation" for her lack of success in those areas considered feminine - motherhood and homemaking.

Zaharias understood that to exploit the marketing value of her celebrity she would have to make it easier for the press to accept her. That understanding forced her to spend much of her life "adjusting" her image. She was "a woman so gifted and so driven that she bore the burden of being a symbol before she could invent a self."[3] Perhaps, it wasn't so much that she did not have time to "invent a self," but that she constantly felt the need to "re-invent" her self as it fit her needs at the time. The Olympic Zaharias of 1932 is a shorthaired "tomboyish" woman who obviously enjoys using her body athletically, and thrives on the "unladylike" thrill of competition. After her marriage in 1938, Zaharias made a point of emphasizing her interest in homemaking. In the early stages of her golf career, when she played as an amateur against the "proper" women of the USGA, she sought the help of a friend in selecting clothes that were more feminine. Yet, as a founder of the fledging LPGA Tour, Zaharias' behavior and attitude were more like her male counterparts in athletics. She would often walk into the locker room before a tour event and announce that since she was there "everyone else was playing for second."

In *This Life I've Led*, when Zaharias writes "my goal was to be the greatest athlete who ever lived," it may be Zaharias' way of finally saying, this is who I really was all along – deal with it.

Mildred Ella Didrikson was born in Port Arthur, Texas. Almost from the moment of her birth, controversy became part of her life. The day was June 26, but the year is fuzzy. There is no official birth certificate on record. A baptismal certificate states the year as 1911. The historical marker near her grave in Beaumont gives the year as 1914, but her gravestone records her birth as 1911. In *This Life I've Led*, Zaharias says it was 1914. On her 1932 Olympic application, for the reason mentioned earlier, she used 1913, and, as an adult who may have wanted to shave a few years, Zaharias listed the year of her birth on a visa application as 1915.

Zaharias created another controversy by spelling her name "Didrikson" – with an "o" – for her entire life. Her parents, Hanna and Ole, were Norwegians who immigrated to the United States in the early 1900's. They and the entire Didriksen family spelled the name with an "e" – except for Babe. "Didrikson" was used on her early school records, and Babe not only declined to correct it, but also took the spelling as her own. Her family accepted her "personalized" spelling of the name, and good-naturedly attributed it to her innate desire to do things differently.

There is no question that Babe was different. Unlike other girls, Babe found joy in sports. In a 1933 interview she said, "As far back as I can remember I played with boys rather than girls.... The girls did not play games that interested me. I preferred baseball, football, foot racing and jumping with the boys, to hopscotch and jacks and dolls, which were about the only things girls did.... I guess the habit of playing with boys made me too rough for the girls' games. Anyway, I found them too tame."[4]

As a child, Babe played sandlot baseball and constantly used the makeshift gymnasium that Ole had constructed for his children in the family's backyard. The classic "young Babe story" told and re-told in the press – probably because Babe herself loved to tell it – was of her jumping neighbors' hedges to practice for the high hurdles. Even before she was a teenager, Babe's athletic ability was compared to the boy athletes her age. In most cases, she was considered their equal. Susan Cayleff in her book, *Babe The Life and Legend of Babe Didrikson Zaharias*, quotes Effie Piland, the principal at the school Babe attended, Magnolia Elementary School in Beaumont. "I remember she could out-play anyone in marbles and out-play them in baseball. She could out-do all the boys."[5]

Most believe that it is from this comparison to the male athletes of her time that "Mildred" became known as "Babe" - that the nickname is a result of comparing the young female athlete to the best known athlete of the era, Babe Ruth. Like so many other things surrounding Zaharias, the root of her nickname is more legend - initiated by Zaharias herself – than fact.

The Didriksen family called Mildred Ella "Baby" throughout her infancy and continued to do so after her younger brother was born. Babe's brother, Bubba, explains that the nickname was a result of Hannah Didriksen's Norwegian accent. "My mother used to call her Baden, which expressed in broken American Norwegian is Babe - baby - and that's where she picked up the name."[6] Zaharias tells it differently. "The 'Babe' came later, when I began hitting home runs in ball games. Babe Ruth was a big hero then, and the kids said, 'She's a regular Babe Ruth. We'll call her Babe.'"[7]

Like listing her age as younger on her Olympic application, Zaharias romanticized the story of her nickname to enhance her image as an athlete. Yet there is no doubt the Zaharias version could be true. Among sports fans, the name "Babe" has always evoked only two athletes – Babe Ruth, and Babe Didrikson Zaharias. Because Ruth and Zaharias were so extraordinary, the sports world developed a way to set them apart from all other athletes by referring to both as "The" Babe. Decades after Zaharias and Ruth's death, "The Babe" still defines the ultimate in athletic greatness – raw talent turned into realized potential.

Zaharias began the quest to realize that potential in 1928. It was then that Babe set her sights on the 1932 Olympic Games.

"In the summer of 1928 the Olympic Games were being held in Amsterdam, Holland," Zaharias wrote in *This Life I've Led*. "Poppa kept reading about the Olympics in the newspaper, and telling us about the star athletes over there.

"I got all steamed up. I was fourteen years old at the time. I said, 'Next year I'm going to be in the Olympics myself.' Poppa said, 'Babe, you can't. You'll have to wait four years.'

"I said, 'Well, why? Why can't I be in it next year?' And he explained to me that the Olympics Games were held four years apart. It sounded like the greatest thing in the world to me - that free trip across the ocean and everything. I didn't know that the 1932 Olympics would be held in this country in Los Angeles - not that it would have made much difference to me. Lillie (Zaharias' sister) and I started in training for the Olympics right then and there."[8]

Zaharias' "training" was makeshift at best.

"Lillie was going to be a runner and I was going to be a hurdler and jumper," Zaharias wrote. "I never was too good at straightway running. I didn't seem to want to stay on the ground. I'd rather jump some obstacle.

"There were hedges in the yards along our block - seven of them between our house and the corner grocery. I used those hedges to practice hurdling. But there was one of them that was higher than the others. I couldn't get over it. That sort of messed up my practicing. So I went to the people who lived in that house. Their name was King. I asked Mr. King if he'd mind cutting his hedge down to where the rest of them were, and he did it.

"I'd go flying over those hedges, and Lillie would race alongside me on the pavement. She was a fast runner, and had an advantage anyway because I had to do all that jumping. I worked and worked, and finally got to where I could almost catch her, and sometimes beat her."[9]

Realizing the Dream

The opportunity to make the Olympic dream a reality came in Babe's senior year in high school. Babe's exploits on the Beaumont High girl's basketball team were chronicled by Beaumont Journal sportswriter (and Babe's friend), Bill "Tiny" Scurlock. The articles Scurlock wrote caught the attention of Melvin J. McCombs. McCombs coached the Dallas based Employers Casualty Insurance Company women's basketball team. McCombs went to Beaumont to watch Babe play and offered her a job at Employers Casualty and a spot on the basketball team.

At Employers Casualty Babe's " day job" included normal clerk/typist duties. Her real "job" was to play on the Employers Casualty Cyclone basketball, baseball and track and field teams. The situation was perfect for Zaharias. As Susan Cayleff points out in *Babe*, Zaharias "thought she couldn't make a living in sports, except perhaps in physical education, so the merger of basketball and secretarial skills seemed an ideal solution."[10]

It was important to Babe to "make a living." The Didriksen's, with seven children, often lived on the edge of poverty. Zaharias began contributing to the family's income with odd jobs after school when she was in junior high. Her first job was in a fig packing plant unloading cans and then placing them on a conveyer belt that would take them to the area where they would be packed with figs. Zaharias soon found that she could make more money sewing sacks at the potato gunny sack factory.

"It was piecework - a penny a bag, or something like that," Zaharias wrote in *This Life I've Led*. "I could sew up those sacks faster than anybody else. I was making sixty-seven, sixty-eight cents an hour."[11]

The full time job at Employers Casualty gave Zaharias more than just an opportunity to help support her family. In the early 1930's industrial recreation teams and leagues were where some of the best athletes could be found. Babe's recruitment by Employers Casualty's coach Melvin McCombs was not unusual for that time. Companies in that era sought out good athletes to fill out the teams that they fielded in local leagues, and more importantly, in Amateur Athletic Union competition (AAU).

In the 1930's the AAU was one of the few, if not the only, highly competitive venues open to women athletes. Working at Employers Casualty gave Babe the opportunity to play with and against the best athletes in the geographic region. It also exposed her to professional level coaching. That aspect of her "contract" with Employers Casualty was as important as the weekly salary. The athletic experiences she could get at Employers Casualty would increase her chances for a ticket to Los Angeles.

As a "worker-athlete" Zaharias was in her element, and she excelled. Employer's Casualty belonged to the Women's National Basketball League. Organized under the auspices of the AAU, the league consisted of forty-five teams. In 1929 the league selected its first All-American Team. Babe joined Employers Casualty in 1930. She was selected as an All-American in her first year as well as in 1931 and 1932. In the 1931 national tournament, Zaharias scored 106 points in five games and Employers Casualty won the national championship.

Babe was not only doing what she wanted to do, and did best, but also her sports exploits gained her national attention and recognition. The rough tomboy from Texas had become national newspaper copy. As a teenager Zaharias' confidence bordered on cockiness. Zaharias biographers Nancy Williamson and William Johnson point out that Babe's rise to national attention did little to change her brashness.

"It was a heavy burden for an unsophisticated, uneducated young woman to carry and Babe did not do it very well," Williamson and Johnson wrote in *Whatta Gal*. "She became more arrogant, more self-centered, than before."[12]

Babe's success at the 1932 national AAU Track and Field Championships - which were also the tryouts for the 1932 Olympic team – in Evanston, Illinois only increased her bravado. As a publicity stunt her coach, Melvin McCombs, entered Babe as a one-woman "team." She would compete against two hundred other women athletes in eight of the ten events at the meet. Because she had to run from one event to another, the judges delayed a few events to give her a chance to rest. The delays and accommodation for Zaharias were not appreciated by some of the athletes. One report of the event points out that Babe's behavior only served to increase the irritation of the other women. "Babe made them madder by going around the infield bragging and hollering, 'I'm going to win everything I enter."[13]

She did not win quite everything she entered. Babe won six events. She set an AAU and U.S. record in the shot put and set world records in the baseball throw and the javelin throw. In the 80-meter hurdles she set a world record in a preliminary heat and went on to win the event. She tied for first in the high jump, setting an AAU record, and she won the broad jump. Babe had earned 30 "team" points. She had won the team title by eight points over Illinois Athletic Club who had twenty-two points.

The feat caught the imagination of the nation, and thrust Babe into the sports spotlight. It also earned her a spot on the 1932 U.S. Olympic Track and Field Team.

The players selected for the Olympic Team left Evanston for Los Angeles by train immediately following the championship. The trip across the country did little to endear Babe to her fellow competitors. Evelyn Hall, an Olympic hurdler, describes Babe's exploits during the trip. "Babe kept running through the train, shrieking and yanking the pillows out from under your head if you were sleeping. Babe was pretty cocky. Everyone was doing things for her. If she wanted a drink of water, someone got it for her. She seemed to have managers; her teammates waited on her."[14]

As she would later do in the locker rooms of LPGA events, Babe warned her fellow Olympic competitors of her impending success. "I came out here to beat everybody in sight and that's just what I'm going to do. Sure, I can do anything. I'm going to win the high jump Sunday and set a world's record. I don't know who my chief opponents are and anyway, it wouldn't make any difference. I hope they are good."[15]

> **BABE DIDRIKSON ZAHARIAS**
>
> Began playing golf: age 13
>
> First tournament win: 1935,
> Texas Women's State Championship
>
> First LPGA victory : 1950
>
> Last LPGA victory: 1955

Babe backed up the boasting with her talent. Although she did not win all three of the events she entered, Babe cemented her status as a star with two gold medal performances and one silver. Her win in the javelin set a world and Olympic record (143 feet 4 inches). She set a world and Olympic record in the 80-meter hurdles (11.7 seconds). In the running high jump she tied fellow American and Olympic Team Captain Jean Shiley at 5 feet 5 1/2 inches, but because of Babe's jumping style (what is now known as a Western Roll), the judges awarded the Gold to Shiley and the Silver to Babe.

From Gold to Golf

The opportunities for today's athletes – including women – to turn Olympic stardom into financial success are unlimited. For Zaharias in 1932, those kinds of opportunities were almost non-existent, but Zaharias was determined to exploit her Olympic success. Next to excelling in athletics, the most important thing to Zaharias was to achieve financial security. Her autobiography is filled with stories about how important it was to her to use the money she earned to shower gifts on her family, especially her parents.

"My first year in Dallas, when I was just making the $75 a month, I remember how happy I was coming home with a new radio for Christmas," Babe wrote in *This Life I've Led*. "I sat up all night on the day coach from Dallas to Beaumont, holding the radio on my lap. I was wishing I could plug it in on the train somewhere to see if it would play.

"The train got into Beaumont about six o'clock in the morning," Babe continued. "I got out to the house and slipped in through the back door, which they always left open for the kids to use. I went upstairs to Momma and Poppa's bedroom. They were sleeping – Poppa was snoring away. I plugged the radio in right by Momma's bed and tuned in Station KFDM, where I used to hear Castor Oil Clarence when I was little. They woke up to the music on the radio, and they were so excited about it."[16]

Money and what she could do with money were important to Zaharias. And, she was never really the "down-home bumpkin" that she liked to present as an image. She knew exactly what she wanted to accomplish financially, and seemed intuitively to know how best to get what she wanted. From the very beginning of her career in athletics, she understood the importance of the media as a catalyst to her goals. Her extroverted personality, and willingness to give the press what they wanted - quotable copy – made her a media darling.

Zaharias cultivated relationships with the press. The most important was her career-long friendship with the most famous sportswriter of the period, Grantland Rice. Rice not only kept her name in print, but also introduced Babe to the celebrities and other people who would be important as business contacts the rest of her life. Zaharias knew that the press would use her. She also knew that she could use them as well, and she never hesitated in getting as much out of her relationships with the media as she gave to them.

Zaharias' first opportunity for exploitation came just after her triumphant return to Beaumont after the Olympics. She received a letter from the Illinois Women's Athletic Club offering to find her a job paying $300 a month if she would play in their athletic program. Zaharias, already a shrewd businessperson, showed the letter to Homer R. Mitchell, Employers Casualty's President. Mitchell did exactly what Zaharias had hoped he would. He matched the offer, and Zaharias returned to Dallas and Employers Casualty. By the final months of 1932, the most outstanding woman Olympic champion the world had ever seen was back at her "day job" desk, and in the middle of the AAU basketball season on the Employers Casualty team.

"After the Olympics and the post-Olympics and all that were over, I got back into the old office and basketball routine at Employers Casualty," Zaharias wrote in her autobiography. "I was still liking it. But the pressure got pretty heavy on me during the fall of 1932. People kept telling me how I could get rich if I turned professional. That big money talk sounds nice when you're a kid whose family has never had much."[17]

The decision to become a professional was not made by Zaharias. It was made for her. An advertisement for the 1933 Dodge automobile appeared in the Chicago Daily Times that featured a picture of Babe hurdling and carried the caption, "Dodge 6 is a real champion. Claims she owns one, her second Dodge. The Stuff That Makes Real Champions - Babe Didrikson."[18] Babe explained that someone had set up the ad at Dodge in Dallas without her permission. Despite her claims that she did not authorize or receive any money from the ad, the Southern branch of the AAU immediately declared Babe a professional.

"I'd already started another basketball season with the Employers Casualty Golden Cyclones," Zaharias wrote in *This Life I've Led*. "This made me ineligible for that. And it meant I couldn't compete in the AAU track meets anymore, either. The Dodge man in Dallas wrote the AAU, explaining that I wasn't to blame, and so did the advertising agency that handled the ad. And later that month, the AAU announced that it was reinstating me as an amateur. But by then I'd decided to turn pro anyway."[19]

The incident was more complicated than Zaharias made it appear in *This Life I've Led*. The media became embroiled in the incident. *The New York Times*, which had downplayed Babe's

Olympic and AAU successes, printed eighteen stories about the controversy. *Coronet* magazine, through the voice of one of its columnists saw it as a gender issue.

"In retrospect, it seems clear that the AAU was determined to eliminate 'muscle molls' from its ranks," the *Coronet* columnist wrote. "No official ever put it that bluntly, of course, but the decision was called 'for the best interest of the game.'"[20]

In her book *Babe*, Susan Cayleff describes the incident as taking "on overtones of class warfare; Babe was the persecuted working woman 'who we shouldn't expect to match wits with fast-thinking men in the business world.' Her plight was compared with that of other shunned athletes, including Jim Thorpe."[21]

Although, in her autobiography, Zaharias never mentions that she played an active part in the controversy, she threw some salvos of her own in typical Babe fashion. In an interview, she said she was suspended "because they didn't want me to beat the rich dames."[22]

After months of controversy and probably out of frustration and anger, Babe resigned from Employers Casualty and the AAU. Within hours of receiving Zaharias' resignation, the AAU cleared her of the charges.

The incident would be only the first of several in Zaharias' career that focused on her status as an amateur, and it probably was the catalyst for her decision to exploit her fame as a professional athlete. More importantly, the incident is the first real controversy dominated by perceptions that would follow Zaharias for the rest of her career.

The AAU amateur controversy brought to the forefront two issues. First was the global issue of the image of women athletes in terms of gender identification. As *Coronet* pointed out, the AAU would have been much more comfortable with a Babe that did not have the "muscle moll" image. Within a few years of the AAU dispute, Zaharias would begin to emphasize the feminine aspects of her personality and distance herself from the tomboyish girl who took the Olympics by storm.

Second, is the personal struggle that Zaharias would wage much of her life with her own personality. The incident shows the dichotomy that was Zaharias. The brashness of the "rich dame" remark and the courage of her ultimate decision to leave amateur sport behind were juxtaposed against Babe's repeated attempts to appease the AAU. In a statement made mid-way in the controversy, Zaharias said, "I will do everything that I can to be reinstated in the AAU and I don't want to turn professional. I have only played three years of basketball and I'm not ready to quit as an amateur."[23]

Zaharias was in a position that made it hard for her to know what to do. She had been successful. She was well aware that she was an outstanding, if not the best, female athlete in the world. Yet, there was no place for a woman athlete to compete in professional sports. As for amateur sports – the only place women could compete – the organizers seemed to be bent on taking that away from her.

Zaharias, probably because of her self-confident personality and her understanding that the time was right to turn her fame into money, allowed the incident to push her to professional sports. For Zaharias, the transition from Olympic hero to professional athlete was not at all like the transition of women Olympic basketball players in 1997 who found two professional basketball leagues waiting for them after the Games.

For Zaharias, "turning professional" did not mean competing in her sport at the highest level. It meant being a sideshow-like attraction competing against no one, and being a celebrity whose fame was used by others as a promotional gimmick.

"I started out by doing some work for the Chrysler Motor Company...," Zaharias writes in *This Life I've Led*. "They were sorry about what had happened, and they wanted to make it up to me....

"They hired me to appear at the Dodge booth at the Auto Show in Detroit," Zaharias continued. "I signed autographs and talked to people. I even played the harmonica to attract the attention of the crowd and draw people over to the booth."[24]

According to Zaharias the Chrysler people introduced her to George P. Emerson, an advertising executive, who negotiated a contract for her to do "stage appearances on the RKO circuit after the Auto Show was over."[25]

These "stage appearances" found Zaharias doing an 18-minute act in which she traded quips with a comic, sang a take-off on the song "Fit as a Fiddle and Ready for Love," and then did a series of athletic demonstrations.

Zaharias began her show business career in Chicago, and Emerson had booked several engagements in New York at $2500 a week. Zaharias played Chicago for only one week when she began to have second thoughts.

"Before the week was out I was beginning to enjoy myself," Zaharias wrote. "I liked the feeling of that crowd out there.... And yet it was still in my craw that I wanted to be a champion golfer. I could see I'd never get to do that with these four or five stage shows a day."[26]

Zaharias canceled the New York engagements and returned to Beaumont. By the spring of 1933 she was ready to commit herself to golf.

"In the spring I went out to California," Zaharias wrote. "I was going to do nothing but learn golf.... I told a reporter out in Los Angeles, 'I have enough money to last me three years and I intend to win the women's amateur golf championship before those three years and my bankroll are gone.'"[27]

When Zaharias began working on her golf game, she did it with no professional help. She found the "three year bankroll" she talked about to the Los Angeles reporter was a miscalculation.

"I was right about it taking your full time to become a top golfer," Zaharias wrote. "I soon found out that I was wrong about how long $1800 would last. I was practicing my golf out at a driving range, trying to hold down those expenses."[28]

Eventually, Lou Nash, a friend Zaharias had met on the golf course, convinced her that she needed to get professional instruction. Zaharias hesitated because she felt she could not afford to take lessons. Nash introduced her to Stanley Kertes, a young golf pro based in Los Angeles, who agreed to teach her at no charge.

Zaharias' first lesson lasted all day and Kertes took Babe out to dinner. After dinner, Kertes asked if she wanted to quit for the day. Zaharias replied that she was ready to hit more balls, and she and Kertes stayed at the driving range until midnight. Kertes invited Zaharias back the following day offering to give up his other lesson to work solely with her.

"The next morning I couldn't wait to get there," Zaharias wrote. "I had my shower and breakfast and was ready to leave for the driving range by five o'clock in the morning. It wasn't daylight yet, but rather than just sit around, I went out there. I had a golf club, and I practiced what he'd told me about the grip and the stance. Finally they came and opened up the place, and Stan and I hit balls all day long."[29]

By the fall of 1933, Zaharias' $1800 had run out and she knew it was not fair for her to take up all of Stan Kertes' time. Zaharias returned to Dallas and to her $300 a week job at Employers Casualty. In early 1934, Zaharias left Employers Casualty to accept an offer to play basketball. A promoter, Ray Doan, from Iowa put together a woman's team called Babe Didrikson's All-Americans. The team traveled to different cities and played against local men's teams. In the spring, Doan arranged for Babe to play baseball with the House of David baseball team. The House of David was an all-men's team. The players all had long beards – the team's trademark – and the team was the best known "barnstorming" baseball team in the nation. Although the "barnstorming" built up Babe's bank account, her financial position was still not secure and she was no closer to breaking into world class golf.

"These years I'm talking about were a mixed-up time for me," Zaharias wrote about the mid-1930's. "My name had meant a lot right after the Olympics Games, but it had sort of been going down since then. I hadn't been smart enough to get into anything that would really keep me up there.

"I had to find some way to build my name up again so I could make some money," Zaharias continued. "At one point I thought maybe tennis would be the answer. I figured there could be money in that. If I got good enough at the game, I thought perhaps a lot of people would pay to see me play tennis matches."[30]

Zaharias began to work on her tennis game, but never got the chance to play competitively. During the Olympic javelin competition, she had torn the cartilage in her right shoulder and the injury interfered with her ability to serve.

"The shoulder trouble didn't bother me on any of the other tennis strokes," Zaharias wrote. "It was just the serve that it interfered with. But that was enough to kill me for tennis.

"The shoulder didn't interfere with my golf swing," Zaharias continued. "And, golf was still my real objective. All I wanted to accomplish with these other things was to get in a financial position where I could concentrate on golf. That was my big sports love now."[31]

Again Employers Casualty gave Zaharias the opportunity she needed. They brought her back to Dallas and her job. This time they also added a membership at the Dallas Country Club and paid for golf lessons with club pro George Aulbach.

By November of 1934, Babe was ready to test her golf skill. She entered her first golf tournament – the Fort Worth Women's Invitation. In the qualifying round she shot 77 and was the tournament's medalist.

"It did me good to see the headlines in the Texas newspapers the next day: WONDER GIRL MAKES HER DEBUT IN TOURNAMENT GOLF: TURNS IN 77 SCORE," Zaharias wrote. "It was like 1932 all over again. I guess the qualifying medal was as much as I could expect to win my first time out. Anyway, I got eliminated in an early round of the tournament match play that followed."[32]

The Babe was on her way to what would be the final goal of her life – a career in golf. But it would not be as smooth a journey as it appeared. Once again the issue of professionalism would keep Zaharias in the headlines, but off the course.

Zaharias entered the 1935 Texas State Women's Golf Championship in April. As Susan Cayleff relates in *Babe*, her reception by the best players in the state - players who were also well known national competitors - was anything but warm.

"When she entered the event, Peggy Chandler, a Texas Women's Golf Association member announced, 'We really don't need any truck drivers' daughters in our tournament,'" Cayleff writes. "Several women, insinuating that Babe was too masculine to compete against, withdrew from a pre-tournament driving contest. Babe responded by clowning. She feigned exaggerate femininity, taking intentionally ludicrous, 'girlish' swings at her balls. Except one. She stopped clowning long enough to rocket one ball 250 yards. She won."[33]

When Babe played her way to the finals, writer Paul Gallico - often a Zaharias critic - added a psychological component to his reporting of the event. He described Peggy Chandler, who would be Babe's opponent in the final as the player "who had snubbed Babe and was one of the more feminine and well-dressed golfers on the women's circuit." He went on to write "The Texas Babe seems to be working out a life long vendetta on sissy girls."[34]

Vendetta or not, Babe won. The 36-hole match was tight with no player ever more than 3-up. The turning point came on the thirty-fourth hole. With the match all even Babe eagled the par five from the fairway to go 1-up. The two players halved the next hole, and Babe won the final hole to take the championship.

"I was on top of the world that day," Zaharias wrote. "It had taken me longer than I originally figured to get going in golf, but I was rolling at last. I had the Texas Championship, and now I was ready to shoot for the national championship. I wanted to hit all the big women's tournaments around the country. I already had my entry in for the Southern Women's Amateur at Louisville on May twentieth."[35]

On May 14 the Untied States Golf Association ruled, after an investigation, that Zaharias was ineligible to compete in the Women's Southern Championship and the national championship because she had played other sports professionally. The investigation of Babe's status came as a response to a request from Mrs. Willard Sullivan, the secretary of the Women's Southern Golf Association. In June the USGA issued their final ruling, and "for the best interest of the game," banned Zaharias from amateur golf for three years.

Although Zaharias had support in the press and from several Texas golf officials, she remained surprisingly quiet and philosophical about the setback.

"Of course, I was disappointed when they told me I couldn't compete as an amateur," Zaharias is quoted in *Babe*. "But I admire them for barring me too. They were big enough to adhere to their rules."

"I didn't do any sounding off," Zaharias wrote in *This Life I've Led*. "When you get a big setback like that, there's no use crying about it. You have to face your problem and figure out what to do next."[36]

What she did was exactly what she did when the AAU banned her. She became a professional. She signed a contract with P. Goldsmith Sons, a sporting goods company for $2500 a year. Goldsmith merged with MacGregor Golf Company, and brought out a line of Babe Didrikson golf clubs. The company also arranged for Zaharias to play a series of exhibitions with one of the best men players of the era, Gene Sarazen.

From 1935 until 1938, Zaharias played exhibition golf – as a professional – and competed in the few "open" tournaments available for women. In January of 1938 Zaharias entered the Los Angeles Open. It was one of the most prestigious tournaments on the men's circuit, but there was no rule that barred women from entering.

"I knew I wasn't going to beat the top men pros, but I was still trying to establish myself as the greatest woman golfer," Zaharias wrote. "I wasn't the only one who didn't have any business being in it."[37]

Babe's entry was accepted and she was paired with two other players who "didn't have any business being in it." One was a minister and professor at Occidental College and the other was a well-known professional wrestler who had entered on a dare.

Enter George

George Zaharias was twenty-nine years old. He had achieved financial success and celebrity through his on-stage wrestling "bad-guy" persona. Wrestling was entertainment; although it required athletic talent. George, at a husky 235 pounds made the perfect villain. The son of Greek immigrants, who eventually settled in Colorado, George was dubbed by sportswriters "The Crying Greek from Cripple Creek."

On that January day in Los Angeles when George and Babe were paired together, it seems that a relationship between them developed almost immediately.

"What an introduction George and I had," Babe writes. "One minute we were saying hello, and the next minute photographers were crowding around and calling for him to put wrestling holds on me. He put his arm around me, pretending to apply neck holds and stuff. And I didn't mind it at all.... I already had the feeling that this George Zaharias was my kind of guy, and it turned out that he was thinking I was his kind of girl."[38]

Despite a travel schedule that kept both George and Babe on the road, the two were able to see each other often during 1938. In July, while both were in St. Louis the couple announced their engagement.

"We wanted to have a wedding with both families present," Babe wrote. "But one or the other of us kept having to take off for an appearance some place else. What with this commitment and that, we never could seem to work out a date for the wedding. Finally it was December. We were both in St. Louis again, and George got real stern with me. He said, 'We're going to get married this week or call the deal off.' I said, 'It's a deal. Let's go.'"[39]

Babe and George were married on December 23, 1938. Baseball great Leo Durocher, who at the time played for the St. Louis Cardinals, was George's best man and Durocher's wife, Grace, was Babe's maid of honor. The couple was married at the home of wrestling promoter Tom Packs, with a few friends in attendance. Because the decision was made so quickly, no one from either Babe's or George's family attended.

The marriage of Babe and George resulted in the union of two professional athletes with much in common. They were both attempting to use their athletic skill to produce income in any way that was open to them. In *Babe*, Susan Cayleff describes Babe and George as "hustlers" and "working class sports entertainers." She also describes the way in which the marriage benefited both.

"His exaggerated manliness contrasted favorably with Babe's attempted womanliness," Cayleff writes. "He softened her image, she heightened his.... There was more than a little of each in the other. Both knew that a well-executed show, be it in the ring or other arena, was a performance, a pageant, a ritual."[40]

If Babe improved George's image in the sports world, George did the same for Babe. Writers who six years before had included descriptions of her tomboyish appearance and mannish athleticism as a way to explain Babe's athletic success, now used George as proof of Babe's femininity.

Paul Gallico wrote "For many years until the Babe met and married her big, hearty, and adoring wrestler husband, George Zaharias, she was a pathetic and solitary figure, neither one thing nor another in the average normal world of ordinary men or women or even, for that matter, of athletes."[41]

Babe had reached her goal of Olympic domination; she was beginning to find financial security with her career in exhibition golf. Her marriage to George gave her the one thing she had not yet achieved – an appearance of normalcy in terms of her gender and with it a new sense of respect.

From the very beginning of their marriage Babe emphasized her interest in the domestic chores associated with femininity.

Babe made a big show of decorating and furnishing the couple's first house in Los Angeles. In the Spring of 1939 Babe and George traveled to Australia. In *This Life I've Led*, Babe describes the stopover in Hawaii by recounting the couple's domesticity.

> **BABE DIDRIKSON ZAHARIAS**
>
> **Amateur Career Highlights**
>
> **First American to win British Championship: 1947**
>
> **Establishes record for winning most consecutive tournaments: 17**

"On the way over we stopped off at Honolulu for three weeks," Babe wrote. "We rented a place where we could keep house. We loafed around the beach, and I tried out recipes for Hawaiian dishes and everything. And I rented a sewing machine and ran up half a dozen Hawaiian-style shirts for George, with those short sleeves and the fancy patterns."[42]

It seems odd that the woman who set out to be the greatest athlete in the world should focus on her ability as a wife. But, an image of normalcy would be crucial for entering the world of golf and exploiting her success financially. In the 1930's successful women were feminine women. Beginning in the mid-1930's Babe began the process of repairing the damage done by her masculine tomboyish image of the early 1930's. She purposefully began what Susan Cayleff calls a process of "feminization." In addition to emphasizing her interest in domestic activities, Babe began talking publicly about her teenage "boyfriends," began wearing make-up and allowed her short cropped hair to grow.

In 1975, biographers William Oscar Johnson and Nancy Williamson commented in their book, *Whatta-Gal* that during the mid-1930's Babe was "obviously, a more womanly new woman in the making. The fiercely sheared bob was gone and the vendetta against femininity was at an end."[43]

Although, at the time, her career in golf was a non-competitive one, Babe seemed to intuitively understand that competitive golf lay on the horizon, and that a more feminine image would better fit a world class golfer. Perhaps, as Johnson and Williamson suggest, her more feminine image touted the end of her "vendetta against femininity." But, an alternative analysis could see Babe's remaking of her image as an attempt to beat everyone at her own game. Perhaps her memory of Peggy Chandler's "truck driver's daughter" comment and the withdrawal of long drive competitors at the Texas Women's Championship encouraged a sense of over-kill in terms of Babe's "make-over". She probably hoped the time would come when she would meet those women and others like them on the golf course. Perhaps she was laying the groundwork for another type of revenge. When they met again, Babe's feminine image would allow her to make a subtle statement - "Now I'm just like you, and I still beat you."

Whatever the reason for the makeover, Babe's marriage to George made it complete. In addition her marriage also put George in a position to take on the role of Babe's business manager. George began that role with the Australian tour in 1939 and he would remain in control of her business interests for the rest of her life.

In the fall of 1939, Babe and George began the process of getting Babe back into amateur golf.

"Here I'd been practicing all the time, and developed this fine golf game, and about all I could do with it was play exhibition matches," Babe wrote. "I wasn't getting a chance to show whether I was the best woman player, because I was barred from practically all the women's tournaments as a professional."[44]

In 1940, Babe applied to the USGA to reinstate her amateur status and began a three-year waiting period. She dropped all her professional appearances and contracts, and for the next three years played only the two events open to either amateur or professional women golfers – the Western Women's Open and the Texas Women's Open.

Between 1940 and 1943, Babe and George lived in California and Babe continued to be involved in sports. She began playing tennis again, learned to bowl, and, during World War II, played a number of exhibition golf matches (unpaid) with Bob Hope and Bing Crosby. In

This Life I've Led, she emphasized that during this period her focus was on being George's wife.

"All the time I was doing this sports stuff out there on the West Coast, I was also enjoying being Mrs. George Zaharias," Babe wrote. "That's what I've been ever since we were married, whether I was keeping house or playing in a golf tournament. I've always competed as Mrs. Zaharias, not Babe Didrikson. George and I are a team."[45]

Finally... Back to Golf

On January 21, 1943, "Mrs. Zaharias" was reinstated as an amateur golfer. With most events not being held because of the war, her career remained on hold until 1946. Yet, in 1945 on the strength of her Western Women's Open victory, a second place finish in the Western Amateur, a win in the Texas Women's Open, and a victory over Betty Jameson in a 72-hole benefit challenge match, Babe was named Associated Press "Woman Athlete of the Year." It was her second AP Athlete of the Year award, and it made her what she most wanted to be – the number one women athlete in the world.

"I'd won it back in my Olympic year of 1932," Babe wrote. "But, this was the first time I was picked since then. During all those years in between, what with my troubles over professionalism and everything, I hadn't been able to compete enough to establish whether I was the No. 1 woman athlete."[46]

Babe wasted no time in affirming her number one status, or in resuming her habit of boastful predictions for her future success. With a full schedule of events for the summer of 1946, Babe was quoted in *Coronet* as wanting to "establish the longest winning streak in the history of women's golf."

Once again she fulfilled her own prophecy. The streak started in August of 1946 with a win at the Trans-Mississippi Championship in Denver. By October of 1946, the end of the women's amateur competitive schedule, she had entered and won four more – the Broadmoor Invitational, the All-American Championship, the U.S. Woman's Amateur and the Texas Women's Open. The women's amateur circuit began again in Florida in January 1947, and the streak continued. Babe won the Tampa Women's Open, the Helen Lee Doherty Invitational, the Florida Mixed Two-Ball Championship, The Palm Beach Women's Amateur, the Women's International Four-Ball, the South Atlantic Championship, and the East Coast Women's Championship. In early spring Babe won the Titleholders Championship in Augusta, GA., the North and South Championship at Pinehurst, NC, and win number 15 was the Celebrities Tournament in Washington D.C.

Babe's 16th win was one of her most famous. In June 1947, Babe became the first American to win the British Women's Amateur Championship. After a triumphant return to the United States in July, Babe won the Broadmoor Invitational for the second straight year. In the course of twelve months, Zaharias had won 17 events.

The streak was phenomenal, but like Babe's birth date, perhaps a bit controversial. There is one event that Babe, husband/promoter/manager George and some of the press seem to have passed over – the 1946 Women's National Open Championship.

The National Open was in its inaugural year in 1946. It was the showcase event of the newly organized professional golf tour for women – the Women's Professional Golf Association (WPGA) – the brainchild of Hope Seignious, a young woman determined to bring women's professional golf to the world. The tour played only a few events and had very few professional players – Patty Berg, Betty Hicks among the best known – filling out its fields with top level amateurs. At the 1946 National Open one of those amateurs was Babe Didrikson Zaharias. Babe lost a first round match to amateur, Grace Lenczyk of Connecticut, and Patty Berg emerged as the inaugural winner. The event eventually was taken over by the USGA, is today's U.S. Women's Open and one of the four major tournaments on the LPGA Tour.

Babe hardly mentions the event in her autobiography – mentioning it only in passing when describing the importance of the Women's Amateur.

"In 1946 all the golf tournaments started up again," Babe wrote. "There was a whole string of them during the summer, ending with the National Women's Amateur the last week in September. That was the biggest one. The National Women's Open was just getting started. It hadn't become the top tournament that it is today."[47]

Betty Hicks states in no uncertain terms that "Babe sorta repressed that match as she counted to 17."[48]

Without the National Open, Babe's streak would have been a legitimate record at 13 entries and 13 wins, which was still phenomenal. Combined with her British Open win, the streak was the catalyst that pushed her one more time – and this time permanently – into the ranks of professional golf.

The Babe and The LPGA

As the first American to win the British Amateur, Babe returned to a hero's welcome and offers for endorsements and exhibitions. Babe, of course, was on the wrong side of the amateur/professional fence. As an amateur none of those offers could be accepted.

"All sorts of offers kept coming in," Babe wrote. "It got to the point where I stood to make a fast half-million dollars if I'd turn professional. It's pretty hard to say you don't want the kind of money I was being offered. It nearly killed me to throw over the amateur standing I'd struggled so hard to get, but I couldn't see any other choice. On August fourteenth we called a press conference in New York, and I announced that I was turning pro. I signed with Fred Corcoran to be my business representative."[49]

Corcoran was a former Professional Golf Association (PGA) official who worked for Wilson Sporting Goods Company and also represented Ted Williams and Stan Musial. Corcoran arranged for Babe to be part of Wilson's advisory staff and the company began marketing a line of Babe Zaharias golf equipment. He also negotiated a deal for an instructional book with A.S. Barnes, and set up exhibition dates.

The exhibitions were "side-show" type activities, but they were a far cry from Babe's early 1930's shows of singing "Fit as a Fiddle." Corcoran was an experienced promoter with contacts among both athletes and the press. Babe now did exhibitions with the world's best known athletes.

"One was Yankee Stadium in New York," Babe wrote. "I think there were about 60,000 people there that night. I had to stick to demonstrating short stuff. I wanted to take a seven or eight-iron and hit the ball clear over the stadium roof, but they wouldn't let me."[50]

At that exhibition, Babe, in her own typical cocky fashion, coaxed the shy Yankee Clipper, Joe DiMaggio, to hit against her.

"I went over to the Yankee dugout to get him," Babe wrote. "'Come on, Joe,' I said. 'I'm going to pitch to you.' He didn't want to come, but I took him by the arm, and I grabbed a bat and handed it to him. I walked Joe out to home plate and bowed low.

"All I was afraid of was that I might hit him with a pitch, or that he might hit me with a batted ball," Babe continued. "'Whatever you do, please don't line one back at me,' I said to him just before I went to the mound. I did hit him right in the ribs with one pitch, although I don't think it hurt him. But I guess he was being careful about his batting. He skied a few, and then finally he took a big swing and missed and sat down."[51]

Corcoran also arranged a golf exhibition for the ever-exuberant Babe with the other quiet baseball legend of the era, Ted Williams.

Like her description of her encounter with DiMaggio, Babe tells it with her coming out on top.

"Ted doesn't play too much golf, but he's capable of hitting a golf ball just as hard as he is a baseball," Babe wrote. "He was rusty and erratic that day on the driving range in Sarasota. When he topped one that just dribbled off the tee, I called to him, 'Better run those grounders out, Ted! There may be an overthrow.'

"During the five minutes or so that we took turns hitting the ball, most of my shots went further than his did," Babe continued. "But I'll have to admit that every so often he whaled one that traveled a longer distance than any tee shot of mine."[52]

The business relationship between Babe, George and Corcoran did more than make Babe a "respected" marketable sports personality. It is what ultimately led to the founding of the LPGA.

In 1948, Hope Seignious and her Women's Professional Golf Association still held a few events, and the WPGA still organized the Women's National Open. But, despite Seignious' determination to create a viable professional outlet for woman golfers, she did not have the marketing skill or the sports contacts that were needed to make the organization grow. The WPGA was dying, but its short life had shown some of the most important people in the golf world that the time might be right for women to play the game professionally.

Babe claims the idea for a professional tour came from George.

"The amount of competition available to a woman golf pro was still pretty limited," Babe writes. "That was the only fly in the ointment for me. George realized this, and he started thinking about the problem, the way he had been when I was up against the same situation during my earlier pro period. And once again George came up with an answer. He got the idea that there should be a professional tournament circuit for women, just as there was for men."[53]

Certainly, George was involved in the LPGA's founding, but Babe's version enhances the role that George played.

With Babe and Patty Berg and several other women on Wilson's advisory staff, the company had a decided interest in seeing that women's golf thrived. Wilson president, L.B. Icely asked Corcoran to take an active role in developing a tour for women. The deal Icely agreed to was that Corcoran would manage and market the tour, and Wilson would pay his salary. With that kind of strong corporate backing the tour had a good chance at success.

In January 1949, Babe, George, Corcoran and Patty Berg met at the Venetian Hotel in Miami and hammered out the basic tenets that would form the organization.

Babe suggests that Seignious gave the group her blessing. "We called her (Seignious) up and invited her to be president of our new association," Babe writes. "She had been ill, and said she wouldn't be able to take on the job, but she wished us luck."[54]

But the transition was not quite that smooth. The WPGA had all but ceased to exist in late 1947 as the frustration of the struggling players turned to bitterness. When approached, Seignious would not give up the name of the organization and its charter to Corcoran because much of her money was invested in the WPGA magazine. Corcoran made an end run around the problem by calling the new organization the Ladies Professional Golf Association.

Betty Hicks is one of the few to actually record Seignious' reaction to the coup.

"In 1949 Babe and George Zaharias pounced on women's professional golf," Hicks writes in her book *Travels with a Golf Tour Gourmet*. "'Ladies' golf belongs to me!' Wrestling promoter George Zaharias decreed. Elbowing Seignious out of the picture, the Zahariases were major factors in the formation of a new organization which Babe's manager, Fred Corcoran, quaintly named the 'Ladies Professional Golf Association.' 'Ladies!' sniffed Hope Seignious indignantly. 'Lady' is what they take out of the inside of a lobster.'"[55]

> ## BABE DIDRIKSON ZAHARIAS
>
> **Professional Career Highlights**
>
> **Led in money earnings four consecutive years: 1948-51**

With Wilson's corporate money, Babe's star status and Corcoran's experience and contacts, the LPGA began a very slow, but always steady march to becoming, 50 years later, the largest professional sports organization for women in the world. Hope Seignious, the founder of the U.S. Open and the first women's professional tour, faded from the golf scene, and with a friend managed a trucking firm in Greensboro, NC.

When the LPGA incorporated in 1950 it had only eleven charter members, and there is no doubt that Babe was the "franchise." She was the most recognizable woman athlete in the world, and her fame - along with her personality - brought spectators to the golf course. As it had in 1932, that fame and personality brought mixed reviews from her "fellow-competitors."

"According to Peggy Kirk Bell, her color, humor, and sense of fun, while antagonizing a few, 'didn't do anything but help the LPGA,'" Susan Cayleff writes. "(Patty) Berg and Bell were adamant that Babe presented the 'right kind of image for golf.'"[56]

Others were not so pleased. Betty Jameson believed the LPGA "didn't want everybody to be Babe. They wanted some color in some other areas."[57]

Betsy Rawls felt Babe lacked dignity. "She really was a rather crude person," Rawls is quoted in Susan Cayleff's *Babe*. "She added a lot of color to the tour at a time when it was needed, but she did not add any dignity to the game."[58]

Babe's biggest critic was Betty Hicks. "Babe gave them the show they wanted, and she in turn was assured center stage," Hicks wrote. "But in seeking the limelight in this way, she was helping to perpetuate a cruel myth about women athletes - the myth that they weren't quite women."[59]

Reminiscent of her boasting before the 1932 Olympics, Babe's sometimes off-the-cuff comments could be beyond cruel and border on hurtful. She was sometimes her own worst enemy. "Where I go the galleries go," Susan Cayleff quotes Babe as saying. "Let the rest starve."[60]

By making comments like that, it may be that the bitterness of some of the tour players toward Babe was more than normal competitive jealousy. "Babe's supremacy would be easier for us if she didn't cram it down our throats," Hicks wrote.[61]

Babe may have "feminized" herself, but in those early years of the LPGA Tour she had changed little from the girl who ran down the aisle of the train on the way to Los Angles knocking pillows from under the heads of her teammates. She was still Babe and she did what she always did as a response to the consequences of her interpersonal behavior. She simply continued to win.

In her eight-year career with the LPGA she entered 128 events and won 31 to establish a winning percentage of almost 25%, winning almost every fourth time she played. She held ten major championship titles – three U.S. Opens (1948, 1950, 1954), three Women's Titleholders (1947, 1950, 1952), and four Western Opens (1940, 1944, 1945, 1950).

After a lifetime in sports she had not learned humility, and continued to be the brash, boastful "Texas Tomboy." But, no matter how boastful, she could still back up the boasts with performance. Babe was going as far as she could, and she would take all her fellow woman athletes, including her critics right along with her.

"Babe Didrikson Zaharias is my personal Gargantua," Betty Hicks wrote. "She ate little girls who couldn't drive the ball more than 225 yards."[62]

But Hicks also admitted, "Babe Zaharias is Mrs. Golf. She's the big drawing card.... Even though she annoys us at times with her egocentric attitude, we have twice elected her president of our association. We grin at her antics, tolerate her demands for favors from sponsors, sincerely wish her speedy recoveries from illness, take our beating from her routinely – and thoroughly enjoy beating her."[63]

The "Team" Erodes

As the LPGA Tour grew, Babe's respect as a sport's star was only enhanced. It was at this time that Babe's relationship with George began to show signs of eroding. Babe wanted desperately to settle in one area and own a home. George resisted.

In *Babe*, Susan Cayleff documents George's restlessness. "His wanderlust was legendary amongst those who knew him well," Cayleff writes. "(Bertha) Bowen (a life-long friend) said simply, 'George liked to ride the road.' He'd pack himself and his belongings into his Cadillac and drive off for weeks at a time.... This conflicted terribly with Babe's love of domestic security and signaled their growing dissatisfaction with the marriage."[64]

Babe, like many athletes, was constantly concerned about her physical condition and her body. George, after retiring from wrestling, ballooned to almost 400 pounds.

"Didrikson's affection and even tolerance for Zaharias had disintegrated considerably since the early days of their marriage," Cayleff writes. "George's appearance was a source of constant friction between them.... Babe, ever body-proud, found his eating habits repulsive."[65]

George had few social graces, while Babe, also not terribly socially adept, was trying to absorb the social niceties that she needed in her new role as the Tour's star.

George still had almost total control of Babe's finances, and he fought against giving that control away - even to Babe. "Several women on the tour were aware of how much George controlled the money even though Babe earned it," Cayleff writes. "His control of the money was 'hard' on Babe, yet, (Betty) Jameson commented, 'Babe in a way liked that, she trusted him.... She coped with George."[66]

Like many couples the Zaharias' were experiencing "growing pains," and for Babe it created a void. Into that void came a young, talented woman named Betty Dodd.

Dodd and Babe met in 1950. Dodd was nineteen – twenty years younger than Babe – and was touted as one of the Tour's brightest young stars. Babe asked Dodd's father if Betty could spend some time at her home in Tampa. "I want to work with her on her game," Babe explained.

Dodd points out that although the press labeled her as Babe's protégé, from the beginning, the relationship was not about Dodd's golf game, but about Babe's need to have some fun. "Well, she just wanted somebody to play with," Dodd said in a 1987 interview for *Babe*. "I sort of just admired her. She was my idol sort of. Not sort of – she was."[67]

"What began as a youthful admiration for a charismatic idol on Dodd's part and desire for a 'running buddy' on Didrikson's grew into a mutually enriching and satisfying intimate relationship," Cayleff writes. "She and Babe became constant companions. Dodd lived with the Zahariases in their converted clubhouse-turned dreamhouse in the midst of the Tampa golf course from 1950 until Babe's death in 1956. Although a sexual relationship was never publicly acknowledged, they became each other's primary partner.[68]

"Peers and friends openly acknowledge Dodd's centrality in Babe's life," Cayleff continues. "[Betty] Hicks, who described Dodd as 'the gangly Texas redhead and long-ball hitter,' said 'the companionship, competition, adulation, loyalty and solicitude of Betty Dodd were deeply meaningful to Babe.' (Betty) Jameson deemed them confidantes who 'had each other's ears.' (Peggy Kirk) Bell felt Didrikson really needed Dodd and that Dodd was wonderful to her.'"[69]

Babe, writing in 1955, is understandably vague about Dodd. Even if the relationship between the two was a committed one, the 1950's was not an era that would easily accept such a relationship. Babe, very much a product of that time was not about to take the risks faced forty years later by women athletes like Billy Jean King and Martina Navratilova in honestly talking about their sexuality.

By calling her 'my buddy,' Babe acknowledges the presence of Dodd in her life, but never describes the nature of the relationship. Yet, in Babe's detailed description of recovery from her first cancer operation and the onset of the second cancer battle, Dodd is prominent as "always being present." And, as Susan Cayleff points out, talking about Dodd as part of her support in dealing with her illness made the relationship between the two much more palatable and understandable to the public and the press.

Babe's silence about the relationship with Dodd was matched by her silence on her feelings toward George. In *This Life I've Led*, George is also a constant presence during her illness. Babe fueled the public image of a perfect marriage. Yet Cayleff uses Dodd's comments to paint a much different picture.

"Betty Dodd recognized that Didrikson often felt ambivalence and hostility for her husband, but she never allowed it to show," Cayleff wrote in *Babe* and then quotes Dodd. "She was very loyal to George," Dodd said. "She didn't want the world to know that she had those kinds of feelings about George because it had always been the other way."[70]

Certainly the relationship between Babe, George and Betty Dodd is complex. Its being cloaked in silence and innuendo is understandable given the time in which it took place. Babe's avoidance of "telling the whole story" is also understandable considering her experience with the press early in her life in terms of her gender and sexuality, and her obvious deep feelings for both George and Betty Dodd.

Illness

Babe was diagnosed with colon cancer in April 1953. Her doctors knew that her chances of recovery were very slim. Although they told George that the chances of her attaining full recovery were slight, they never voiced that prognosis to Babe. Only fourteen weeks after a colostomy she was back on the golf course. She went on to win four LPGA events that year, including a dramatic and decisive twelve-stroke victory over Betty Hicks in the 1954 U.S. Open. Babe won the Vare Trophy for the low scoring average that year, and was awarded the William D. Richardson Trophy for "her outstanding contributions to golf within the past year." In 1954 she was voted Associated Press Female Athlete of the Year for the sixth time.

In 1955, Babe won three more events. She was making one of the most spectacular comebacks the sports world had ever known. In early spring she began experiencing severe back pain which she attributed to shoveling out a car that had been stuck in the sand on a fishing trip. The diagnosis was a herniated disk, and in June she had surgery to remove the disk. In August Babe was told that cancer was again found – this time in the pelvic area – and on August fifth, radiation treatments were begun. It was the same day that Babe completed the tape-recording of her memoirs that would be used in *This Life I've Led*.

Like the rest of her life, Babe's illness was played out to the entire nation. In 1953, the press covered her surgery, recovery and return to the golf course. In 1955, Babe's condition was again part of daily news reports.

Babe detractors had often characterized her as self-centered and childish, yet in dealing with her illness, Babe showed both maturity and concern for others. She purposely allowed the press to follow every detail of her struggle against cancer in an effort to generate an understanding of the disease and those who suffered from it. At the time, cancer patients were often hidden and their fight against the disease were battles waged alone and in private. As a public person who seemed unafraid of the dreaded "Big C," Babe's honest and open approach helped to bring the disease out of the shadows. The publicity she generated led to further research funding. Her personal approach to dealing with the disease – as with almost everything else in her life - was often to express things with a sense of bravado rather than expressing her real emotions and fears. Although that attitude may have set unrealistic standards for other cancer patients, she gave an awareness that had not been present before; it was possible to live with the disease.

"There are several reasons why I didn't retire from golf after that 1953 cancer business - and still don't intend to retire – in spite of my 1955 ailments," Babe said in an interview in 1955. "One reason is that every time I get out and play well in a golf tournament, it seems to buck up people with the same cancer trouble I had."[71]

Babe also put "her money where her mouth was." In September 1955, she and George formed the Babe Didrikson Zaharias Cancer Fund. The fund, in Babe's words, was specifically designed "to help the needy people who are not able to pay to find out if they have cancer."

Babe's illness also brought her to personhood. For her entire life, her gender was constantly in question. News reports of her athletic successes were almost always sprinkled with references to her appearance, body type or clothes. She had spent her life trying to "appear" feminine while she thrived in the most masculine arena there was – sports.

As a cancer patient, Babe was just a person. News stories of her recovery did not describe her as "button-breasted," "tomboyishly thin," or a "muscle moll" - all phrases used to describe her in stories about her sports feats. None of the stories talked about her use of lipstick, her ability to cook, or her interest in gardening - subjects often found in stories about her exploits on the golf course. Cancer gave Babe what she had been striving for her whole life. It made her a person.

"The Babe" Legacy

Babe was more than a pioneer in women's sports. Her brashness, her boasting and her bravado forced the world to look not only at her but also at the other women with whom she competed. She simply would not be the quiet, humble hero that the sports world loved. She made the world take notice of this woman who was so bold as to think that she could perform at the same standard as men in their most revered arena – sports.

Her legacy is Title IX – the federal legislation formulated and pushed by the women athletes just a generation after Babe. It opened opportunities in sports for every other generation of women athletes to come.

Her legacy is the 1996 U. S. Olympic Softball team – described as power-hitters and base-runners, not "ladies in cleats" and "distaff shortstops."

Her legacy is the 1999 U. S. World Cup Women's Soccer Champions – embraced by the world as "true athletes."

Her legacy is the WNBA – a place where women can make an excellent living doing what they do best, not in a side-show atmosphere, but with respect.

Her legacy is the LPGA – an organization that sanctions over forty tournaments a year with over $30 million in prize money, and in its teaching division, thousands of women "teaching" professionals who work, and make a living, at golf clubs nationwide bringing golf to all people regardless of gender.

Her legacy is the ten-year-old girl, blond ponytail flying from her baseball cap sliding into second base and being tagged out by another ten-year-old girl with short brown hair. Neither ever concerned about their appearance, and both scowling at each other, anticipating their next confrontation as they brush the dirt from their uniforms.

Babe Didrikson Zaharias died on September 27, 1956. She was forty-five years old. She was also the greatest athlete who ever lived.

Chapter 2

Golf's first 'Glamour Girl'...
Betty Jameson

The golf clubs under the tree weren't shiny. They were a friend's well-used hand-me-downs. But, to the 10-year-old Elizabeth May Jameson, they seemed like the most extravagant gift imaginable that bleak Christmas of 1929. She had asked for nothing else. But, she made sure that her parents heard her request daily from early November until she went to sleep on Christmas eve in that first year of the Depression.

Betty's eyes were bright when she saw the clubs Christmas morning. Her eyes were brighter still when she swung the cut-down beat up used clubs for the first time. She was on her way. She would be just like the young 19-year-old Betty Hicks whom she had seen defeat the much older Collett Vare in the newsreel at the movies.

Betty Jameson did not really know who these women were, but she knew that with her own set of not quite brand new golf clubs, she would be like them. She would be a golfer – maybe the best there was.

Eighteen years later, the 28-year-old Jameson was the best. At the 1947 U.S. Women's Open Championship, Jameson – now a professional – won with a 72-hole score of 295. She was the first woman golfer in history to score lower than 300 in any 72-hole event. The feat was, for women's golf, what breaking the four-minute mile was for track and field.

Elizabeth May Jameson was born in the spring of 1919 in Norman, Oklahoma just as World War I was ending. Her family relocated to Dallas, Texas and it was there, at age 10, that Betty began a golf career that would make her one of the youngest prodigies the game has produced, and then one of the games' women pioneers as a founder of the LPGA.

On the eve of one of the most historic events in golf – the opening of the World Golf Hall of Fame at World Golf Village in 1998 – Jameson reminisced about her start in golf.

"I saw a newsreel one afternoon about Betty Hicks beating Collett Vare in the national amateur championship," Jameson said. "Betty was only 19 and she had beaten the best player in the world. I really did not know anything about golf, but the story of Hicks' win impressed me. That this young girl could dethrone the national champion caught my attention."[1]

That day Jameson asked her father, who was a recreational golfer, if she could play with him. Busy with his job as an advertising executive with the Dallas newspaper, Jameson's father kept putting the date for the golf course off. Jameson, however, was determined. After days of "talking golf up" around the house, Jameson's mother finally gave her the carfare to get to the course.

BETTY JAMESON

Began playing golf: age 10

First Tournament win: 1932, Texas Women's Publinx Championship

First LPGA victory: 1952

Last LPGA victory: 1955

"It was a little course with sand greens – my father called it 'Cow Pasture Country Club,'" Jameson said. "It cost fifty cents to play and fifty cents to rent clubs. There was no one there for me to play with, so I played the first nine holes by myself. I just sort of did what I had seen on the newsreel. On the tenth tee, I was joined by a man. He was the only other person there. He was a fireman and he had his days off.

"I loved the game immediately," Jameson continued. "I played that first round in November, and I wanted to keep going back to the golf course. My father was left-handed. I kept looking around the house for clubs that I could use so that I would not have to pay the fifty cent rental fee, but they were all for left-handers. Just as I had continued to ask to go to the course, I talked about nothing for the next month except getting a set of golf clubs. My parents found an old set of clubs that belonged to a friend and cut them down. They appeared under the tree on Christmas morning and I could not have been happier."[2]

The following summer Jameson played as often as she could. In one of her earliest rounds she shot 39. Her father was so impressed he talked to the editor of the newspaper, and Jameson, at just over 11-years-old, had her first "ink" as a golfer.

On summer evenings the local driving range held long-drive contests. The young Jameson was often a competitor. One evening local golf professional Francis Scheider happened to watch as she hit balls. Scheider immediately saw Jameson's potential, and offered to give her lessons. Scheider was well-known in the area and Jameson jumped at the chance to finally learn the nuances of the game.

"To get to Francis' course, I had to take two buses," Jameson said. "It did not matter to me, I think I probably would have walked if I had too. I was just so happy to be working with him. He would give me a lesson, then some cookies and a glass of ice cold milk, and then send me off to practice. I was never a milk drinker, but to this day I still remember how good that milk tasted."[3]

Through Scheider, Jameson learned what she says was her first lesson in how to hustle opponents. Scheider introduced her to another one of his students, a young boy of 10. The two youngsters spent almost everyday that summer on the golf course.

"I can't remember that boy's name," Jameson said. "I do remember that the first time we played he asked me what I shot. I increased my normal score by five strokes. Even then I knew there was such a thing as first tee talk. You learned quick in this game."[4]

Whatever "first tee talk" Jameson used, she was able to back it up. At age 13 she won the Texas Women's Publinx Championship, at age 15 the Southern Women's Amateur Championship and, in 1938, the Women's Texas Open. At age 19, she had accomplished much of what she set out to do after watching the movie newsreel nine years earlier. Although she was one year older than her idol Betty Hicks when she won the U.S. Amateur title, Jameson became the national champion in 1939 at age 20. In 1940, she won again, and became one of the few women to hold back-to-back U.S. Amateur titles.

Jameson was publicized as "golf's glamour girl." Her platinum blond hair, clear blue eyes and graceful athleticism made the image a natural for her. Jameson never shied away from the image, but her own self-concept was one of much greater depth. Unlike Babe Zaharias who would mold her gender image to what the public wanted, Jameson appeared comfortable with her role as athlete and woman. She is almost a solitary voice among women athletes of her generation to speak about both the "place of women" and her personal beliefs on "a woman's place."

"My mother and grandmother were great figures in my life," Jameson said. "My mother knew I could be a world beater – that was the old fashioned term – and my grandmother, on the other hand would say, 'Are you still playing golf?' As a woman I always thought I was swimming with the tide. I thought women could do anything and I still do. Women's place in the world meant something to me. I was not active in the women's movement because I did not mix with many of those people, but I supported it."[5]

In the midst of World War II, most major golf events were suspended beginning in 1942. Without golf, Jameson turned to writing.

 "Because of the war tournaments stopped," Jameson said. "I was on the city desk at the Dallas Times Herald. I liked the idea of writing, but I was not a good typist, and I could not meet the deadlines; so I went to an Army depot and drove generals around in trucks in San Antonio. I had to earn a living."[6]

Jameson as a "truck driver" is far removed from "golf's glamour girl." The way in which she spent that downtime from golf implies that her view of herself was closer to the "world beater" her mother saw than the "glamour girl" golf fans knew.

Golf for Jameson was always about drama. When the war ended, Jameson looked again to the golf course. Older now, she needed to make golf an income-producing activity. The natural place for her was in the professional ranks. But, for Jameson, the professional game – played at stroke play instead of the match play format of amateur golf – did not hold the same sense of drama.

"I thought if I wanted to be the best in the world, I should turn professional," Jameson said. "At least I would be making money. I could not afford the amateur game. I did not dream that without match play the whole essence and drama of golf would disappear. I did not realize how humdrum it is, playing hole-after-hole and not daring to take chances. I love match play. The fact that you knew you could make six on one hole and not be out of the match made you a little more daring – you were never protective. For me, it was just a little more exciting."[7]

Jameson may not have liked stroke play, but as the first woman to break the 300 mark in a 72-hole event, she proved that she could play the "humdrum" format successfully.

All her life Jameson had been interested in art and painting. If golf were drama for her, it also represented the touch and sensitivity of art as well.

"I would have liked to paint before I played golf," Jameson said. "I think I am as good a painter as golfer. The two are very similar. There is a touch that you must develop to be a painter that is very much like the touch that is part of every good golf swing."[8]

> **BETTY JAMESON**
>
> **Career Highlights**
>
> U.S. Amateur Champion: 1939 & 1940
>
> First woman to score lower than 300 (295) in a 72-hole event.
> U.S. Open Champion:1947
>
> Won four LPGA events in a single year: 1955

Jameson used the terms of art to describe the respect she had for the premier player of her era, Babe Zaharias. "Babe had great hands and eyes," Jameson said. "She played the game with touch and sensitivity."[9]

Jameson and Zaharias were not the best of friends. The two approached life, and golf, from opposite ends of the spectrum. Jameson was soft-spoken and dignified. Zaharias boisterous and always playing for a laugh. Yet in a 1998 interview on The Golf Channel, Jameson seems to have put her differences with Zaharias to rest and from the perspective of 50 years, see the humor in Babe's personality.

"Babe always made me laugh," Jameson said. "She was always on stage whether there were thousands of people or just an audience of one. My favorite memory of her is of one Sunday morning when we were all sitting around waiting for our tee times. It was too early to go to the course. Several of us decided that we would attend church. Babe kind of looked around to find that she would probably be left at the hotel on her own. 'What the Hell,' she said standing and striding to the door. 'Let's go to church.'"[10]

In that same Golf Channel interview, another women's golf pioneer, Peggy Kirk Bell, described Jameson, not as a "glamour girl," but as the "lady of the links." That description of her is probably more accurate than the one given by the media and public relations people. Jameson represented the values of her time, but her belief that she could be a "world beater" kept her always just on the edge of radicalism. If she hadn't had the ability to carve a sand iron out of a bunker and nestle the ball next to the pin, she might have been living in a loft in New York City and showing her artwork in Greenwich Village galleries.

Chapter 3

The Consummate Performer:
Patty Berg

The crowd of almost 200 spectators jockeys restlessly for position around the first tee. Standing sentry over a neat pile of shiny-white, brand new golf balls is a huge red and white golf bag. "Wilson" is boldly embroidered on the bag in black, and underneath, "Patty Berg" is written in italics.

With no fan fare, a short, stocky white-haired woman muscles her way through the spectators and marches to the bag – arms swinging purposefully, head jutting forward and focused straight ahead, each staccato step hard against the velvet green grass of the tee. The three young women who are escorting her almost run to keep up.

The crowd quiets as the woman grabs a driver out of the bag and dons a red "Wilson" baseball cap which she wears just ever so slightly askew. With no introduction she turns to the crowd. "I met this guy the other day," the woman says in a loud voice, with a sharp clipped cadence. "He told me he just got a new set of clubs for his wife. I said, 'Good Trade.'"

There is laughter but it is a bit tentative. Before the laughter has stopped, the woman takes a few short swings with the golf club, and looks at the crowd from under the brim of her hat. Continuing the monologue she says, "Hey, it's an old joke, but so am I."

The laughter is more natural this time. Without waiting for the laughter to end, the woman says, "I saw that baseball player, George Brett, the other day. He said he shot three over – one over the clubhouse, one over the front patio and one over the swimming pool."

Now the laughter is uproarious. The spectators are shaking their heads in disbelief that they are actually laughing at this "cornball" stuff. But, the laughter stops quickly. The crowd has learned that the woman will just keep talking, and if they laugh too long they might miss what she says next.

"This is how you play this game," the woman says as she drags a ball into position with the club and sets it up on a tee. "Finish high and let it fly." She addresses the ball, takes a smooth relaxed swing, and sends the white sphere soaring against the blue sky. It lands dead center well down the fairway. "Yes sir," she says turning back to the crowd. "Finish high and let it fly."

The crowd applauds wildly, everyone is smiling. The woman paces up and down the tee keeping up a constant chatter of jokes, stories and tidbits of golf knowledge.[1]

The woman is Patty Berg. The year is 1982. She is 64 years old. This is just one of over 10,000 clinics she has done over her 40-year career. It is obvious that she loves every minute of it. She loves to be in front of an audience, she loves the applause, and most of all she loves to perform. It is vintage Patty Berg, and the audience loves her for it.

Above all else, Patty Berg is a performer. Fellow Hall of Famer Kathy Whitworth describes Berg as a "frustrated actress." In any situation, if there is an audience, Patty Berg will tell jokes, relate folksy stories, or resort to a bit of slapstick comedy – anything to get a laugh. Berg's ability to be comfortable in front of a crowd and her desire to entertain is probably one of the qualities that allowed her to achieve "star" status in women's golf. It endeared her to the public. More importantly, it was the "niche" she found that would allow her to establish her own personality and take her out from the shadow of her much more charismatic colleague and competitor – Babe Didrikson Zaharias.

Patricia Jane Berg was born in 1918 when, in Europe, the "war to end all wars" was drawing to a close. The befreckled daughter of Minneapolis grain merchant and 10-handicap golfer Herman Berg, Patty was a "tomboy" right from the start. Her early fame was as the quarterback on the 50th Street Tigers, a pick up football team put together and coached by Berg's young neighbor, Bud Wilkinson. Wilkinson would stay with football, and as an adult, become the head coach at the University of Oklahoma.

PATTY BERG
Began Playing golf: age 15
Wins first tournament: 1934, Minneapolis Ladies Amateur
Declares herself a professional: 1940
First LPGA victory: 1950
Last LPGA victory: 1962

Even as an adult, Berg never tired of telling "Tiger stories."

"We had only one signal – 22 – and everyone ran every which way. We didn't have any wide ends, or tight ends, we just had a lot of loose ends. We never lost a game just teeth."[2]

Although Berg loved the rough and tumble competition of football, her youthful chubbiness and the concern of her mother ended her career as a quarterback.

"Bud told me I was a little slow and that there wasn't any future in football for me. I was also tearing my clothes and hurting my legs. Finally, my mother told my father, 'we have to get her into something else.'"[3]

The Bergs seemed intuitively to understand that their daughter's main interests revolved around sports, and offered amazing support and encouragement in a time when it was unusual to allow a daughter to be an athlete. The alternative to football became speed skating. Berg skated for the Minneapolis Powderhorn Club, and won several national events. Berg also ran track, and it may be that her interest in golf was first ignited from a track experience.

"I skated in many national championships and won some medals. But the first athletic event I ever won was in track at the John Burroughs school in 1930. Bobby Jones had to go right by that school to go out to the U.S. Open, which he won at Interlachen. (Berg's father was a member at Interlachen, and Jones' win in 1930 was part of his Grand Slam) At the same time, I was running in the 30-yard dash at school and I won it. I really wasn't into golf at the time, but I read about Jones in the papers. We were so happy that he won at our club."[4]

The very next year, when Berg was 13, and without any parental prodding, she began swinging a golf club in her back yard. Her father could not have been more pleased. As soon as Patty showed an interest in golf, Herman got Willie Kidd, Sr., Interlachen's head professional to give her lessons. Patty worked with Kidd, and his assistant professional Jim Pringle. But soon Berg found the mentor, University of Minnesota Golf Coach Lester Bolstad, who would shepherd her golf game for her entire career.

"I went to Les Bolstad for trap shots. I watched him play one time and he holed two of them. I said, 'Well, that's for me.' I started taking lessons from him and stayed with him for my whole game. I stayed for 40 years."[5]

Berg was drawn to sports for the competition, and it was her first competitive experience that solidified her commitment to golf. Berg's rendition of her first tournament is typical of her self-effacing humor. But, the story, and her telling of it, also gives a deeper look at the personality and character of the young athlete.

"In 1933, at age 14, I had played in my first Minneapolis City Championship. I remember on Sunday night, before qualifying on Monday, I went into the living room with my golf bag. I had a towel here and a towel there on my bag, and I said to my dad, 'How do I look?' He said. 'Are you going to go swimming or are you going to play in a golf tournament?'

"The next day I qualified with 122 strokes. In that 122 I was lucky. I had a lot of lucky things happen to me. It should have been about 140. On one hole I chipped in. It was kind of like a beeline shot. Then on another hole, I was in the bunker, and I shanked the ball. It grazed the top of the bunker, hit the flag, and jiggled down into the cup. I was really very, very lucky because I hit a lot of bad slices that were headed out of bounds – but hit something and stayed in.

"Another lady shot 121, and we were placed in the last flight – the tenth flight – just the two of us. She proceeded to beat me like a drum. I lost every hole. I congratulated my opponent and she said, 'You didn't play very well.' My caddie said, 'That's all right. You just didn't have any luck today.'

"As I walked back to the clubhouse, all I could think about was next year's Minneapolis City Championship. I decided right then that I was going to devote the 365 days to improving my golf game. So I practiced all day and went to the driving range at night. I thought if I worked every day, and if I had the will to win, and the desire, drive, determination and self-control, and the patience, and the will to strive for perfection and conquer all the pitfalls, and if I had the spirit and faith and enthusiasm and a winning attitude with positive thoughts then maybe I could do better in 365 days. I didn't believe that I would win in 1934, but I hoped I might move up a flight or two, and not shoot 122 and be defeated on every hole."[6]

At age 15, Berg did win the 1934 Minneapolis City Championship. She calls it the "turning point" of her career.

"I don't think I would be in golf today if I hadn't improved that much. When I went on to win after dedicating 365 days to a goal, I really started to dream. Maybe someday, I could have golf as my livelihood.

"And that's the way it turned out. I'll never forget those 365 long days from 1933 to 1934. That's a long time to work on just one endeavor after such a shaky start."[7]

Both funny and inspirational, the story is still a regular part of Berg's speeches. Berg plays up the inspirational tone when she tells the story, and uses it to punctuate her emphasis on the importance of persistence. The story also tells a lot about the girl Berg was, and the woman she was to become.

Patty and "The Babe"

In the mid 1930's the only "golf game in town" for women was amateur golf. There were no professional tournaments. A few events were "opens," which allowed anyone – amateur and professional – to compete. But the world of professional women's golf was limited to good players giving exhibitions – and those players were few – and even fewer women who taught golf at clubs.

One of the few true women golf professionals of that era was Helen Hicks. In 1935, Wilson Sporting Goods Company, in an effort to market their line of golf equipment, employed Hicks to host golf clinics and play exhibition matches. Hicks was women's professional golf, and women's professional golf was basically public relations and marketing – it was not competition or tournaments. Tournament golf in the 1930's was amateur golf.

It was into this world of amateur woman golfers that Patty Berg emerged in 1934. After her Minneapolis City Championship win, Berg began to play what was then called the "amateur circuit." She not only played, but she won – just about everything.

Between 1934 and 1939, Berg won twenty-nine championships, including the U.S. Amateur and three Titleholders (the most prestigious event for women at the time). In 1938, Berg was named to the Curtis Cup team. Playing on the team that competed against Great Britain every two years was an affirmation of our American woman golfer's skill and her position as a "star" within the world of amateur golf.

The three best-known American women golfers in the 1930's were Didrikson, Hicks and Berg. Didrikson and Hicks were committed to professional contracts. They played matches against male

---

PATTY BERG

Amateur Highlights

U.S. Amateur Champion: 1938

28 amateur championship titles 1934-40

Curtis Cup Team: 1936 & 1938

pros and each other, as well as the few other women professionals – Helen McDonald, Opal Hill, May Dunn, Bessie Fenn, and the British golf legend, Joyce Wethered.

Berg, on the other hand, spent the 1930's in competition. By the end of the decade she had compiled a winning record that should have qualified her as being at the top of her field. She was respected, and had a certain level of name recognition, but she and her record were overshadowed by the woman who literally "grabbed" all of the interest in women's sports, Babe Didrikson. Because of the lack of tournament play for women professionals, the two very seldom played against each other. Toward the end of the 1930's, when they did play, it was usually in an exhibition format – never under the pressure of a competitive event.

Interestingly, Berg turned professional in 1940, when she signed a contract with Wilson Sporting Goods. In that same year, Didrikson would leave the pro ranks and apply to be re-instated as an amateur. For the next five years the two best women golfers in the world would still not compete against each other. It would not be until the formation of the LPGA in 1948 that Berg and Didrikson would finally compete head-to-head on a regular basis under the stress of tournament conditions. The shear charisma of Didrikson's personality would still overshadow Berg, her accomplishments, and her own naturally outgoing character.

"Patty Berg got kicked under the rug because of Babe," Mickey Wright said. "As a player, as someone who knew golf, all aspects of it, I really don't think she got her due as the fine golfer she was."[8]

Didrikson would dominate golf headlines, and Berg would play the supporting role until Zaharias death in 1956. Yet, Berg showed no resentment, and Zaharias seemed to know that in Berg she had an equal.

"She was really one of my idols," Berg said about Zaharias. "I just thought she was terrific. She was a great, great friend of mine, too. I had lots of fun with her. I thought she had a great sense of humor and she got a charge out of everything."[9]

In 1951, Berg and Zaharias played on a team of American professionals who toured Great Britain. In one match they played the British Walker Cup Team – Great Britain's best amateur male players. In the morning events, the American women lost two matches and tied one. They trailed the men by 11/2 points.

"At lunch, our table had little American flags on it," Berg relates. "I said, 'All of those who expect to win their singles, follow me.' Babe says, 'Come on, follow Napoleon!'"[10]

The American women did win all their singles matches and beat the men from Great Britain, 6 1/2 to 2 1/2. The story points out that not only did Berg have natural leadership qualities – which may have been underrated by the force of Zaharias personality – but that Zaharias acknowledged, respected and used those qualities in Berg to augment her own leadership ability. In the press and in the public eye, Berg may have played "second fiddle" to the maestro, Zaharias, but it seems apparent that Zaharias was well aware of Berg's abilities and had no problem using them to her advantage.

Although Zaharias got more "ink," the two are relatively equal in terms of their golf accomplishments. Because they did not play amateur golf at the same time, and Zaharias' death cut short her professional career, the parity between the two gets lost. Because of the timing of Zaharias' shift from professional to amateur and back to professional, she and Berg never really competed against each other as amateurs. When they both played professionally after 1948, the record until Zaharias' death in 1956 is almost exactly even. Their amateur and professional major tournament wins are presented to show that Babe and Patty equally dominated the game in the 1930's and 1940's.

AMATEUR EVENTS

U.S. WOMEN'S AMATEUR:
  Berg wins in 1938 (Zaharias is a professional, and cannot compete)
  Zaharias wins in 1946 (Berg is a professional, and cannot compete)
WOMEN'S WESTERN AMATEUR:
  Berg wins in 1938
  Zaharias does not hold this title
NORTH & SOUTH AMATEUR:
  Zaharias wins in 1947
  Berg does not hold this title
WOMEN'S SOUTH ATLANTIC GOLF CHAMPIONSHIP
  Berg wins in 1938 & 1939 (Zaharias is a professional and cannot compete)
  Zaharias wins in 1946 (Berg is a professional and cannot compete)
BROADMOOR LADIES INVITATIONAL
  Zaharias wins in 1945, 1946, 1947 (The event was not played between 1929-41; therefore, Berg did not have the chance to compete)
HELEN LEE DOHERTY INVITATIONAL
  Berg wins in 1936, 1937, 1938, 1939 & 1940 (Zaharias is a professional and cannot compete)
  Zaharias wins in 1947 (Berg is a professional and cannot compete)
WOMEN'S TRANS NATIONAL AMATEUR CHAMPIONSHIP
  Berg wins in 1938 & 1939 (Zaharias is a professional and cannot compete)
  Zaharias win in 1946 (Berg is a professional and cannot compete)
CURTIS CUP TEAM
  Berg is member in 1936 & 1938
  Zaharias is a professional in the 1930's, and again in 1948 when the competition resumed after World War II. She did not have the opportunity to be chosen.

PROFESSIONAL EVENTS

(Berg serves in the Marine Corps between 1943-1945, begins competing again in 1946)
U.S. WOMEN'S OPEN
  Berg wins the first Open in 1946 (Zaharias does not compete)
  Zaharias wins in 1948, 1950 & 1954
WOMEN'S WESTERN OPEN
  Berg wins in 1941, 1943, 1948 & 1951
  (Berg also wins in 1955, 1957 & 1958. These wins occurred during Zaharias' illness or after her death)
  Zaharias wins in 1940, 1944, 1945 & 1950
TITLEHOLDERS CHAMPIONSHIP
  Berg wins in 1937, 1938, 1939 (as an amateur), 1948, 1953 & 1955
  Zaharias wins in 1947 (as an amateur), 1950 & 1952

Of the two players, Zaharias seemed most interested in maintaining her position as "star," and did show a little "revisionist history" in her autobiography, *This Life I've Led*, when she claimed Berg was the inaugural LPGA President, and Zaharias held the office from that point on. In fact, Berg was LPGA President from 1949-1952. Zaharias took over in 1953 and served until 1955, when Louise Suggs took the reins.

A case could be made that Zaharias' mis-rememberance of the situation may show a bit of uncomfortableness with Berg as a "golf insider," because of Berg's long amateur career. It may also reflect just a bit of resentment on Zaharias' part for Berg's natural leadership qualities that the Berg Presidency affirms.

On Berg's part there is no indication that she ever resented her position of supporting player to Zaharias' starring role. Berg, naturally self-confident, just kept playing and winning. She allowed Zaharias to take the competitive limelight. She had an intuitive understanding of how important Zaharias' charisma was to fostering women's golf.

Berg simply found a place for herself – where she could be the "star." That place was in giving clinics. Within the clinic format, Berg, the performer, could be the "headliner." In front a crowd in a clinic, Berg could shine in her own right, without any reflection at all from the Zaharias star.

The "Personhood" of Patty Berg

Patty Berg is a "person." She presents neither a dominantly female nor dominantly male image. Babe Zaharias spent a good part of her energy creating a "female" image. Berg is in a sense genderless. She is in no sense severely "masculine," and yet, makes no outstanding effort to appear overly "feminine." As an athlete, the scale might easily be tipped toward the "masculine," but Berg's innate attitude of not taking herself too seriously seems to keep the gender scale balance. Her image is neither masculine nor feminine; it is that of a person.

Berg's image as "person" with minimal gender identification may be a result of her "Tomboy" childhood. Not only did the "girl" quarterback of the 50th Street Tigers collect scrapes and scratches on her knees, she collected something more important – the respect for her own worth as a person from others, especially boys. Berg did not have to fight her way onto the neighborhood football team. She had the ability, and the boys on the team knew it. That early experience was one that fostered her feelings of self-worth. Even when she stopped playing, it was not because she was a "girl," it was because of her ability.

The story she tells about the young Bud Wilkinson "cutting" her from the team is important. Wilkinson told her she was a "little slow" for the game. So if it was disappointing to her – which did not seem to be the case – it was not a reflection on her gender, only her physical skill as it related to football. In addition, Wilkinson told her that she couldn't go anywhere in football. When telling the story, Berg never implies that this was a derogatory comment, just simply the truth as it was in the late 1920's. The comment implies that Wilkinson thought she had good athletic ability that could be used in other sports – those that girls could play.

This experience seems to be one in which she learned to be accepted for her abilities regardless of gender.

In relating the story of her "retirement" from football, Berg also mentions her mother's attitude. Berg's mother did not want her to stop because football was "unladylike" or "unfeminine," but simply because Berg was continually tearing her clothes. Berg's mother further suggested that "we get her into something else," not stop her from "playing" all together. It is significant that Berg's mother held this "open-minded" attitude toward her daughter and her interest in sports. Again, Berg experienced respect as a "person."

Finally, there is Berg's early experience in golf. Her weekends were spent with her father and other youngsters – again mostly boys – traveling throughout the area playing golf and doing charity events. It is the definitive experience of Berg's life.

"I played eight years of amateur golf and every Saturday and Sunday, when I was home; my father had me play some exhibition for charity. He said, 'If you're going to play the game, you're going to do some charity work for people. So get started, you're not just sitting at home.'"[11]

This early exposure to charity work stayed with Berg her entire life. At almost every interview she relates this story, and at age 80 she is still heavily engaged in work for several charities. But the exhibition tours set up by her father also furthered the basic concept of her own self-respect as a person. It was a concept she has carried with her throughout her life.

"We had a regular schedule. We'd leave Friday night or early Saturday morning, and sometimes we rode the train, especially if we went up through Duluth to Superior. Every time we went on these trips we took the poem, 'Casey at the Bat.' Everyone would do a dramatic reading and then we'd all cheer."[12]

Once again, Berg was in the company of all boys and was treated as an equal. Once again her "personhood" and her athletic talent was affirmed.

These childhood experiences gave Berg a strong sense of self-worth that was not gender connected. Her gender was never an issue. She was who she was based on what she could do. It was an attitude toward herself that she would carry with her for her entire life.

Berg presented herself to the world just as she was. She never expected not to be respected for her abilities. She never made excuses or exceptions for her gender – she did not think she needed to. She was, and still is, simply a "person."

Patty the Persistent

Even with her strong self-concept, strong sense of self-worth and strong background of equality, Berg would eventually meet the "glass ceiling" of sports that all women athletes in the 1930's and 40's had to face. Berg and her contemporaries of the 1930's played the "Broadway" of women's golf. But, it was still "Off Broadway" because it was amateur golf. It was not until the late 1940's that the idea of a professional women's golf tour could take hold – and it was not an easy process. The number of professionals in the game was so small at the time, that amateur players played an important role in the tour's survival. Berg was understanding and sensitive to the inclusion of amateurs.

"We have to thank all the amateurs of that time because whenever we went into their area, they'd play in our tournaments. They helped us get publicity. A girl is going to bring out a lot of people. You go down to Fort Worth and Polly Riley is going to bring out a lot of friends. We'd go to Minneapolis and Bea Barrett would draw a lot of people.... So we have to give them a big, big, big thanks because they did a lot for us."[13]

The problem was that often an amateur would win the event. That would take away from the publicity for the professionals, and also affect the tour's ability to attract sponsors and other financial support.

Hope Seignious, through the WPGA, did succeed in founding the U.S. Woman's Open Championship. But by 1949, it became clear that the WPGA tour effort was doomed.

Sports writer Bud Harvey wrote, "The professional golfing ladies, after a number of starts, have not succeeded in organizing an open tournament circuit, patterned after the PGA's round-the-calendar schedule. The women have a first class show, but they seem to have trouble in masterminding themselves into the lucrative position their skill is worth on today's bullish sports market in the United States."[14]

The simple fact was that it was difficult to get financial support for women athletes.

Berg, now the tour's president, had been a professional for nine years, and the organization in which she played was about to fold. But, on the horizon lurked the fame of Babe Didrikson Zaharias who had again joined the professional ranks in 1948, and the support of Wilson Sporting Goods Company. In January of 1949, Berg attended a meeting with Babe, Babe's husband George, and Babe's manager Fred Corcoran (also a Wilson employee) to look at forming a new professional tour. Corcoran had instructions from Wilson chairman, L.B. Icely, to help organize the new tour. Berg remembers what it was like to be part of the transition.

"I think you have to give a lot of credit to Hope Seignious and her dad, because they helped us a lot. She had tremendous vision, but I thought that we just had to get going, that's all. We had to get somebody with Fred's background."[15]

Corcoran had been an official with the PGA tour. He had an understanding of publicity, marketing principles and, more importantly, the blessing of Wilson Sporting Goods. Corcoran agreed to manage the new women's tour for one dollar a year (he would retain his position at Wilson), until the tour became stable. Berg recalls Corcoran's first move.

"The first thing he did was change the name from Women's Professional Golf Association to Ladies Professional Golf Association. Fred felt 'Ladies' sounded better than 'Women,' and he thought the name change would give us a little publicity. And that's what happened."[16]

Despite Berg's characteristic enthusiasm, Corcoran found the response to the fledgling LPGA among the people who counted – potential sponsors – was less than overwhelming.

"The announcement that we had formed the Ladies PGA touched off a national storm of indifference," Corcoran said in his book, *Unplayable Lies*. "Potential sponsors were polite when I called them, but you could hear them stifling a yawn at the other end of the line." [17]

Through the efforts of Corcoran, the charisma of Zaharias, the skill of the small group of professionals, and the persistence of Berg, the LPGA took hold and succeeded.

The Berg Legacy

Patty Berg is a hero for many women. But, it is the woman athlete in the 50 year old age group who is most appreciative of Berg's accomplishments. This generation of women recognize Zaharias as a sports legend, but their connection to her is tenuous. These women never had the chance to really know Zaharias. She died before most reached their 10th birthday. Nancy Lopez is not a hero for women in their 50's. Lopez is a source of pride, but not a player with whom they identify. When this age group was leaving college, Lopez was entering first grade.

For the generation of women athletes now in their 50's, it is Patty Berg who represents their golf heritage. Patty Berg is their hero. These woman, like Berg in the early part of her career, always played "Off Broadway." They were highly skilled competitors, but played to no crowds, and received little recognition. It is Berg, with whom these women – some thirty years younger – can identify. It is Berg whom these women chose as a role model.

> **PATTY BERG**
>
> **Professional Highlights**
>
> Six of her 57 professional wins came before the founding of LPGA
>
> Won seven events:1948
>
> Recorded hole-in-one: 1991, age 73

These women and Berg saw themselves within the athletic framework as genderless. Their sense of self-worth allowed them to view the gender issue in sports as an irritating obstacle that had to be lived with, and "worked around." They had the dogged persistence to not only keep playing, but to make things change. That persistence formed the structure that would give more opportunity to future generations of athletes.

Berg – through her personality and attitude – paved the way for the current prestige, acceptance, and success of women's professional golf. Those women, now in their 50's, who made themselves Berg's proteges paved the way for the factor that would bring prestige, acceptance and success to all women's sports – Title IX legislation.

Berg's legacy has a significance and influence that goes beyond just golf. Berg's legacy includes all of women's sports.

Chapter 4

Quiet Hero:
Louise Suggs

I believe I may have arrived twenty years too soon, but the day is dawning for women golfers."[1] Louise Suggs spoke those prophetic words in 1949 as she took her place as one of the original nine members of the LPGA.

Suggs was right on both counts. She did arrive twenty years too soon. During the first season of the LPGA in 1950, Suggs and her fellow professionals played for $34,000 in total prize money. The fledgling Tour could put together just eleven events, each of which was played before small groups of fans in towns like Niles, Illinois, Carrollton, Georgia and Newton, Massachusetts. Suggs, in 1950 – her inaugural season as a professional – won $3000 in official prize money. Twenty years later, in 1970, rookie JoAnne Carner finished 11th on the money list with official winnings of

$14,551. The Tour conducted 21 events with total prize money of almost $500,000, and Carner, a future Hall of Famer, was seen by millions of fans who watched several events on television.

Suggs was also right when she characterized the founding of the LPGA as the dawn of women's golf. In 1950, the name "Louise Suggs" might have been familiar to the few "hard core" golf enthusiasts, but it was far from a household name. The Tour in 1950 had less than 20 members. Often, LPGA officers had to cajole talented women amateur golfers to join the small band of professionals who toured the country in almost "gypsy-like" fashion in campers and cars.

Today, even non-golfers recognize Nancy Lopez's smile, and little girls at golf courses across the country make sure their pony tails peek out of their golf caps, imitating Annika Sorenstam and Karrie Webb. In 1998, the LPGA received over 500 entries to the Tour qualifying school. Those who are successful will gain a spot within the 400-member LPGA roster. They will play for more than $30,000,000 in prize money. The life-style is still gypsy-like, but the number of events and the wide range of cities make traveling by air almost imperative.

Louise Suggs saw the future and played a dominant role in shaping it. Suggs' playing record equals her two more recognizable contemporaries – Patty Berg and Babe Zaharias. Her fifty tournament wins include eight majors. She has two U.S. Open victories, an LPGA Championship win, three Titleholders Championships, and she served three terms as LPGA President. Yet, among today's average women golfers, Suggs is virtually unknown. The reason could be that the controlled, reserved, quiet, dedicated and hard working Suggs not only saw the future but also was the future.

Fellow Hall of Famer Betsy Rawls describes Suggs as "somewhat withdrawn." Rawls also states that Suggs "never emoted much on the course or empathized with the gallery. She was very sensitive...."[2]

Suggs competed against and often beat the boisterous Zaharias and the comedic Berg. She succeeded in the flamboyant, sometimes sideshow atmosphere of the early tour, but it was never comfortable for her, and she often resented it. Suggs is more in the mold of the current tour and tour player – sports as business, and the athlete's persona as that of a calculating corporate executive. Suggs would probably be comfortable with the stoicism of Annika Sorenstam and the reticence of Betsy King.

A Dichotomy

Mae Louise Suggs was born and grew up just outside Atlanta in Lithia Springs, Georgia. In the early 1920's her father, Johnny Suggs, was a talented pitcher who played baseball for the Atlanta Crackers. Johnny left the field for management when he met and married the Crackers owner's daughter. On September 7, 1923 two events occurred almost simultaneously and changed Johnny's life. A fire destroyed the Crackers stadium and with it Johnny's front office career in baseball. On that same day he became the father of a daughter – Louise.

The Suggs family moved from Atlanta to Lithia Springs where they owned and operated a golf course and picnic ground. At age three, Louise tagged along as her father redesigned and made improvements to the golf course. At age ten, during the height of the Depression, the young Louise found that golf was one of the few forms of entertainment easily available to her.

"In those days Lithia Springs was out in the country; there were no neighbors or anything. Since our house almost had the golf course for a backyard, I just started hitting golf balls."[3]

Johnny Suggs gave Louise the benefit of both his athletic experience and his golf knowledge. Her approach to the game became a combination of her innate reserved and precise personality, and the instinctual natural movement patterns of an athlete. Ben Hogan, whose reserved personality mirrored that of Suggs, described the precision aspect of her game.

"Her game shows the benefits of a great deal of intelligent experimenting, study and practice. Her timing and her consistently high standard of play, stay with her for the reason that she has got the fundamentals and the refinements down to where they reduce the margin of error to about its minimum."[4]

Suggs herself described her alter ego – the "feel" player – in her book, *Golf for Women* published in 1960.

"When somebody asks me how hard I stroke a sixteen foot putt, I've got to answer, 'I don't know. I look at the ball; I look at the cup; I take in the kind of lie I've got. And when I've done that, I just feel I've got to hit the ball in a certain way.'"[5]

Like Berg, Suggs played against and defeated older and more experienced women amateur players as a teenager. She won her first major competitive event at age 16 – the 1939 Georgia Women's Amateur Championship. From that point on, Suggs dominated women's amateur golf.

Because Patty Berg had become a professional in 1940, Suggs and Berg would not meet head-to-head until ten years later within the competitive environment of the struggling LPGA. Between 1940 and 1944, Zaharias was waiting out the lay-off imposed by the USGA that would return her to an amateur. With no fanfare, the reticent Suggs quietly slipped her almost perfect golf game into the void left by the two most famous women players of the previous decade. In 1941 she won the Southern Amateur Championship. In 1942 it was the North and South Championship. Suggs was proving that she could play, but the combination of her quiet personality and the chaos of World War II that had engulfed the world kept her greatness hidden to all but a few golf insiders.

During the early 1940's, Suggs' access to tournaments was limited. Many events – including the most prestigious of all, the U.S. Amateur – were not held because of the war. By 1947 the 24-year-old Suggs was back to playing a full amateur schedule.

That year, the Amateur crown was up for grabs. Babe Zaharias had won in 1946, and shortly after left the amateur ranks to turn pro for the second time in her career. According to *Time* magazine, Suggs was not favored to win. Instead, another Atlantan, Dorothy Kirby, was considered the better player. After 34 holes of the 36-hole final round, the match was dead even. Suggs won the 35th hole to go one up. On the final tee, Suggs lost her drive to the right and was faced with

LOUISE SUGGS

Began playing golf - age 10

First tournament win: 1939, Georgia Women's Amateur

First LPGA victory: 1951

Last LPGA victory: 1962

an almost impossible shot to the green from the rough. *Time* describes the final two shots that brought Suggs to national prominence.

"Calmly she selected a club, wiggled once and sent a tremendous wood shot to the green. Then she curved a putt around a partial stymie and the ball dropped into the cup. That gave her the match and the title...."[6]

With that win Suggs became the third member of the women's golf "Big Three" – Patty Berg, Babe Zaharias, and now Louise Suggs. In another two years, the woman who had shunned the limelight would find herself part of the publicity seeking environment that the founding of the LPGA would bring to women's golf. Not unlike her golf game, Suggs' life would become a dichotomy – the private, retiring woman would be thrust into a world that required public exposure and an extroverted personality.

Suggs' Struggle

The LPGA Tour brought Louise Suggs face-to-face with two challenges – competition against the greatest women players in the game, and dealing with those players' personalities. Suggs met the first challenge with ease. In the 1950 season, Suggs won more prize money than either Berg or Zaharias, and her scoring average was lower than Berg's and less than half a percentage point higher than that of Zaharias. In fact, Suggs was the low scoring professional – finishing second – in the very first LPGA event. In an effort to increase the size of the tournament fields, the new tour allowed amateurs to play. Ironically that first event, the Tampa Open, was won by an amateur, Polly Riley. In the first six years of the tour, prior to Zaharias' death, Suggs earned $55,374 in prize money. Berg won $49,151, and Zaharias $34,984.

The real challenge for Suggs was personal. She had great difficulty finding a place for her quiet, stoic personality within the boisterous, publicity driven atmosphere defined for the tour by its star personality Babe Zaharias. Patty Berg had found a niche in hosting clinics and depending on her sense of humor to offset the sometimes irritating gregariousness of Zaharias' personality. It was not as easy for Suggs. For someone as sensitive as Suggs, "The Babe" could be hard to take – especially when as golfers they were "more than equal."

The rivalry between the two was probably very real. Although she never commented on her relationship with Suggs, Zaharias was adept at finding ways to irk the more sensitive woman. Fellow Hall of Famer Betty Jameson recalls Zaharias' habit of announcing to the press her practice-round scores as lower than she actually shot just to make it look like she had played better than Suggs.

"When she (Zaharias) would come in from a practice round she'd give them a good newspaper score," Jameson said. "Louise would just be livid about it. She'd say, 'Oh, that liar.'"[7]

Suggs has not commented publicly about her feelings toward Zaharias. Betsy Rawls believes Suggs had a difficult time dealing with Zaharias.

"Louise respected the game, but she didn't like or respect Babe because Babe disregarded the rules. Louise also resented the tremendous publicity given to Babe. She couldn't laugh at it."[8]

In *The Illustrated History of Women's Golf*, Rhonda Glenn, who came to know Suggs personally, expressed Suggs behavior best. "Her stoic approach was in direct contrast to the Babe's flamboyance, and some have said there were hard feelings between Babe and Louise. Typically, Miss Suggs remains silent on the matter."[9]

Change

Although Suggs found "life with the Babe" difficult, she continued to play a brand of golf that was outstanding. Eventually, she also began to feel comfortable in the public eye, and to understand that public recognition could help her to define her values and ideas for future generations.

The change occurred for Louise Suggs when she was elected LPGA President in 1955.

"When Louise was president of the LPGA from 1955 to 1957, she was at her best," Betsy Rawls said. "She felt she had the respect of the players. She did an excellent job, which gave her a little more self-esteem."[10]

That new found self-esteem, her willingness to share the spot-light, and her life-long reticence is reflected in her book, *Golf for Women*, published in 1960. Suggs is the book's editor, not its author, and although she does author four chapters, the rest of the book is a collection of golf instruction by several of her contemporaries. Suggs, uncharacteristically, takes a hard-line, strong position on participation in the game by women.

Similar to her statement in 1949 about the future of women's golf, Suggs, with her encouragement of women as golfers, again sees the world, not as it is, but as it will be. Her position foresees the trend 30 years in the future – when, in the 1990's, women would become the fastest growing segment of the golf population

"When it comes to this fascinating and frustrating game, there are a few convictions I hold that are based on observation and are not to be classified as prejudices," Suggs wrote. "One of these convictions has to do with women and golf. There's been far too much of this nonsense, so far as I'm concerned, about women being inferior on the golf course, the people who make this claim usually basing their argument on the female's physical structure. To them I say: 'If a woman can walk, she can play golf.'"[11]

This statement is a departure for the reserved, unemotional Suggs; her arch rival Babe Zaharias would have been proud. But, typical of Suggs, she slips back into character, and hedges the power of her conviction. Like the dichotomy of her intuitive yet precision-based

---

LOUISE SUGGS

Career Highlights

British Amateur: 1948

Curtis Cup Team: 1948

Set a 72-hole scoring record (291 at the 1949: U.S. Open), 14 stroke victory margin set a record that held until 1986

Hole-in-one (unofficial and first) at age 68, practice round, 1991 Centel Senior Challenge

golf game, Suggs recognizes that women participants in golf may find themselves engaged in the age-old dichotomy of the "iron fist in a velvet glove."

"Perhaps the first consideration for a woman golfer is the reaction she will suffer from walking into this man's world," Suggs wrote. "She will feel diffident about taking up a game so long dominated by the male sex. There isn't really very much I can say about this. The only mistake I'd caution against is the natural one a woman can make under these circumstances: over-aggression. Play the game as well as you know how and think of the initial breakthrough much as you would if you were moving into a new community. It seems unfriendly – at first. There is resistance – at first. But the opposition will melt before two positive qualities: the ability to play and the grace you would manifest in any social situation."[12]

In May 1998, Suggs attended the opening of the World Golf Hall of Fame in St. Augustine, Florida. The event and the World Golf Hall of Fame itself was a milestone in golf history – and, in particular, the history of the LPGA. The World Golf Hall of Fame is the permanent home for the LPGA Hall of Fame – complete with player memorabilia and interactive visitor exhibits.

Throughout the weekend, Suggs declined invitations for interviews. She showed an intense curiosity about the exhibits and the technology that made them work, but her natural shyness kept her on the fringe of the festivities. But, on the morning of the induction of Johnny Miller and Nick Faldo, a ceremony at which Suggs and the other LPGA Hall of Fame members would be honored as well, Suggs visited some of the exhibits. One is a putting green where "tournaments" for visitors are staged. The exhibit allows visitors to act out roles as players, TV announcers, cameramen and producers as the staged event is shown on televisions surrounding the putting green. It was at this exhibit, by a quirk of fate, that Suggs was thrust into a situation reminiscent of the "carnival-like" atmosphere of the early tour.

Suggs, Nancy Lopez and top ranked amateur Carol Semple-Thompson all happened to arrive at the exhibit at the same time. The three were persuaded to "be the players" in the "tournament" while visitors acted out the other roles. Semple-Thompson was eliminated when she took three strokes to get the ball in the hole, while Suggs and Lopez took two. That left Suggs and Lopez in a deadlock, and the rules dictated a "play-off."

Lopez was first to putt and put the ball within four inches of the hole. Suggs then stepped up to the 25-foot putt. She firmly stroked the ball. It broke just ever so slightly from left to right and softly dropped into the hole. The crowd went wild! Lopez embraced Suggs, and a small smile appeared on Suggs' face.[13]

It was a nice moment. Two players from different eras, and with different personalities – both having made a huge impact on the game – going head-to-head, the "veteran" coming out on top, and the younger, much more "famous" player showing a deep respect for the pioneer.

Louise Suggs may have been born 20 years too early to enjoy the personal recognition and financial reward that was part of the future she accurately foresaw in 1949. Yet, with that putt at the World Golf Hall of Fame almost 50 years later, she proved it would not have mattered when she was born. Suggs had the ability to compete in any era – and win.

Whatever the club, the distance "The Babe"
hit the ball, was legendary.

Babe Didrikson Zaharias

Her standard advice to any and all players:
"Finish high and let it fly".

Patty Berg

Babe Didrikson Zaharias

Patty Berg (right) talks with
LPGA teaching professionals
Peggy Kirk Bell (left) and
Annette Thompson (center).

Louise Suggs (left) putts at the
Hall of Fame Induction in 1998.

(below) Babe Didrikson
Zaharias' Memorial Center,
a museum in Beaumont, Texas

1998 World Golf Hall of Fame
Dedication and Induction Ceremonies

Betty Jameson

1994 Sprint Senior Challenge

Louise Suggs

Patty (center) is in her "element" giving a golf clinic.

Patty Berg

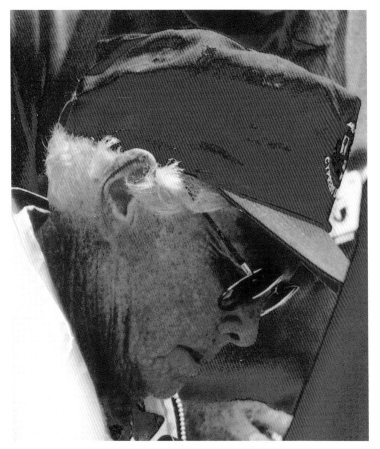

Surrounded by friends, Patty signs autographs
at the 1995 Sprint Senior Challenge.

Patty Berg

Being interviewed in 1998 at the
World Golf Hall of Fame.

Louise Suggs

COURTESY LPGA.

Louise Suggs (left) and Patty Berg

1932

The Babe

Circa 1950

Circa 1950

Part II

COMING OF AGE

1960's - 70's

Setting the Scene

The LPGA Tour began its eleventh year in 1960. In the first ten years, the Tour struggled to survive, but in 1960 the Tour not only was alive, but began to thrive. Both the Tour and its players showed a new confidence reflected by more tournaments, increased purses and most important, quality play. Betsy Rawls and Mickey Wright were the first players inducted into the Hall of Fame who were not among the original founding members of the LPGA Tour.

Rawl's and Wright's induction into the Hall of Fame was of major significance for the LPGA. They were the first in the modern era of women's golf to meet the difficult induction criteria. Literally, they had played their way in. Their induction confirmed that professional women's golf was a viable presence in the sports world. Their success demonstrated that, along with baseball players, football players, basketball players and men golfers, women could make a living in professional sports. The success of Rawls and Wright also cemented the future of the LPGA Tour. It was alive, well and ready to take its place alongside all other professional sports.

The induction of Kathy Whitworth, Sandra Haynie and Carol Mann into the Hall in the 1970's gave the LPGA and the Hall legitimacy. Their qualification for the Hall showed that while the Tour grew in numbers it was not being diluted in terms of talent level. Their induction gave the Tour what every competitive sports organization needs to continue to grow – depth and parity.

Rawls, Wright, and youngsters Whitworth, Haynie and Mann saw fellow woman golfer Babe Didrikson Zaharias named the Female Athlete of the 20th Century in 1949 by the Associated Press. They watched as Althea Gibson broke the color barrier in tennis in 1950, and Jackie Robinson did the same in baseball in 1947. Whitworth, Haynie and Mann watched as the LPGA was formed. Their "heroes" became the young Rawls and Wright.

Rawls and Wright grew up in a pre-war "black and white, good against evil" world. Their values, standards and personalities had been formed by that world. It was the gray, "whose the good guy?" world in which they honed their talent, and it was the materialistic, consumer-oriented world of the 1950's and 1960's into which they brought their skills. They may have been part of a generation "in the middle," but as individuals Rawls and Wright proved to be definitive and spectacular.

Whitworth, Haynie and Mann grew up in the confusing world of the 1950's. They had to pick their way through far too many choices on the way to making decisions, yet they saw a world in which those choices seemed more limited for some than others – especially women. Their life on Tour was lived in the turbulent era of the 1960's and early 1970's. Their generation had to be flexible enough to keep up with a world that was turning upside down. Whitworth, Haynie and Mann became part of that process. They responded by embracing the new interest in mass communication that characterized the era to make themselves more visible. In the process, they gave new definition to what women could be.

Chapter 5

The Academic...
Betsy Rawls

I n 1996, Betsy Rawls was the recipient of the United States Golf Association's Bob Jones Award. The USGA states that "the award is given in recognition of distinguished sportsmanship in the game. The award seeks to recognize a person who emulates Jones' spirit, his personal qualities, and his attitude toward the game and its players."

The Bob Jones Award is golf's most prestigious honor. It recognizes the recipient as bringing a quality to the game that emulates golf's greatest hero – Bobby Jones. It salutes the recipient for contributing to the game. Rawls' selection for the honor is distinctive because she is one of only nine women who have received the award in its forty-four year history. To receive the Bob Jones Award – especially as a woman – is to be recognized as one of golf's "inner circle."

When Rawls received the award at age 67, she had spent a lifetime in golf. Her twenty-five year playing career from 1951- 1975 had spanned the most important years in the history of the LPGA. She had played a major role in the growth of the LPGA Tour while she served as its first paid Tournament Director from 1976-1980. As executive director of the McDonald's LPGA Championship since 1981, Rawls has shaped this tour event which is the LPGA's greatest contributor to charities. The winner of this event is the LPGA Champion.

Certainly these are amazing accomplishments. But what is more amazing is that Betsy Rawls never intended any of it. Rawls – now one of golf's "inner circle"- never intended to be a golfer at all.

Elizabeth Earle Rawls was born on May 4, 1928 in Spartanburg, South Carolina. She was the younger of the two Rawls children; her brother had been born two years earlier. Just after Betsy's first birthday, the family moved to Texas, settling near Austin.

Unlike so many of her fellow Tour professionals, Rawls did not play golf as a child, and by the time she was seventeen, Rawls had enrolled in the University of Texas as a physics major. It was then that Rawls developed an interest in golf.

"My father was once Indianapolis city golf champion, but then he didn't play much until I was 17 and became interested in the game," Rawls said. "I had a lesson from Harvey Penick in Austin for $1.50, and then he never charged me again. I became good pretty quickly, got hooked on golf, and won some amateur tournaments."

Rawls' description of her beginnings in golf makes it sound routine. But it was hardly that. Living in the Austin area, Rawls had access to golf's most respected guru – Harvey Penick. She obviously sought him out, and he – as is often the case with great teachers – recognized her talent, and was willing to develop it "pro bono."

Rawls understates the speed and quality of her progress – "I became good pretty quickly...and won some amateur tournaments." The facts are that Rawls began to play the game in 1945 and just four years later the "some amateur tournaments" she won were actually among "the" amateur events in the nation. Rawls, with only four years experience, won the 1949 Texas Amateur and one of the most prestigious events for women at the time, the Trans-National Championship. Rawls repeated her win in the Texas Amateur in 1950 and backed that up with one more national victory, the Broadmoor Invitational.

Rawls was also "pretty good" at physics. In 1950 – the same year the LPGA was founded – Rawls graduated, Phi Beta Kappa, from the University of Texas with a degree in physics. The fledgling women's golf tour was almost unknown to Rawls, and a career in golf was the furthest thing from the young graduate's mind.

"Having majored in physics at the University of Texas, I had every intention of being a physicist," Rawls said. "I grew up isolated from the world of women's professional golf; there was no publicity about them. I didn't identify with them, and I hardly knew a tour existed. I played golf for fun and never considered turning professional, where there was no money and no glamour."

Less than a year later, all that changed. In the spring of 1951, Wilson Sporting Goods approached Rawls with an offer to become a member of its professional golf staff. She accepted the opportunity, and the "studious" Rawls used it to open up a less serious side of her personality.

"I decided it would be more fun to be in golf than physics," Rawls said. "Wilson paid me a salary and all my expenses and travel for the exhibitions I did for them."

There was more than fun that attracted Rawls to professional golf. Rawls saw the tour as an opportunity to constructively use her fiercely competitive nature.

"There were enough tournaments to play, and I liked golf so much that the motivation was the tournaments and the competition," Rawls said. "No one who turned professional at that time did it to

BETSY RAWLS

Began playing golf: age 17

First tournament win:1949, Texas Amateur

First LPGA victory: 1951

Last LPGA victory: 1972

make money, to get endorsements, or to be on television. It was purely for the sake of playing competitive golf and wanting to prove yourself."

Rawls did not have to wait long for success. Her first professional victory came less than six months into her career – in September 1951 – and it was one of the most coveted titles in golf – the U.S. Open. The twenty-three year old Rawls finished five strokes ahead of her nearest rival, Louise Suggs.

Rawls may have been a newcomer, but her victory at the U.S. Open was not a total surprise to either Rawls or her fellow players. The year before, in the 1950 Open, as an amateur, Rawls was runner-up to Babe Zaharias.

"I wasn't surprised that I won the U.S. Open in my rookie year," Rawls said. "I had quite a bit of confidence. When you start out, you think you are supposed to win. Only later are you surprised at important victories."

Rawls would win the Open three more times (1953, 1957, 1960) to share the record for the most Open wins with Mickey Wright. In just her second year on Tour, Rawls was the leading money winner, and over the course of her career, went on to accumulate a total of 53 LPGA victories, including eight Major championships.

Rawls played to win – literally. Winning was most important to her. Yet her calm, unflappable behavior deceptively concealed the steely resolve which personified her game. Women's golf historian Rhonda Glenn in her book *The Illustrated History of Women's Golf* describes Rawls as "a woman of endearing shyness, she was a great competitor through sheer strength of will. When Betsy played you could almost see her mind working, and seldom did she fail to find a way out of trouble. Not the longest hitter on the tour, her understanding of the game was nearly unmatched."

For Rawls the end justified the means, and that end was always to win.

"Although I always read a lot and was interested in other things, all I wanted to do was play golf, think about it, and practice," Rawls said. "It's not necessarily a good thing to be so totally absorbed because it's very narrow and limited, but winning makes it all worth it. Nothing can make you feel quite as good as winning a golf tournament. You've done the entire thing yourself. No one can help you. It's totally you. You get great satisfaction when you win, and you're rewarded directly according to your performance. I had a lot of drive, and any great player must have an obsession with winning and a need to win... I didn't set myself targets. I set out to win every tournament I could, which was the only goal I had."

Rawls' wanted to win because she wanted peer recognition and over her twenty-five year career that is exactly what she gained. Rawls, a self-described introvert, found that life on tour enhanced her ability to relate to others, and they looked to her for leadership.

"Golf changed me a lot as a person," Rawls said. "When I started out, I was reluctant to talk, but as time went on it became easier to relate to people."

Two times the players elected Rawls president of the organization (1961 & 1962), but more importantly, they often turned to her for advice about their game.

"I learned that one bad shot does not mean the whole tournament," Rawls said. "And then I learned the knack of not letting disappointment or frustration show, of not expressing anger. I turned negative feelings into determination. I didn't give up or feel sorry for myself."

Rawls passed on her understanding of taking personal responsibility for your game to one of the tour's greatest players, Mickey Wright. Wright looked up to Rawls and turned to her for advice early in her career. Wright credits Rawls' response as the one factor that kept her on tour at a critical time.

"Early in my career, I was a spoiled brat as far as golf was concerned," Wright said. "I thought the idea was to hit perfect shots and the natural result would be success. I would get mad when one did not always follow the other. I would hit a bad shot, feel sorry for myself, and get angry.

"Betsy Rawls took me aside one day for a discussion," (early in the season of 1958) Wright continued. "Betsy Rawls was the hardest working, never quit golfer I've ever known, and she got sick and tired of my whining. It may not have been what I wanted to hear, but it probably was the most important golf lesson I ever had. She told me that I'd better give up golf if I could not stop that thought pattern.

"Betsy said that I'd have to take responsibility for every shot – good or bad. She said the name of the game was to get around the course, not just hit the ball, and that I'd better gain some respect for the short game. I started watching other good players, and I began to see how they behaved. I started to learn the most important thing – how to play the game."

According to Tour chronicler Betty Hicks, Rawls early on gained the respect of the LPGA's biggest star, Babe Zaharias.

"Betsy Rawls was the woman who frustrated Babe perhaps more than any other," Hicks said in her book, *Travels with a Golf Tour Gourmet*. "She refused to let Babe intimidate her."

BETSY RAWLS

Career Highlights

Won multiple events every year from 1951-1962

Won 10 events in a single year:1959

Afterlife

Although Rawls earned and enjoyed the respect of her colleagues, she found joy in playing the game, and her desire to win never faded. She won multiple events every year from 1951-1962, and she won at least one event each year from 1951-1966. Rawls led the Tour in victories three times (1952, 1957, and 1959). In 1959 she won ten times and received the Vare Trophy for low scoring average.

By 1969, after eighteen years, Rawls' career was winding down, but the desire was still as strong as ever.

"I joined the tour in 1951; I thoroughly enjoyed it then and all of the 25 years that I played," Rawls said. "I never got tired of it, never woke up and said, 'I hate having to go to the golf course this morning.' I always looked forward to playing.

"My biggest thrill was the last LPGA championship I won, which was in 1969," Rawls continued. "I had reached a point where I wasn't sure I could win again. It was on the toughest course on our schedule, which was Concord Country Club, New York. I played really well. I didn't have one bogey in the final round. I got a great kick out of that. I probably enjoyed that win the most."

Rawls won two events in 1970, and her last win came in 1972. Like many world class athletes, Rawls delayed the decision to leave competition. She, unlike other athletes, was lucky. She waited until a new challenge presented itself, and the transition away from the competitive arena was much easier.

"When you feel your ability slipping, there is a gradual change, a desperation at first that you're not winning," Rawls said. "I was able to tolerate not winning, but I didn't like it, and I knew it was happening. I didn't suffer, but I don't think any athlete wants to quit. I didn't come to terms with it until the LPGA offered me a job as tournament director, and then I had to face it squarely. I wasn't ready to quit, but my better judgment prevailed. I knew it would be only a short time before I'd have to quit."

Rawls took over as LPGA Tour tournament director in 1975. She was the first person to hold that position as a salaried employee of the Tour. Rawls as tournament director reflected just how much respect and recognition she had gained from her peers. In the position, Rawls brought a sense of continuity to the organization during a critical transition period because her experience reflected almost the entire history of the Tour.

"There were about 20 players when I joined (the Tour), and 20 tournaments," Rawls said. "The players made the pairings, kept statistics, had a staff including a treasurer and secretary. Altogether, we did a lot of hard work. We made all the policy and procedure decisions as a group. We would get in a room and sometimes with great trauma we would thrash it out."

Once Rawls had decided to leave the Tour as a player, she brought all of her energy and organizational skill to the job of tournament director. She served in that position until 1981, and saw the organization through the greatest growth spurt in its history.

"I was proud to contribute to the beginning of the organization, not only the growth of it but the survival of it," Rawls said in 1996. "All of the players had to take pride in doing things right so the organization could grow and thrive the way it did."

In 1981, the fifty-three year old Rawls took on a new challenge. She was named as executive director of the McDonald's LPGA championship. Rawls still holds that position, and under her leadership, the event has raised well over $23 million for charities.

In 1980, Rawls earned another first among women in the golf world. She was the first woman to serve as a rules official at a men's U.S. Open. In the conservative world of golf, Rawls was placed in the vanguard of breaking the all-male domination of the USGA. It was an unusual role for a woman who never considered herself close to being a feminist.

"I didn't relate my own lifestyle to that of women in general because I was not concerned about my role as a woman or what other people expected women to be," Rawls said. "There was never much talk about the women's movement on the tour, where the whole world is reduced to what's happening on a particular green at that moment."

Rawls' life choices demonstrate the purest form of feminism. Hers is unconscious feminism. A lifelong, extremely firm understanding of herself as "person" – capable of anything. And in the end that may be her legacy.

She is a woman who, as a youngster, chose to study physics, a field dominated by men at the time. It did not seem to matter. Her intelligence and determination allowed her to gain a degree, with honors, in that field.

Her burning desire to compete led her to professional golf. With hardly a look back she threw herself into a competitive arena, not only dominated by men, but so new for women, that its very existence would remain in doubt for at least the next five years. It did not seem to matter. Her skill and dedication brought distinction and respect.

In Rhonda Glenn's book, Rawls commented on the essence of golf. Taken in the context of her career and her accomplishments, it is not hard to broaden the interpretation beyond just golf.

"For most golfers there is a never-ending struggle to improve and to learn the secrets of this complex sport," Rawls said. "There are many more failures than successes and many more disappointments than joys. To all people who have played professional golf over the years, however, one thing is certain – the struggle has been worth it."

Chapter 6

The Innocent Challenger...
Mickey Wright

The ball flew – much further than the 11-year-old ever expected. With eyes shining, the young player carefully placed another small white ball on the soft green grass, and put the club behind it. The club was swung – another solid click. The ball flew again – further than the time before.

A spark ignited in the slim, tall, slightly awkward body of the 11-year-old.

The girl turned to her father and asked if they could go play. He smiled, but never answered her question.

The spark within the young woman, fueled by the thrill of hitting a golf ball far, was not dimmed by momentary disappointment. Instead, it would turn to a blaze and never be extinguished.

"My father was a 15 handicap," Wright remembers. "He spent a lot of time at the driving range, and he would take me with him. I loved hitting golf balls, and I began pestering him to play with me. He was not real excited about playing with an 11-year-old who just wanted to swing as hard as she could, and hit the ball far. He told me I had to take lessons first."[1]

Wright's father, Arthur, a San Diego attorney, led her to Johnny Bellante, the golf professional at La Jolla Country Club. Bellante, well known as a teacher, had already developed the game of PGA Tour great, Gene Littler.

In her book, *Play Golf the Wright Way*, Wright describes that first encounter with Bellante.

"I'll never forget that first lesson. Like an overwhelming Newfoundland puppy, not quite housebroken but willing to make up in floppy affection what I lacked in behavior, I showed up on the practice tee wearing sneakers and pedal pushers and an 'I'll-show-you-how-far-I-can-hit-the-ball' expression.

"Johnny had trained puppies before; a soothing voice, a kind word, but you must obey the master's commands. I obeyed."[2]

That is how the career of Mickey Wright, believed by many to be the greatest woman golfer ever, began in post-World War II San Diego in 1946. Wright would go on to collect eighty-two LPGA Tour victories between 1955 and 1973 – the most ever to that point in LPGA Tour history. She would become a member of the LPGA Hall of Fame in 1964 at age 29, win four U.S. Opens, and retire from the game prematurely at age 35.

Not One of the Boys

Wright would play most of her career at the same time that the triumvirate of Arnold Palmer, Gary Player and Jack Nicklaus dominated the PGA Tour. In fact, Wright and Palmer joined the professional ranks in the same year – 1955. In a sense, Wright played in the shadow of these male players who ushered in the new "televised" golf era. It was the raw power of Palmer, the finesse of Player and the brashness of young Nicklaus that were seen in the homes of millions of Americans. To almost every golfer in the ten-year period from 1955-1965, "Arnie" was a household name. The name Mickey Wright could very well stump those same golfers.

In another sense, Wright, typically unassuming and almost shy, quietly showed her underlying strength of character by using her skills to play her way outside the Palmer – Player – Nicklaus shadow. Wright played so well that she cast a long shadow all her own.

Forced to acknowledge Wright's talent and success, the golf world – tournament organizers, national organization, sportswriters and players – seemed to be struggling in its attempt to find a way to include this new golf phenomenon. Wright was a woman who had the capability to singularly dominate the game, exactly as extraordinarily talented men dominated. In actuality, the struggle was not what it seemed – an attempt at inclusion. It was an attempt to understand and resolve a contradiction.

Wright was a woman, and a serious athlete. Through athletics, she found self-expression. Wright was different from women athletes of earlier eras. Wright, unlike her contemporary, Babe Didrikson, did not downplay her athletic skills by wrapping them in a delightfully irreverent personality.

Wright's never intended to challenge cultural perceptions.

MICKEY WRIGHT
Begins playing golf: age 11
First tournament win: 1949, Southern California Junior Girls Championship
First LPGA victory: 1956
Last LPGA victory: 1973

For her, golf was an intimate personal quest. It was not a public demonstration. Her success in golf was the manifestation of her personal integrity focused on achieving her own goals.

"I wanted to be the best at something," Wright said in a 1997 interview. "Even now, I still find joy in hitting golf balls. It is a form of self-expression."[3]

Golf was Wright's life. Wright took golf seriously. She put her athleticism in front of the world unencumbered – not downplayed by humor, or wrapped in a "personality." It was real, and she was a skilled athlete.

Like her "I'll-show-you-how-far-I-can-hit-the-ball" attitude at age 11, the adult Wright was just as honest. She presented to the golf world – quietly, naturally and with no harm intended – a "This-is-who-I-am-and-what-I-do" attitude toward golf.

For others, whose perceptions were based on hard and inflexible gender rules, dealing with Wright's honesty was confusing and uncomfortable. Wright's ability was admired, and the golf world wished to acknowledge it. They just did not know how to express that acknowledgement without diminishing standard gender concepts – Wright's and other woman player's femininity, and male player's masculinity.

Wright was about as far from being "radical" or "feminist" as any one person can get. Although she was gracious and kind to golf fans, her basic instinct was to shun publicity and notoriety.

In a 1997 interview, Wright explained the way she saw her life during the 1950's and 1960's.

"I never felt a second-class anything. My father was a respected, prominent attorney in San Diego. I had always been a good student, and I had the opportunity to play the best golf courses in the area. I thought I was the luckiest person in the world.

"I ran into my share of the 'she's good for a girl' mentality. It was a little aggravating, but it spurred me to be even better. Mainly, I remember support and encouragement from most people I met or got to know."[4]

Wright had no "private agenda" to challenge accepted gender roles. Wright's talent and hard work, and possibly fate had put her in a position that made her a threat – albeit, an unknown one – to conventional thought. Wright's ability to play golf at a phenomenal level forced others in the golf world to deal with the issue as best they could.

The solution was to describe "the Wright phenomenon" through comparisons. Wright was compared to other women golfers – the two most frequent were Didrikson and Joyce Wethered, the outstanding woman player who dominated women's golf in the 1920's. More often, Wright was compared to male players – possibly because of her strength, power and distance. The one group of players that Wright was seldom compared to was the three great men players who were her contemporaries – Palmer, Player and Nicklaus. Instead, the comparisons would almost always be made to male players of a more classical era – golf's "golden era" of Jones, Hogan and Snead.

One of golf's greatest writers, Herbert Warren Wind, described Wright's swing as having "the same decisive hand action that the best men players use... combining her hitting action smoothly with the rest of her swing, which was like Hogan's in that all the unfunctional moves had been pared away. And like Jones' in that its cohesive timing disguised the effort that went into it."

It was as though Wright was acknowledged, but with a qualification. She was talented. She was a player. But, and it was a big but, not a player of today. She was a player more like those of the past. By comparing Wright to the great male players of the past, the golf world could lessen Wright's threat to standard gender roles.

Wright, through her golf game, put herself on the line. She showed she could equal, or surpass, the accomplishments of her contemporaries, both male and female. Others put her in a category that kept her from challenging the supremacy of her male contemporaries. It was not until 1988, that Ben Hogan, to his credit, changed that perception. Hogan characterized Wright as having "the finest golf swing I ever saw, man or woman."

For Wright, the only thing that ever mattered was to hit the ball far, with the most perfect of swings – and to be the best.

It is ironic that this quiet, shy, young woman, with high personal standards and a well-developed sense of personal values, was thrust to a position that would turn the golf world upside down.

Mickey Wright did not seek this role. Once placed in the situation, Wright demonstrated that she had the intelligence and courage to play it out with grace and honesty. In doing so, she unintentionally played a key role in unlocking a door which future women golfers would more easily open.

85

The Time, The Place and The Person

As an expectant father, Arthur Wright was certain he would soon have a son. He planned to name the new baby Michael. On February 14, 1935, Arthur Wright had to change his plans. His wife Dorothy gave birth to a girl – Mary Kathryn Wright. Undaunted, Arthur simply adjusted by nicknaming his baby girl "Mickey."

> ### MICKEY WRIGHT
>
> ### Amateur Highlights
>
> ### U.S. Girls Junior Champion: 1952
>
> ### World Amateur Champion: 1954
>
> ### U.S. Open - Low Amateur: 1954

Mickey grew up in a world that had changed – almost overnight – from being simple to being complex.

For Mickey Wright, it is that time just before, and during World War II that remains most vivid in her memory.

"The 1940's in San Diego were an idyllic time in many ways. The most beautiful spot in the world: unspoiled by tourists, Sea Worlds and freeways; a wonderful school system, and a relatively safe place to live by today's standards. I never remember having the doors locked in our house, day or night.

"This atmosphere was spoiled only by the fear of the war coming to our shores. My two brothers both enlisted in the Army Air Corps while they were in their teens. Two stars in our window were a constant reminder that the war was real. The dirigibles over the city, the spotlights searching the skies, and the blackout curtains on windows also were a constant reminder.

"For parents who had survived the depression, the added inconveniences of "A" cards for gas and meat and butter were never considered a 'big thing.' Mother's daily concern for my brothers, Herbert and Carroll, in the Pacific Theater was stressful, and the writing and receiving of their letters was a big event.

"For me life was pretty simple; playing hide and seek, capture the flag, kick the can, roller-skating on our newly put down sidewalks, and going to school was what life was all about.

"The things I liked most about that time was the simplicity and order of everything. Plus, the carefree safety of the period. I can not really think of anything I remember disliking about it."[5]

Wright's childhood world also included golf. The game totally engaged her.

"It was important for me to play golf. At first, I am sure, to please my father. He loved golf, and was delighted in my interest in it. As I discovered, I had some talent – greatly encouraged by my teachers Johnny Bellante and Fred Sherman. I just got the 'bug' as most golfers do, and wanted to do it better and better.

"After winning the Southern California Junior Girls Championship in 1949, Harry Pressler took me as a student, and really inspired me to be the best. Harry's first wife, Leona Chaney Pressler had won the Western Amateur in either 1937 or 1938 – that was an inspiration – not to mention the thrill for a youngster to be able to play golf with Randolph Scott, Mickey Rooney and Johnny Weismueller when they came to vacation at Mission Valley Country Club. Fred Sherman (Mission Valley's owner and professional) always made sure I played with them."[6]

Because of Wright's intense interest in golf, her young adulthood was a bit different than other young people her age.

"I did feel different as an aspiring golfer as a youngster. I never had the feeling that I was treated differently because I was a woman athlete. Being a golfer was not really being an 'athlete'. You were a golfer. I was never treated [differently from others in] any way in high school. I was there for an education. I do not know if the other students at the school knew that I played golf.

"My life was at the golf course. My father got me a car when I was 16, and I spent all of my time at the course. I knew no one my age who played golf. There were no junior programs, with the exception of one tournament a year sponsored by the Brietbard Association. All my best friends were in golf, and all of them were much older than me.

"Bertha and Hank Wohlers, members at the San Diego Country Club took me under their wing and played with me, and encouraged me. At La Jolla Country Club, Gene Littler's mother, Dorothy, and several others – Margaret Allen, Mrs. Coe and others whose names I have forgotten were wonderful to me."[7]

Like other youngsters Wright had childhood heroes, but hers were all golfers – at least two were actually her friends.

"I lived golf, breathed golf, and thought of not much else. My heroes were Gene Littler and Billy Casper in person (who Wright knew through her association at La Jolla Country Club). Through magazines, Louise Suggs, Patty Berg and Marge Ferrie – the California State Champion – were my idols, and symbolized my goals."[8]

At a time when high school sports were available to young women on a limited basis, there was no opportunity for Wright to play high school golf. That, however, was not much of a deterrent to Wright's plans. In 1952, she won the U.S. Girls Junior Championship, and in 1954, the World Amateur Championship. Also in 1954, Wright was the low amateur in the U.S. Women's Open.

Those victories challenged Wright to move to the next level. She was ready to test her game against the players, who had been her idols, and now were part of the fledgling LPGA Tour. It was then that she ran into a snag.

"I was ready to play professionally. My father was not that enthusiastic. He believed that women should have something that would offer security if they were unmarried. To him, security meant a teaching certificate. He insisted that I attend Stanford. Stanford is a great school, but my mind was on golf."[9]

After one year at Stanford, the inner drive that pushed Wright to excel overwhelmed her and Wright made a "deal" with her father.

"My father agreed to give me $1000 to finance a try at the Tour. If I did not do well, and ran out of money, it was back to school.

"In my first tournament I won $500. That was good enough for me. Although my father was still a bit skeptical, I was not about to quit. At that point, I knew I would succeed."[10]

Succeed she did. Between 1955 and 1964, Wright established herself as a force on the LPGA Tour. She won four U.S. Women's Opens in that period – 1958, 1959, 1961 (narrowly missing four U.S. Open wins in a row when she faltered on the last day of the 1960 tournament, and finished third to Betsy Rawls) and 1964. In 1958 and 1961, Wright won the U.S. Women's Open and the LPGA Championship in the same year. She is the only woman golfer to accomplish that feat twice.

In 1963, Wright won 13 of the 32 Tour events played. In that year, Wright won 40.6% of all the tournaments played.

By 1964, Wright had proven her instincts right in the $1000 deal with her father. More importantly, she had achieved what she set out to do – at age 29; she was unquestionably the best woman golfer in the world.

Growth

Success for Wright was complete, but it was not overnight. Although Wright did win at least one tournament per season between 1956 and 1969, it was not until 1958 that Wright began to take command as the Tour's leading player. She joined the Tour at age 19, and Wright needed to do some "growing up."

Wright's growth as a player was quick for two reasons. First, she was in her element. She was doing what she wanted to do, and her intelligence gave her the ability to intuitively understand that if she wanted to achieve her goals she still had some things to learn. Second, she did not resist the learning process.

Accomplishing most of what she set out to do, Wright, after suffering a severe wrist injury, in 1965, decided to "semi-retire" from the Tour. Her plan was to continue the education she had started at Stanford by matriculating as a sophomore in psychology at Southern Methodist University (at the time, she made her home in Dallas). Wright planned to attend classes during the fall and winter months, and play on Tour in the summer. The "semi-retirement" lasted only one year.

"I like to go to school. But, when I went back in 1965, the students were not what I expected. They were all younger than me, and they did not seem to have the same understanding of responsibility that I had."[12]

Wright had dedicated her life to one specific, intensely personal goal. She always understood realizing that goal was her personal responsibility. When she returned to the academic world, having spent the previous 10 years highly focused and dedicated to hard work, it seems it was difficult for Wright to accept the "laissez faire" attitude of the mid-1960's college student.

The 1960's were a time of discontent – especially on college campuses. College students often were more interested in expressing their discontent than in setting, and achieving, personal goals. Wright had been part of a micro-society (professional golf) in which everyone was just as focused and dedicated as she was.

The essence of Wright's personality centered on seriousness and responsibility. To be in a situation in which people devalued these qualities was unacceptable to her.

Wright's venture into academic life was another period of growth. She learned that not everyone had the same values and worldview that she had. Wright now understood that for her to be comfortable and effective, she must be around people who saw life as she saw it. Perhaps, she also learned that, at age 30, she was not looking for "retirement," but a new challenge. In the world of the 1960's it was difficult for her to find that challenge. Responsibility, hard work and dedication were not part of the 60's mentality. The one familiar place that Wright was sure would offer her what she wanted was the Tour. Therefore, Wright turned again to golf.

The Best

Between 1966 and 1969 Wright added fifteen more LPGA Tour victories to boost her winning record to 81 events. In 1970 health problems began to affect her ability to play golf. Wright had developed an extreme sensitivity to the sun, and she was diagnosed with neuromas (abnormal growth of nerve fibers) in her feet. Between 1970 and 1979 her tournament playing schedule stayed below ten.

Wright's health kept her from winning any events between 1969 and 1972. But, there would be one more win for Wright. Although it would be her last, it would also be symbolic.

In 1973, Wright won the Colgate Dinah Shore Winner's Circle Championship. The Dinah Shore event was only in its second year, but it would change women's golf forever and bring the LPGA to its rightful position as an "equal sister" of the PGA Tour and all other professional sports. In 1983, the Dinah Shore would be designated as a LPGA "Major." Eventually, the event would develop a tradition, respect and significance that would make it known as the "Women's Masters."

Wright's 1973 win at the Dinah Shore gave her career a significance it did not have previously, and one that was fitting for a player of Wright's magnitude. The Dinah Shore win allowed Wright to be connected, not only with women's golf's past, but linked her directly to the future. She had competed against all of the LPGA founding players and met unparalleled success. With the Dinah Shore win, she had shown that she could also compete against future generations of golfers – and win. She had passed the test of athletic greatness. She had demonstrated the ability to compete and succeed, against all generations that spanned her athletic life. The win at the Dinah Shore gave Wright the assurance of what she had always wanted. She was the best. There were no qualifications. There were no asterisks in the record book. For all players to come, the standard to shoot for would be Wright's.

Along with the Dinah Shore, two other events give Wright's career a sense of timelessness. One occurred in 1954 at the U.S. Women's Open. Wright was playing in the event as an amateur. It was her first appearance as an Open competitor. She was 19 years old. On the last day (on which two rounds were played), Wright (who was in contention) was paired with Babe Didrikson Zaharias (who was also in

> ### MICKEY WRIGHT
>
> **Professional Highlights**
>
> **Shares record for most U.S. Open victories (four)**
>
> **From 1959-68 won 79 events for an average of 7.9 victories per year**
>
> **Thirteen victories in 1963 (out of 32 events) is the Tours leading winning percentage at 40.6%**

contention). It was the last Open in which Zaharias would play. Zaharias won. The 19-year-old Wright broke 80 in each round, hit her drives even with the "Babe's" all day long, and finished fourth.

Although the two were not close friends, and certainly represented opposite poles in terms of personality, the incident takes on significance as a symbolic "passing of the torch." This is especially true, since Wright had so often been referred to as "the next 'Babe.'"

The second event took place 25 years later, in 1979. For all intents and purposes it was Wright's last season on Tour (She would play only two events in 1980). Wright was playing in the Coca-Cola Classic in Upper Montclair, New Jersey. It was one of her last tournaments. The weather that week was typical of northern New Jersey in early May. Every day brought soaking rain and chilly temperatures. Wright sloshed through the wet fairways wearing sneakers because her foot problems had reached a level that eliminated the possibility of wearing golf shoes.

Even with the end of her career in sight, Wright's swing was as solid that week as it had been in 1964. She was hitting her trademark towering iron shots close to the pin, and she was not only in the hunt, but also very close to the lead. After the final round she found herself in a five-way playoff for the championship title. One of the players in that playoff was a third year Tour member who was beginning to cause a stir in golf circles. She was a young, brown-haired woman with a quick smile – Nancy Lopez.[13]

The memory is so vivid for Wright; it's as though the years since that day have melted away.

"I was 44 or 45 at the time. I was tired. The rain had kept us on the course close to eight hours. We got to that final par-3 of the playoff, it was just Nancy, and me left. I put my tee shot on the green in good position and made par. I stood there and watched her make that 25-footer to beat me. Right at that moment, I knew it was the changing of the guard, and it brought a feeling of sadness."[14]

It was the second "changing of the guard" in which Wright had been involved. She had eagerly accepted the responsibility for being "the best" from the best – Zaharias – in 1954. In sadness, 25 years later, Wright gave that responsibility to the next in the line of "bests" – Lopez.

Who is the "best of bests?" A very good case can be made for Wright. Zaharias accumulated only 31 wins (Although her life was cut short at age 42, it seems impossible that she would have reached an over 80 wins mark.). Lopez currently has 48 wins, and at age 40, reaching Wright's mark seems unlikely. Lopez has yet to win a U.S. Women's Open, although that possibility does exist. Wright accomplished all of those things – 82 wins, four U.S. Open titles, and a victory at the Dinah Shore. She accomplished them by age 45.

The only other contender is a player of Wright's generation – Kathy Whitworth. Whitworth's 88 victories is a record that may never be challenged, but among those victories there is neither a U.S. Open title nor a Dinah Shore Championship.

Suspended in Time

Today Mickey Wright applies her intelligence, intensity and sense of responsibility to challenging the world of investment. She lives on a golf course in a quiet neighborhood, in the town of Port St. Lucie, Florida. Wright involves herself in the stock market, cooking and reading. She often hits golf balls, but seldom plays golf.

In a 1994 interview, Wright described herself as being "suspended in time." She explained it this way.

"There is really nothing that can give me what golf gave me. I can never replace it. I am grateful just to have had it. It's necessary to go to another reality, one that includes watching the stock market, cooking my favorite meals and still finding the joy in hitting golf balls."[15]

In a more recent interview, Wright elaborated on her feelings.

"I feel somewhat of an anachronism, in that I relish golf as it used to be. I still play with 35 year old clubs; I still wear 60's style glasses, and really still see golf as something you enjoy the joy of, not how much money you can make from it. I see it as a sport and an art form, not as big show business."[16]

Although Wright has respect for today's players – especially Lopez and Laura Davies – she willingly shares her thoughts on golf's current trends.

"In 1978 I was paired with Nancy Lopez in the first round of a tournament in South Carolina, and she shot 80 that day. Yet, I was never so impressed by anyone. I knew she would be the next great golfer because of the way she handled herself during a bad round and the look in her eyes when she finished. Whatever 'it' is, she had it."[17]

Perhaps what Wright saw in Lopez was what had always been most important to her – personal responsibility and intensity.

In an interview with Rhonda Glenn for *Golf Magazine*, Wright answered the question of which player she felt had the greatest potential to take the role of "outright best."

"Laura Davies. She's the only one I have seen [with the potential] since I left the Tour, or when I was on it. She's gone a step beyond the long hitters of my time – [JoAnne] Carner, me and whoever else was long.... I haven't seen Laura play enough and I don't think she's played enough to know if she has all the other things. She looks like it, though."[18]

In that same interview Wright commented on the LPGA Tour.

"Monetarily, LPGA officials probably have done everything possible, but in the pure sense, they've hurt women's golf by playing the courses so short and by not allowing potentially great players to fulfill their potentials.... If the pros had to hit every club in the bag and take three shots to get to every par five, which is why they're called par five's, three to get there and two putts, then the truly fine players would win the most. Those who have the potential to be the best would have a chance to fulfill that potential."[19]

As it was in 1946, Wright's concept of golf is still that of self-expression and realizing personal potential. What about her strong interest in responsibility? Perhaps her comments about Tour prize money shed some light.

"Apparently no one under 40 realizes that in the mid-50's, school teachers started at $2,000 a year and secretaries made $50 a week. In my first year on Tour (1955), I made about $7,000. So I was well paid for what I did. It was enough to allow me to retire at age 35....

"What I won is about 50 times less than the amount pros get now. I think they're grossly overpaid; all athletes are. It's gotten to the ridiculous stage. I've been saying that for 10 years. The idea that an athlete is worth more than a research scientist! I thought things were a little screwed up when I came out on Tour. I could make $7,000, and if I'd done what my father wanted and gotten my teaching certificate, I would have started at $2,000 a year with a college degree. I thought it was distorted, even then."[21]

The biggest mystery surrounding Wright's career is why she left the Tour when she did with so much of her playing life ahead of her. The answer may lie in her acknowledging the distortion that she saw. Wright's physical condition certainly played a part. But, she also left college when she realized her values did not apply in that world. Perhaps she foresaw that, in sports, the distortion of values would only grow, and so would her discomfort.

Wright has found a life that closely resembles her early childhood in pre-war San Diego, and for her it is satisfying because it conforms to her standards. When asked if she would do the whole thing over again – exactly as she had done it – Wright's answer was quick.

"In a New York minute."[21]

Chapter 7

One Determined Lady...
Kathy Whitworth

Whit." It is the name by which Kathy Whitworth is known to her fellow Tour players, and it fits Whitworth perfectly. "Whit" is direct and concise, strong yet simple, and implies respect. It reflects the determination that pervades Whits' personality, golf game and life. "Kathy" is nice – a term that can also describe Whitworth – but "Whit" is a winner. And, that is the essence of what Whitworth has always been.

Whit's determination was tested at the very start of her career. At age 19, Whit won the New Mexico Amateur State Championship. The win opened the doors to "big time" golf as it existed in 1958. As an up and coming player, Whit was invited to play exhibition matches with LPGA Tour stars.

"Wilson Sporting Goods often sent Betsy Rawls and Mickey Wright to small towns to play exhibitions," Whitworth said. "A young player who showed some promise was big stuff back then, especially in our part of the West, so I was invited to play in those exhibitions. It was nothing to jump in the car and drive 400 miles to play golf, especially if you could play with the real stars of the game. It became like a regular tour. Every time Mickey came to that area, there I'd be."[1]

After a match in Amarillo, Texas, Whit had a chance to talk privately with Wright, and she looked to the game's best player for advice about joining the tour. Wright, not all that impressed with young Whit's game, was not encouraging.

"We went into the pro's office and I told her I was very seriously thinking of turning pro," Whitworth said. "Mickey thought, however, that, at nineteen, I was still too young for the tour. She advised me to wait a year and to continue to work with Harvey (Penick) on my swing."[2]

That same year, Whit was invited to play in the prestigious Titleholders Championship, the LPGA Tour's equivalent to the Masters, in Augusta, Georgia. Whit and her mother traveled 42 hours by bus to get to the event. The first person Whit encountered as she walked out to the course was Wright.

"What in the world are you doing here?" Wright said. It was not a reception that built Whit's confidence, and the young player asked herself the same question. Her play in the event confirmed Wright's opinion that Whit's game needed more work.

Whit had a group of backers ready to finance her start on Tour, and the young player was torn between Wright's advice and her own desire to get on with what she was determined to do with her life.

"I believed [Mickey]," Whitworth said. "If she said it, then this was the way to go. But, when we discussed my career at home, Mother and Dad said, 'Well, let's just do it.' I agreed. And that was it."[3]

Whit joined the LPGA in 1959 and played her first event, the Mayfair Open in Sanford, Florida, in January of that year.

In 1983, after Whit had broken Wright's record of 81 tournament wins, and on the eve of breaking Sam Snead's win record of 84, her parents, Morris and Dama Whitworth were asked what most contributed to their daughter's success. "Luck," Morris said. But, Dama, who had made that long trip to Augusta in 1958 and traveled with her daughter at the very start of her career, saw it from a different perspective, "Determination," she said.[4]

Kathy Whitworth was born in Monahans, Texas on September 27, 1939. She was the youngest of three girls in the Whitworth family. Too young to understand or feel the effects of World War II, Whitworth was a product of a small town environment and a large extended family.

"A lot of people have asked me how to achieve success," Whitworth said. "I tell them, first you have to get yourself born in a small town."[5]

Within a year of Kathy's birth, the Whitworth family moved back to their hometown, Jal, New Mexico. Jal, with a population below 3000, is a community near the Western border of Texas. An oil and gas town, Jal's refineries produced most of the natural gas used in the Southwest. Kathy's maternal grandparents were homesteaders in the area. Her grandfather owned a grocery store and was a farmer. Kathy's paternal grandmother, Jessie Whitworth, owned the town's hardware store, which Kathy's parents eventually bought and operated. Kathy's father was active in town politics and served three terms as Jal's Mayor. Kathy's mother, one of nine children, was active in church work and community and charity organizations.

"At the time, my cousins and aunts and uncles made up about half the population of Jal," Whitworth said. "You could hardly talk to us about anybody in town – they were probably our relatives."[6]

Active in all sports, Kathy's first competitive experience was as a member of the Jal High School tennis team.

"I was fairly proficient at tennis," Whitworth said. "In fact, that is how I started playing golf. Some of my tennis friends one day insisted that we play golf."[7]

With no clubs of her own, Kathy used her grandfather's clubs. A decent golfer who consistently shot rounds in the 80's, Kathy's grandfather was known in Jal by the nickname his granddaughter would eventually make famous – "Whit."

"I'll never forget that first round," Whitworth said. "I was terrible, but that made golf a real challenge. Because other sports had come to me so easily, I was fascinated with this game I could not master."[8]

Whit spent the first year of her golf career walking the fairways and putting the sandy greens of Jal Country Club alone.

"I was fifteen when I played my first round of golf," Whitworth said. "I was so terrible that I played by myself for an entire year."[9]

After that first year Morris and Dama Whitworth knew Kathy was serious about golf. The family joined Jal Country Club so Kathy would have a place to play and practice. Whit's first "fellow competitors" were her aunt and uncle, George and Nell Addison. Both were fine golfers.

"George was a wonderful athlete, a scratch golfer with a beautiful touch around the greens," Whitworth said. "He won almost everything in our area. Nell was a good player too. She won the club championship and a lot of local tournaments."[10]

Whit began to learn the game in earnest when she started taking lessons with Dode Forrester at Hobbs Country Club, about 40 miles from Jal. But, her earliest mentor was Jal Country Club professional, Hardy Loudermilk. Loudermilk made the significant difference in Whit's development. He introduced her to the renowned and revered teacher of the game, Harvey Penick.

"Hardy taught me a lot," Whitworth said. "Then he did something that showed unusual generosity and humility and caused me to take what was probably the most important step of my career. When I was seventeen, Hardy said, 'I don't know enough to take you where you need to be.'"[11]

Loudermilk called Harvey Penick in Austin and made an appointment for Whit. Dama and Whit drove 450 miles to work with Penick. Penick would work with Whit while Dama took notes. After a lesson, Penick would talk to Loudermilk by phone to discuss the things that Whit was working on. The young player and her mother would drive the 450 miles back home and Loudermilk would supervise Whit's practice session according to Penick's instructions.

That year, at age seventeen, Whit won her first event, the 1957 New Mexico State Women's Championship. Two years later, Whit made the decision to take on the best golfers in the world by joining the LPGA Tour.

The New Kid on the Block

When Whit joined the Tour she was young and shy; and her game was immature. But, she had two great advantages. The first advantage was her relationship with a great teacher of the swing, Penick. The second advantage was Whit's understanding that she had a lot to learn about playing the game. She quickly realized she could learn from the players she was competing with every day.

"I loved watching these great women golfers play," Whitworth said. "I learned a lot by studying them carefully, particularly Patty Berg, Mickey Wright, Betsy Rawls and Louise Suggs. I'd watch Louise and wonder, 'How is she so consistent? Why is she always able to hit her shots the same way? Why does she have the same routine while putting, chipping, and hitting full shots?'

"Betsy had a great mind and her short game was exceptional," Whitworth continued. "She could get the ball up and down from almost anywhere. In one event at

> **KATHY WHITWORTH**
>
> **Began playing golf: age 15**
>
> **First tournament win: 1957, New Mexico State Amateur**
>
> **First LPGA victory: 1962**
>
> **Last LPGA victory: 1985**

Esmerelda Golf course in Spokane, Washington, Betsy cut the corner on a par-4 dogleg a little too closely and the ball landed on the side of a hill. We weren't even sure we could find the ball. When we did find it, Betsy analyzed the situation and proceeded to create some type of shot, managed to hit the ball close to the green, then chipped it close to the hole and made her putt for par. There was no quit – as long as she saw some way to do it. You could just see her mind clicking away. That was early in my career and it made a big impression on me."[12]

Whit had all the advantages a young player could ask for, but the amount of time required to gain experience and maturity was a bit more than she had bargained for. During that first year she became so discouraged that she thought about quitting.

"I was playing terribly and not making any money," Whitworth said. "I drove home to discuss the future with Mother and Dad. They convinced me to give it a little more time, to keep trying. The next week, in Asheville, North Carolina, I tied with two other players for the last prize check. We split $100. I had won $33. I called home, feeling as good as if I'd won the tournament."[13]

Whit's check for $33 kept her coming back. For the next two years Whit and her game were still in the formative stage. Whit ended the 1959 season with an unimpressive scoring average of 80.30. She practiced constantly, but more importantly continued to watch – and learn from – the other players. By 1961 Whit's scoring average was down to 76.05, and in both 1960 and 1961 she collected second place prize money in at least one event.

It was in 1962 that the practice and observation paid off. Her golf game was finally solid, and she made the breakthrough that every great player makes – she learned how to win. She won not once that year, but twice. Her first win was the Kelly Girl Open and her second was the Phoenix Thunderbird Open. Once Whit learned to win, she never forgot. For the next sixteen seasons – from 1962 through 1978 – Whit won at least one event every year. Between 1962 and 1985 she won an event every year except two – 1979 and 1980. During those years Whit was ranked number one on the money list eight times, and until 1974 she never ranked lower than third.

The shy, small town girl, with only a slightly better than average golf game, had transformed herself into a confident, competent woman with a golf game that was the best in the world. But, unlike the Horatio Alger stories, Whit's rise from golf's rags to riches was not consistently smooth.

She hit two very big "bumps" along the way, and each time she had to look deep inside herself to start over.

In 1964 Whit found herself a star in a game that was beginning to get some notice. She was making money. The small town girl was, at least in golf circles, a real celebrity. Whit came off the 1963 season ranked number two on the Tour money list. In the short span of her five-year career she had accumulated ten LPGA victories – eight of them in 1963. By the last event of the 1964 season, Whit had not won a tournament, and her game seemed to be deteriorating.

The Tour finished that year with an event in San Antonio. Whit's life-long mentor, Hardy Loudermilk had moved to San Antonio, and just before the event began, the two had dinner together. Loudermilk listened as Whit talked about how her season had been filled with bad luck, and uncharacteristically "whined" about her poor play. After she finished, Loudermilk asked only one question. "Did it ever occur to you that you have a big head?"

The question hit Whit, always modest, like a ton of bricks.

"I was destroyed," Whitworth said. "Of course he was right. It was one of the great lessons of my life."[14]

Whit learned the lesson quickly and well. She won that event – the San Antonio Civitan Open – finished the year third on the money list and, in the next four consecutive seasons, she finished as the Tour's leading money winner. Fourteen years later, at the end of the 1978 season, Whit had won 80 LPGA tournaments, had been the leading money winner eight times, was Player of the Year seven times, and was the Vare Trophy winner (for the lowest scoring average) seven times. She had been inducted into the LPGA Hall of Fame; an honor she considers the highest the sport has to offer. She was 39 years old and a legend.

Then suddenly, like a marathon runner, she "hit the wall." Everything became not just a run to the finish line, but a struggle to survive.

In 1979, for the first time in eighteen years, she did not win an event. Whit was ready to consider retiring. The small family, "we're all in this together" atmosphere of the early Tour had been replaced by a slick, business-like "big-time" sports environment. The Tour was in a growth spurt, and it was no longer a place where a small town girl could feel comfortable. Whit – who had helped the Tour grow and then seen most of her colleagues and friends from those early days retire – was feeling the pressure created by this new "big city" sports organization. It had taken a toll on her game. To add to the problem, Whit began to tinker with her swing. The swing change was not a step in a positive direction.

"It got worse and worse," Whitworth said. "It got to where I just hated to go out to the golf course because I knew I couldn't play anymore. There was panic and fear because I didn't know where the ball was going or whether I'd even hit it. To actually fear playing golf after having done so well is a horrible experience."[15]

Whit knew this was not like her slump in 1964 – the result of an immature ego. This was the result of everything changing – the Tour, her swing and Whit herself. But, Whit had experienced the same discouragement before – in her very first season on Tour, and she had thought about quitting then as well. As she had done two decades earlier, Whit went to the only place where she could sort things out – home.

"Out here it's run, run, run and go, go, go," Whitworth said. "You don't have a chance to sit back and reflect on it. You don't have time to really know where you're going or how you're going to get there or even recognize when you get there what you've got."[16]

Back in Jal, Kathy, Dama and Morris talked things out. In her book, *The History of Women's Golf*, Rhonda Glenn, quotes Whitworth's account of the conversations with her parents.

"Dad has a lot of common sense," Whitworth said. "He parallels things so I can understand. He never told me what to do, but he made me see both sides and told me what I might think about. I'm still their little girl, you know, and if anything is wrong they're always interested and want to help."[17]

After spending some time at her home in Dallas, Whit wanted to play again. The second step to a comeback was a trip to see Harvey Penick. Under his guidance her game began to reform itself. Whit played the 1980 Tour season, but it was another year without a win.

"I was looking forward to the 1981 season," Whitworth said. "I hadn't run out of motivation. I still wanted to play but I hadn't been able to play. Now I felt like I had turned it around. It was just a question of doing it enough times so that I wouldn't fall back into old habits."[18]

Whit started the 1981 season well. Her scoring average was down, and in May she broke the two-year winless streak with a play-off victory over Alice Ritzman at the Coca-Cola Classic in Ridgewood, New Jersey. She also finished third in the U.S. Open – a title she has never won. The U.S. Open third place finish and its $9000 paycheck made her the first LPGA player to go over the million-dollar mark in career earnings. Pat Bradley won that Open, but Whit's accomplishment was quite a story. As she finished her final round, she was met on the 18th green by a contingent of players popping champagne bottles, and ready to celebrate with the LPGA's first millionaire.

The slump behind her, Whit was ready to make more golf history. The win in the Coca-Cola Classic was her 81st, just one short of Mickey Wright's record of 82 LPGA wins. The next challenge for her would be to break that record and then close in on the victory record of 84 wins held by Sam Snead. With a win in the 1982 season, Whit broke Mickey Wright's record. Then two years later, in 1984 she surpassed Sam Snead when she recorded her 85th win. Whit had become the player to hold the most professional tournament titles in all of golf – man or woman. In 1985, at age 46, Whit got her 88th, and last, LPGA victory. Those 88 wins remain the record other tour players shoot for.

Whit continued to play on Tour until 1991. In a career that spanned five decades, Whit never finished lower than 31st on the money list. Her close observation of her fellow players when she first arrived on tour had paid off. She had learned from each of them, and then used those lessons to surpass their achievements. Like Betsy Rawls, who had so impressed the young Whitworth in 1959, "there was no quit" in Whit either.

Eighty-Eight

One of the legacies of Kathy Whitworth is her record of eighty-eight career victories. Along with being a remarkable accomplishment, the achievement represents the end of male dominance in the game of golf. Whit, and her eighty-eight wins, define the birth of a new era in women's golf. Whitworth's accomplishment brought women's golf fully out of the "side-show" era and into a time when it is considered a "main event." It forced the entire sports world to take women's golf seriously.

> ### Kathy Whitworth
>
> ### Career Highlights
>
> **Leading money winner eight times**
> **Player of the Year seven times**
> **Vare Trophy winner seven times**
>
> **First LPGA player to surpass**
> **one million dollars in**
> **career earnings (1981)**
>
> **All-time male and female**
> **record wins: 88**

Yet in typical Whitworth fashion, Whit deflects the significance.

"I can't say I did this all by myself," Whitworth said. "I had some wonderful people in my life. I practiced and played, but I had a lot of help. I never thought of myself as a great player. I don't think we thought in those terms. You just do what you want to do and enjoy the challenge."[19]

Whit also has a tendency to share the honor.

She beat Alice Ritzman at the 1981 Coca-Cola Classic, ending a two-year winless streak and gaining her 81st victory, putting her just one behind Mickey Wright. Whit received several congratulatory letters after that win, but there was only one that she wanted to keep. It was from Mickey Wright.

"I know there's no feeling quite like a win after a dry haul," Wright wrote. "You're truly a great player. You've worked very hard for many years and most justly deserve every good thing that comes your way."

Then Wright commented on the pressure Whitworth would be under to achieve more victories – wins that would exceed the record she held at eight-two.

"I would think if your sights are set way beyond that, at ninety or even 100, they [the pressures] might not bother you," Wright wrote. "I would want to set a record of my own that no one would touch, and I would think ninety wins would do it."[20]

Wright, who almost 25 years earlier suggested Whitworth choose school over the Tour, had graciously said, "don't stop now" – and Whitworth did not. The next year she tied Wright's record and then broke it. Whit was just as gracious in return. She sent Wright a dozen roses, and in her comments to the press acknowledged the significance of Wright's achievement.

"The win is great," Whitworth said. "I am not putting it down. But, as far as Mickey is concerned, it doesn't demean her or her record at all. I think she respects me and she knows how much I respect her. So many times we played together going head to head."[21]

The accomplishment of 88 wins is only one part of Whitworth's legacy. The other part of the legacy is the clear understanding of athletic competition that both Whitworth and Wright showed as Whitworth challenged and then broke Wright's record. These two legendary women showed that they could not only perform under pressure, but that they could respect each other and their role as competitors. They demonstrated that women do understand the essence of athletics and that women, as well as men could be athletes.

The Bridge Between Then and Now

Kathy Whitworth leaves one other legacy. It is her role as a key transition figure between the early years of LPGA and today's tour. Whit's career spanned five decades, and her "sphere of influence" in terms of her relationships with players spanned almost the entire history of women's professional golf. Whit played with the original legends, and, thirty years later, she played with future legends. Babe Zaharias is the one player Whitworth never knew personally.

The history of the LPGA played out before Whit's eyes, and she is acutely aware of her role as both an observer and chronicler.

"When I look back on my life in golf, what satisfies me most is that the length of my career has given me the opportunity to play with so many of history's greatest players," Whitworth said. "I was there when the greats of yesteryear were playing, so I got to know Patty Berg, Sam Snead, Byron Nelson, Louise Suggs, Betsy Rawls, Mickey Wright, Betty Jameson, Mary Lena Faulk and Jackie Pung. In my own era, I've played with the greats like Jack Nicklaus, Carol Mann, Sandra Haynie, Donna Caponi, Marlene Hagge and Judy Rankin. I know an era of golfers who will still be playing when I quit. I'm sure Nancy Lopez will be there as well as Beth Daniel, Betsy King and Pat Bradley. I also know the younger players who are just coming into their own, the champions of the future. Years after I retire, some of the people I've met will still be playing and I'll be able to watch their careers."[22]

Whitworth is currently involved with some of those "champions of the future." She teaches and mentors young women who are part of a golf development program in Japan. Perhaps this involvement with future players allows her to talk wistfully about the LPGA's past, and comment honestly on the differences between the Tour's past and its present.

"Those were great times." Whitworth said. "Our purses were meager by today's standards, but you could make a living, and the top players made a very good living. Of necessity, because we were always on the road and there were only a few dozen players, we were closer too. After a tournament, we'd always sit around together and have a party. Usually the winner would buy the drinks because she was the only one who had any money."[23]

One of Whit's favorite stories about those "great times" involves fellow Hall of Famer Betty Jameson. Jameson was noted for her peripheral vision, and because of it other players in her group could easily distract her.

"Betty had a reputation of moving her playing partners around," Whitworth said. "She'd stand over a putt, head anchored, eyes looking straight at the ball, and without moving, she'd gesture frantically for some player thirty yards away to move.

"Years later, Betty remarked, 'Too bad I never played with you,'" Whitworth continued. "'Yes you did,' I replied. 'I just stayed in the trees on every hole so I wouldn't bother you.'"[24]

Because she lived a large part of golf's history, Whit can accurately relate what it was like to be on Tour in those early days.

"The courses were never closed down," Whitworth said. "We played our practice rounds between the members; they teed off behind us during a tournament, and we shared their locker room.

"The sport was the thing," Whitworth continued. "We enjoyed the competition and money was a necessary evil. We never thought of making a lot of money, neither in golf nor in other jobs. The opportunities for women were very limited in all fields."[25]

Whit is one of the few players who comment openly and honestly about what it was like to be a woman and an athlete.

"When I turned professional, women playing sport were not looked on as ladylike," Whitworth said. "My family backed me because they thought I should express my talent, and they felt it was possible to be a lady and still play golf. The stigma was there, but we were a strong group; so we survived.

"Some of the people I've met have asked me if I have regrets," Whitworth wrote in her book, *Golf for Women*. "They have been concerned that my involvement in my career has caused me to give up the idea of having a family. It wasn't any great sacrifice. I didn't give up a family. I decided I didn't want one. I freely made the decision to dedicate myself to professional golf. No one held a gun to my head; the hours that I spent on the practice tee were hours I wanted to spend on the practice tee. I wanted to be a good player, I wanted to get better, and I didn't mind putting in the hours to get there."[26]

Whit played at a time when the players themselves administered the LPGA. Her impact was not only as a player, but also as a leader of the organization. She served three terms as President of the organization – two terms in the mid-1970's and again in 1989. She guided the Tour through some of its most difficult transitions and her opinions about the responsibility of players to the organization remains strong.

"When you become a top player, the responsibility of leadership lands in your lap, whether you like it or not. We've had a sort of backsliding in that area in the LPGA, and I'd like to see more of our good young players assume the responsibility.

"Today's players have a different attitude than the players of years past," Whitworth continued. "This is not a criticism, it's just a fact. In earlier days, we played every week because we wanted to play. The money wasn't that great. We had to play just to make a living. Even if we won, we weren't going to make a fortune. The pace wasn't as fast, the pressure wasn't as intense, but you played for the love of it. When you see today's players quoted, it is evident that money is very much on their minds. Today, money is a big motivation, which is why we have so many more players."[27]

One More Challenge

In 1990, Whit retired from LPGA Tour competition for good. Her retirement would bring another challenge. The financial management company she had invested with for several years filed for bankruptcy, and eventually its president was convicted of fraud. The incident left Whit facing the most serious financial challenge of her life. At age 52, she lost most of her savings and the home in which she planned to retire.

Whit faced the problem much like she faced the two playing slumps that threatened to end her career. She turned to what she did best – golf. And she worked as hard as she could. In the past eight years she has rebuilt a portion of her financial reserves, and is now involved in several stable golf business ventures.

The drive that Kathy Whitworth brought to the LPGA Tour almost forty years ago is still serving her well. In a recent television interview on the Golf Channel, Whitworth was asked how she developed that competitive drive.

"I don't know where I got my competitive drive," Whitworth said.

She thought a moment, shifted in her chair and then leaned forward intently.

"What you really do is put yourself on the line," Whit said. "You simply can't be afraid to try really hard." [28]

Chapter 8

The Comeback Kid...
Sandra Haynie

Twelve-year-old Austin, Texas native Sandra Haynie had been playing golf for only a year. Interested and talented in all sports, the young Haynie excelled almost immediately as a golfer. With only one year's experience behind her, she was invited to play a practice round in the 1955 Texas Open with the greatest woman golfer and athlete who had ever lived, Babe Zaharias. It was a young athlete's dream.

"Babe hit it so far and was such an impressive athlete," Haynie said. "I went home and said, 'That's what I want to be, a professional golfer.'"[1]

By September of the following year, Zaharias was dead, succumbing to cancer. The teenage Haynie never let the dream that began with the 18-holes played with Zaharias die. Six years later in 1961, Haynie joined the LPGA Tour. She was seventeen years old.

In a career that spanned almost 30 years, Haynie became the eighth inductee to the Hall of Fame. She accumulated 42 victories, and was one of only four players to win the U.S. Open and LPGA championship in the same year. Twice she was sidelined for a year or more with medical problems, but twice she came back to play, and win again.

Haynie would make one other contribution to sports history, and it adds an element of harmonious continuity to Haynie's life story. Much like her brief exposure to Babe Zaharias who focused Haynie on a life goal, Haynie would help, to a much greater extent, another young woman sports star find the path that would lead to "superstardom." That young star was Martina Navratilova.

An only child, Sandra Haynie was born in Fort Worth, Texas on June 4, 1943. By the time Haynie was twelve, the family had moved to Austin where her father was involved in developing a country club.

Sandra began playing golf at age 11, since golf for the Haynies was a family activity.

"I started playing golf at 11, through my father, who was a scratch golfer," Haynie said. "My mother, who did some secretarial work, was also a golfer. We played together."[2]

Haynie's first teacher was A.G. Mitchell. The approach Mitchell took was to train the "whole" athlete not just focus on mechanics.

"I learned how to use my mind, as much as I learned how to use my muscles," Haynie said. "I always picture what I am going to do, and I always like to step behind the ball and look at that picture. I used to get teased on tour because I didn't practice a lot, but I didn't have to, since a lot of my preparation was mental."[3]

At age fourteen in 1957, Haynie won her first amateur event, the Texas Publinx Championship. She followed that with the 1958 and 1959 Texas Amateur Championship, and in 1960 won the Trans-Mississpppi. It was time to do what she had planned when she was twelve.

"I left school at 17, turning professional in December, 1960," Haynie said. "I wanted to play the tour, and I was convinced I would make it, but I had no expectation of winning a tournament. Although I was not intimidated by the women on tour, I had a great respect for players like Mickey Wright and Betsy Rawls because they were so good."[4]

The First Tour

Haynie's first full year on tour was 1961. Her best finish was 10th and for the year she won $3,709.

"In the 1960's you played golf because you loved it, and in the hope that someday the tour would improve," Haynie said. "The money only meant that I could support myself, that I could take a trip or do what I wanted."[5]

It did not take long for Haynie to break into the winner's circle. Her first victory came at home in the Austin Civitan Open, but it wasn't the fact that she had won in her hometown that made the win meaningful. It was the player she beat.

"[It was] the excitement of beating Mickey Wright by one shot," Haynie said.[6]

From that point on Haynie won at least one event every year until 1975. The defining moment of her career, however, occurred in 1974 when she became, along with Mickey Wright, one of two women to win both the LPGA championship and the U.S. Open in the same year.

SANDRA HAYNIE

Began playing golf: age 11

First tournament win:1957, Texas Publinx Championship

First LPGA victory:1962

Last LPGA victory: 1982

1974

The year 1974 was one of discontent for the LPGA Tour. The other highly visible group of women professional athletes, the tennis players, had been embroiled in a fight to increase their prize money to make it more comparable to men in the sport. The philosophical repercussions of what was happening in tennis began to filter to the women playing the LPGA Tour.

Since the women's and men's golf tours were two separate organizations, financial parity for women professional golfers could not be approached the same way it had been in tennis. But, the women of the LPGA began to look critically at their organization, especially the prize money. The players focused their attention on the one event that was run by the same organization for both women and men – the U.S. Open, run by the USGA. The women's U.S. Open purse in 1974 was $40,000. The men's winner was $219,900. The men's winner would receive $35,000. The women's champion would get $6,073.

"I know there's a difference between men's and women's golf, but is it $185,000," LPGA player Jane Blalock was quoted in a Sports Illustrated article in 1974. "That silver cup is hard to eat."[7]

In this controversial atmosphere Haynie kept playing golf. She had a second place finish in the Orange Blossom Classic in March. In April she tied with Jane Blalock for second at the Tour's richest event, the $179,000 Colgate Dinah Shore. The event closest in total purse to the Dinah Shore was the Sears Women's Classic at $100,000. All other Tour events had purses under $50,000.

Haynie won her first event of the 1974 season in mid-June at the Lawson's LPGA Open. One week later she went back-to-back in wins when she won her second LPGA Championship (her first was in 1965). Less than a month later she teed it up at LaGrange Country Club in LaGrange, Illinois to compete in one of most controversial Women's Opens in the history of golf.

For almost a year, the LPGA players had been threatening to boycott the Open. Sportswriter, Barry McDermott explained the players' concerns in a story for Sports Illustrated.

"They wanted the purse raised," McDermott wrote. "[They wanted] a different method of entry selection, a change in the prize-money distribution, polish added to the television broadcast, the golf course defanged and an improvement in the USGA's 'general attitude.'"[8]

Later in the article McDermott describes the change in the Tour and its players. His description calls to mind Haynie's comment about the players of the 1960's "hoping that someday the tour would improve."

"Years ago the burning issue of women's golf was whether their pet dogs should be allowed in the country club parking lots," McDermott continued. "Now the prosperous ladies are into six-figure purses, tax shelters, gallery ropes, television ratings, business consulting, player performance points, pretournament qualifying, endorsements, commercials, player card review, tour caddies, corporation pro-ams and corporate sponsorships: just like Arnie, Jack and Gary. They did not want a crummy-looking Open."[9]

The LPGA membership decided against a boycott only two weeks before the Open's entry deadline, and only after the USGA made some concessions. The USGA agreed to redistribute the purse, put two women golfers in the TV booth and recondition the course to make it less monstrous and more playable. They also agreed to think about increasing the purse for the 1975 Open.

The issue of the golf course's difficulty was important to the women because the scores they shot were a direct reflection of their ability in terms of the public's perception.

"The public thinks that when the men shoot high scores, it's because the course is tough," then LPGA president Carol Mann said. "But when we score badly, it's because we're lousy golfers."[10]

The La Grange course played exceptionally long, and after the first round, Kathy Ahern, a consistently long hitter, led by three strokes. By the end of the third round, Ruth Jessen held a one shot lead over JoAnne Carner (another long hitter), Sandra Spuzich and Sandra Haynie, with Carol Mann lurking one shot back of that group.

On the final day, Carner, Jessen and Spuzich dropped back, while Mann charged, Haynie stayed calm and held her position. Coming to the seventeenth tee, it had become a two horse

race with Mann holding a one shot lead over Haynie. It was then that Haynie took charge –
Texas style.

She jammed a 70-foot putt into the hole for birdie on the 17th, and then dropped a 15-footer
for birdie on the 18th. Her birdie, birdie finish gave her a one shot win over Mann, and put her in
the rarefied company of Mickey Wright with both an LPGA and U.S. Open title in the same year.
The Open that almost wasn't Haynie had turned into the stuff of dreams.

"The highlight of my career was not in winning the 1974 U.S. Open," Haynie said. "It was the
combination of having won the LPGA a few weeks before and being the only other person since
Mickey Wright in 1961 to win the two titles in a season. That was the top. Also, the manner in
which I won the Open at LaGrange was satisfying. Most Opens are lost, not won, but I made a 70
foot birdie at the 71st hole, and then birdied the 72nd hole for victory."[11]

What is even more amazing is that Haynie played a major role in the boycott controversy.
During the 1973-74 season she served as the organization's vice-president under Carol Mann, and
in that position she was at the center of the political skirmishing. The Open win – in fact the three
wins that Haynie had in a span of less than a month – was a testament to her mental approach to
the game and its effect on her ability to concentrate.

"Winning is 50 percent talent, although it always requires 100 percent concentration, and you
need a lot of discipline and confidence in yourself," Haynie said several years after the 1974 Open.
"The golf course is the loneliest place in the world. You are responsible for every shot, good and
bad. You need to have hit enough golf balls, to know whether you can dig far enough down, to
come up with the right shot at the right time."[12]

Haynie won four times during the 1975 season, but in mid-season of 1976 she was forced to
stop playing her normal schedule of up to twenty-five tour events per year. At age 33, Haynie was
diagnosed with arthritis; the disease made it almost impossible for Haynie to swing a golf club.

In the spring of 1976, just prior to Haynie's decision to stop playing, a chance meeting
determined how Haynie would spend her time away from the Tour.

Martina

Sandra Haynie met Martina Navratilova at the 1976 Superstars competition. Haynie was still competing in golf, but she knew the time was approaching that she would have to stop. She had lost the feeling in the last two fingers of her left hand due to circulation problems.

Navratilova was tennis' rising star. She was nineteen years old, had defected to the United States a year earlier and was suffering from a form of "culture shock" that was affecting the quality of her tennis game. Navratilova had two problems – she was out of shape physically, and she was lonely.

"I just couldn't keep my weight down in the States...," Navratilova wrote in her 1985 autobiography, *Martina*. "And the food was so easy to find.... At Forest Hills, where they used to hold the U.S. Open, there was a McDonald's on Austin Street, on the right side, that I could not pass without going for a Big Mac and French fries. You could have put blinders on me and I'd have found the door....

"I have never felt so alone, and I am a person who does not like to be alone," Navratilova continued. "I had grown up with four in a room for part of my childhood, had always had plenty of company on my first trips out of Czechoslovakia, but now there were times when I was alone in my hotel room, alone in airplanes, not yet twenty, and very much on my own.... If ever there was anybody who needed some help, it was me. Fortunately, I got it from someone who knew how to deal with the hard parts of being a professional athlete."[13]

Haynie and Navratilova talked at the Superstars competition, and Navratilova watched Haynie play in an LPGA event a few weeks later.

"I was fascinated by her play," Navratilova wrote. "As nerve-wracking as golf can be, she was so calm, so cool. When she putted, she used the same routine every time. She was so organized, so orderly, with her beautiful swing. I liked the way she handled herself on the course.... We started talking about my sport and my inconsistency on the court. Right away, I figured she could help me get over my own immaturity...."[14]

Haynie saw in Navratilova a chance to give something back.

"We began to talk about what you have to give to your sport, and in spite of having won the previous week, Martina said she was not happy," Haynie said. "She knew she could do more. She asked me for advice, and I gave her things she could understand and use on court. She did them and liked them. I had always wanted to give something back to sport, and I love working with young people because they are delightfully enthusiastic and flexible. You can mold them a little, give them suggestions, and let them fly. I like to work on the head, on concentration, and not on the game."[15]

Luckily Haynie did not have to work on Navratilova's tennis game. Haynie knew very little about tennis.

"I took a crash course in tennis because I didn't know anything about it," Haynie said. "For weeks I watched every tournament I could, scouting to learn peoples' strengths and weaknesses. Players would come and sit with me, and I learned by listening to them."[16]

Haynie took the role of Navratilova's agent. She set her schedule, took charge of her finances and sat in on conferences with Navratilova's attorney during contract discussions. Navratilova bought a house in Dallas that Haynie shared and the two used it as a mini-corporate office.

Haynie's main role was to "work on Navratilova's head."

"I worked on Martina's weight with a training course, and her weight dropped rapidly," Haynie said. "I found out what she was experiencing on court and would suggest ways to make her more positive. I showed her that is was her perfectionism that made her question line calls or lose her temper.

"The public relations side of it was hard for a while," Haynie continued. "Martina was a tough interview, who would tell someone they had asked a dumb question. She was guarded and felt the press was abusive because of her defection and because she drove a Mercedes, made a lot of money, and liked expensive jewelry. She felt she was always being picked on, and maybe it was true. I worked with her to turn it around; so she could tell people who had been born in the U.S. that they had had the opportunities to enjoy all these things that she had never known, and was finding out about now.... I put her in a position to give something back."[17]

Navratilova had an innate trust in Haynie's judgment.

"After a day of talking with Haynie (I realize I have the habit of always referring to her as 'Haynie,' rather than using her first name, but this is out of fondness for a wise old pro), Navratilova wrote. "I knew she was the friend I needed. She was older, wiser, and a champion in her own right. She didn't need my money or my fame to feel good about herself."[18]

By 1978, Haynie's tutoring began to pay off. That year Navratilova won 37 straight tournament matches. She won her first Wimbledon title by beating Chris Evert and was ranked number one in the world.

"It was as satisfying to me as winning a golf tournament," Haynie said. "To be able to have whatever it takes to bring that out of someone else, was really exciting."[19]

The business/personal relationship between Navratilova and Haynie lasted until 1980.

"I was still evolving, still discovering, and that's how the relationship with Haynie started coming apart," Navratilova wrote. "She was a good calming influence on me for a few years, but I was trying to find the world outside.... She was like a guru to me for three years, and she helped me as much as she could, but I was young and I had to find out about the rest of the world."[20]

> ### SANDRA HAYNIE
>
> **Professional Highlights**
>
> **Between 1961 & 1976 she captured 39 of her 42 victories**
>
> **In 1974 she became the second player to win the U.S. Open and LPGA Championship in the same year.**

The Second Tour – Comeback Number One

Haynie's health improved over the three-year lay-off from the Tour, and in 1981 she returned to a full schedule. At age 38, it took some time for Haynie to get back her competitive edge, but in mid-September she won her 40th LPGA event at the Henredon Classic in North Carolina. Haynie finished the season ranked 13th on the money list with $94,000.

"My wins after my return, and in particular my first victory, gave me giant satisfaction," Haynie said. "I felt very confident and got myself into a position where I could dig down inside and bring to the surface what I needed to make my game work for me.... I had worked hard for it mentally and practiced harder because you need to play yourself back into shape." [21]

Twenty years after Haynie had talked about joining the LPGA Tour not for the money, but in the "hopes that it would improve," the tour had become a vehicle in which women professional athletes could find appropriate financial reward. In 1982 Haynie took advantage of that improvement. Haynie won back-to-back events in late June and early July. At the Rochester International, Haynie, now 39, beat the twenty-five year old Hall of Famer-to-be Nancy Lopez. The next week, Haynie carded her fourth Major tournament win by beating another future Hall of Famer, Beth Daniel, at the Peter Jackson Classic. In September, Haynie with Kathy McMullen as a partner won the Portland Ping Team Championship.

At season's end, just six months short of her 40th birthday, Haynie was ranked number two on the money list with $245,000, and she had recorded the lowest year long scoring average of her career with 71.86.

The "Comeback Kid" seemed ageless. She continued to play well in 1983. Although she did not win any event, she finished second twice. Haynie finished the season ranked 13th on the money list. Between 1981 and 1983, Haynie had never finished lower than 13th on the money list and had averaged over $100,000 in prize money during those three seasons.

The Third Tour – Comeback Number Two

Haynie started the 1984 season ready to continue her domination as one of the top players on tour. But she was only able to complete 17 events. Mid season she suffered a knee injury which required surgery. Once more she was forced to leave tournament golf.

Haynie's arthritic condition made her recovery from the knee surgery slow. For the next four years she focused on the business interests that she had developed through her golf career. She has held major financial interests in a T-shirt manufacturing business, a restaurant design and management company and a golf club repair business. But, no matter how successful the business outside golf, Haynie still wanted to compete. There was one more goal that she had set for herself. She wanted to reach the $1 million mark in career earnings.

At age 45, Haynie returned to the tour in 1988. She played only twelve events that year, but in 1989 she played a full schedule of 23 tournaments. At the end of the 1989 season, Haynie found herself ranked at a respectable 57 on the money list with $50,000. She had also surpassed $1 million in lifetime earnings.

Even with the success of 1989, Haynie knew the time had come to leave for good. At age 46, she was a different person than the seventeen-year-old who had joined the Tour almost 30 years before.

"I don't see myself as a selfish person, except with my golf," Haynie said. "I realized that I had become a bit more giving after being away from golf, and I didn't want to return to that type of selfishness.... I found it hard to be forced into making the decision to leave golf. I did feel deprived for a while, and it is hard to go through the times when you miss the competition. After doing something you love for a long period, you realize there is no feeling to replace the competitive adrenalin and excitement."[22]

Haynie gives a great deal of her time to the local Dallas Arthritis Foundation, working with children who suffer from the disease, and with parents whoses lives are affected. She has also found her way to the teaching tee.

"I have done some teaching locally, also with a few of the players on Tour," Haynie said. "I find it gratifying that they ask my advice."[23]

The advice they get is probably very similar to the advice Haynie once gave to one of the world's greatest tennis players at a time when she was struggling to find herself.

"You measure yourself against the best, and it is a good feeling to play your best against the best," Haynie said. "You don't get that feeling many times in your life, and there is nothing else comparable."[24]

Chapter 9

Activist and Advocate...
Carol Mann

Throughout its early history the LPGA had been a "player" driven organization. It was founded by players. For almost the entire first 20 years, the players handled the Tour's day-to-day operation. By the early 1970's all professional sports were entering an era of big money and bigger corporate sponsorship support. "Eventually dollar-wise executives realized that the LPGA Tour could give their products admirable exposure at bargain prices." [1]

The definitive phrase is "bargain prices." For, while the men's tour rode the wave of the blossoming golf boom with higher prize money and increased tournaments, the LPGA continued to struggle for both an "image" and a solid foundation in the new world of big-business sports. In 1970, the number of LPGA events had dropped from 32 to 21 and prize money had decreased from $536,000 to $475,000.

Under the leadership of Kathy Whitworth, who served as President from 1970-73, the Tour began to get a piece of the corporate pie. In 1972 the big break for the LPGA happened when the Tour developed a relationship with Colgate CEO David R. Forster and Colgate – Dinah Shore Invitational was born. The event brought the Tour to national commercial prominence.

By 1975, the Tour had increased it visibility, but it, and its players, were still "second-class citizen" financially. If the Tour were going to survive, the organization would need a major "make-over." It was probably the most critical time for the organization since its founding. The responsibility for guiding the LPGA through this crucial period fell to its then president, Carol Mann.

Mann was 34-years-old, and was an established Tour star – in fact during the 1975 LPGA season, she had won her 35th event which qualified her for the Hall of Fame. The time frame of her LPGA presidency coincided with an era when many people her age were radically questioning "the system." Mann was in no sense a "radical," and her career was approaching the "wind-down" stage. Although she had little to gain personally, at a time when the Tour needed an activist, Mann – who 14 years earlier joined the Tour as a shy, self-conscious youngster – courageously stepped into that role.

In 1975 the Tour players were angered by the disparity between the $1.7 million prize money on the LPGA Tour and the $7.9 million PGA Tour total purse. They were particularly concerned about the difference between their $55,000 U.S. Open prize money and the $236,300 offered in the men's Open. There was a threat that the women would boycott the national championship, and Mann found herself the spokesman.

"I guess it's a matter of impatience when you get down to it," Mann commented to the press. "We think we should be farther along. I think the pressure of other women's activities in sports – namely tennis – has shaken all of us up. The publicity that other women's sports has gained has also shaken us up.[2]

The players did not boycott, but increasing the prize money and the visibility of the tour remained the most prominent issues for the organization. Mann did not allow it to recede into the background, but instead took the lead in taking a hard look at the organization, its problems, its needs, and a way to bring it into what would become the "modern era" of the LPGA.

"We came up with a plan and found the people we needed with the skills to help us make the plan work," Mann said.[3]

"The plan" included developing an organization that was more businesslike and, most important, changing the executive leadership. Mann was instrumental in the LPGA executive board's decision to fire then executive director Bud Erickson and replace him with former hockey marketing executive, Ray Volpe.

Volpe was named "Commissioner", not executive director. In the next seven years he increased prize money to $6.4 million, established a retirement plan for players, and brought the Tour into the fans' living rooms by increasing the televised events from two to fourteen.

Mann's determination to "fix" the problems, and her total support of Volpe brought the LPGA from the brink of bankruptcy in 1975 to a sports organization that would grow to include some of the best known women athletes in the world.

> ## CAROL MANN
>
> **Began playing golf: age 9**
>
> **First tournament win: 1958, Western Junior**
>
> **First LPGA victory: 1964**
>
> **Last LPGA victory: 1975**

Mann not only played her way into the Hall of Fame, but while she was doing that, she also brought the LPGA through one of the most critical periods of its history. In 1990, 15 years after Volpe turned the organization around and on the fortieth anniversary of the LPGA's founding, Mann again spoke out concerning the organization's future.

"Key players need to step forth and take on leadership roles," Mann said. "Every business needs a strong leadership corps. While I'm extremely respectful of the players today and their playing ability, I question their level of commitment to the LPGA. There are divisive remarks made by the players in the paper. What the organization needs instead is to set common goals and have everyone line up behind them. To expect leading players to also become leaders will be tough, and will take exceptional people."[4]

Mann was asking that the tradition continue. She was asking nothing more than had been asked of the LPGA founders, and nothing more than she had asked of herself.

Carol Mann was born in Buffalo, New York on February 3, 1941. Shortly after her birth the Mann family moved to Baltimore, Maryland, and it was there that Carol spent her childhood.

Mann's father, Rip, as well as her mother, Ann, worked for Chevrolet. The middle income family eventually grew to include Carol's four younger brothers. The age difference between Carol and her closest brother is 16 months. Her twin brothers are five years younger, and her youngest brother was born when Carol was ten.

"I wouldn't speak to my mother for a month when the fourth child was a boy; I wanted a sister," Mann said. "But I was allowed to name him. I called him Bunky, since I had a crush on a boy with that name. Bunky in Baltimore means 'friend.'"[5]

At age five, Mann attended a private Catholic girl's school. Like many children, Mann found the initial transition to school difficult, but she soon acclimated herself.

"By the third grade I had decided to become a nun," Mann said. "I had rosaries and all the works. A year later, it was decided I should leave.

"I missed the place so much that I was sick all the time at the public school," Mann continued. "I was so unhappy that I went back to the nuns half way through the year. It was a good place to learn, where I felt happy and special."[6]

It was important for Mann to feel "special." She was extremely tall – her adult height is 6 feet, three inches. Her height often made her feel awkward, self-conscious and led to a sense of insecurity.

At age nine, Mann began playing golf, and through it she found a sense of accomplishment.

"Both my parents played, and my father bought me some right handed clubs although I was naturally left-handed," Mann said. "They were awkward, but all right. I took lessons and got deeper and deeper into it.

"My mother, who encouraged me, walked the fairways with me to count my strokes. My drive came from wanting to be with my father, who was away working all week. I thought I would be able to play with him weekends, but he didn't pay any attention to me. We weren't close, but I wanted to be."[7]

When Carol was thirteen, Rip Mann was transferred to Chicago. It was there that Carol's golf game began to take form.

"[My parents] decided they needed a great country club for themselves and their brood," Mann wrote in her book *The 19th Hole*. "They joined Olympia Fields Country Club, which had been the site of many historic championships in the past."[8]

Within a year of the Mann's joining Olympia Fields, the club was the site of one more historic event – Carol Mann's introduction to competitive golf. She tells the story as an introduction to *The 19th Hole*, which is a collection of golf stories that are the favorites of famous celebrities.

Carol was fourteen years old and the Women's Western Amateur Championship was being played on Olympia Field's South Course. Although her handicap was twenty-eight – above the limit for entry into the event – tournament officials decided just before the event began that Carol could play.

"I was excited, but scared," Mann writes. "The other young women competitors, a little older than I, had so much poise and confidence. And they dressed very well. I didn't have any clothes that looked really attractive. I went to a private girls' school and wore a uniform. My wardrobe was also limited by my height. Already I was close to six feet tall. I was gawky and quite self-conscious."[9]

Carol's score of 114 in the qualifying round put her in the fifth and last flight, and she lost her first match which put her in the consolation bracket of the flight.

"This is about as low as any competitor can go, but I didn't know that at that time," Mann writes. "All I knew was I got to play again the next day. I won that match, the next, and the next. I was still in it, and thrilled!"[10]

What really impressed the young Mann about the event were the prizes – trophies.

"The evening before my final match, I sneaked a peek at the winner and runner-up prizes for all flights, including my exciting consolation flight," Mann writes. "The trophies were real silver. They sparkled. One of those was to be mine. I didn't care which, the winner or runner-up. I was ready to cherish either."[11]

CAROL MANN

Amateur Career Highlights

Western and Chicago Junior Champion: 1958

Chicago Women's Amateur: 1960

The fifth flight consolation match tee time in any tournament is always early, and Carol's match went off just after sunrise with the championship match teeing off almost three hours later. In her book, Mann explains the drama the logistics of the pairings created and the lasting effect it had on her life.

"When we came around to the long, par-five 18th hole, I was one down. I was over the green in four shots, on a very difficult lie – a downslope with fluffy grass all around my ball. My opponent was on the green in four strokes, about 40 feet away. In the meantime, what seemed like a thousand people were following the big final match between two very good players, Pat Lesser (later, after marriage, Pat Harbottle) and Wiffi Smith. The gallery was moving from the seventh green to the eighth tee. In between sat the eighteenth green, where I was about to play my chip shot. There was lots of shushing for the spectators to be quiet. Many members of Olympia Fields were watching and later I was told what happened next made them very proud of their only representative in the tournament.

"I stole a quick glance at the crowd. I was certain they expected me to dump the ball in the little trap between my ball and the edge of the green. Well, I fooled everyone, including myself: I chipped in! The people went wild with applause. That was my first taste of playing in front of people. I was surprised at how much fun it was to have them watching me. That was my christening at what my father called 'being a ham.'"[12]

Carol's chip in won the hole, and the two fifth flight consolation "battlers" were forced to go to the first tee for a play-off to determine who would prevail.

"No one followed us down that first fairway, so when I won it felt a bit anticlimactic," Mann writes. "Still, as the fifth flight consolation winner, I was presented with the most beautiful silver bowl, a lion head on each side. I slept with it that night and kept hearing the cheers and applause. That lovely bowl adorns my trophy room even today."[13]

Learning to be Confident

Winning the fifth flight consolation bracket at age fourteen taught Mann that golf could be a form of self-expression, and that through it she could find approval. It would take several more years for her to recognize that in golf she could find the vehicle that would bring her a sense of confidence and poise.

Golf intrigued Mann, and she spent most of her time on the golf course. In the late 1950's a golf course was an unusual place to find a young teenage girl, and there probably would not be too many other young girls there.

Mann related a story to golf writer Liz Kahn that demonstrates her feeling of being "different."

"I stayed out a lot playing golf rather than looking after my brothers, who were only to be tolerated," Mann said. "My mother criticized me and said 'Who do you think you are?' It bothered me that I wasn't fitting in, and I thought, 'One day I'll show you.'"[14]

By the time Mann had finished high school she was beginning to "show them" and feel a little more comfortable with herself.

"At 17, when I won the Junior Women's Western Open, I was awkward, shy, without poise, and I giggled," Mann said. "I had a pony tail, wore shorts, and was gawky and ugly, but it changed my perspective to have played so well."[15]

A few weeks later, Mann played in the Western Open and she was paired with one of her idols. The experience drained whatever confidence she had gained.

"I was paired with Mickey Wright," Mann said. "I was scared to death and didn't do well. The women were terrific, fun, smart, and very nice to me. I knew I wanted to be a professional, but I wasn't good enough."[16]

Part of the problem for Mann was her difficulty with competition itself.

"Competing and beating people are not easy for me," Mann said. "I played in the 1960 Women's U.S. Amateur, and in the third round I played a woman on her birthday; when she won at the 17th hole, I said, 'Happy Birthday,' and I felt she should win. I had played a pregnant woman in the second round – it was a wonder I didn't lose to her – as I had felt badly about winning."[17]

The other part of the problem for Mann was that she simply did not trust her own feelings and ability.

"At 19, I was terribly shy, with little public poise," Mann wrote in 1981. "I barely spoke above a whisper and thought my ideas needed constant reinforcement. I actually took a survey to determine whether turning pro was the right decision for me."[18]

Mann's survey must have indicated that an LPGA career was the path to follow, for she joined the Tour in 1960. Success, however, was not immediate. Mann's debut in her first LPGA event was anything but spectacular and showed her inexperience.

"In my first tournament I had the flu, and a 102 degree temperature," Mann said. "It was freezing cold and raining, and I shot 89. I five-putted one green because I didn't know how to take relief from the water."[19]

Mann struggled through two years on Tour and then in 1962 things began to change. She met teaching professional Manuel De la Torre and began working with him on her game.

"He transformed my game," Mann said. "The heavens parted intellectually on the golf swing."[20]

Even with her transformed game, Mann progressed slowly – especially financially.

"There were very dire financial constraints," Mann said. "I went broke probably fifteen times in my first five or six years. It's tough to tee it up in the final round with thirty-five dollars to your name and you've got to pay your caddie and hotel bill."[21]

Mann's perseverance enabled her to move up in the tour rankings. She was 16th on the money list in 1963 and won her first event in 1964. The win came at the Western Open. It was the same event where in 1958 the seventeen year old Mann after being paired with Mickey Wright felt that she wasn't good enough to play as a professional. Mann was so ecstatic with the win that she borrowed the tradition of treating the press to champagne from PGA Tour player Tony Lema.

"There was no information or communications about how the others were doing," Mann said about the event. "After I chopped along the last hole I said, 'Who's doing well?' I was told that I had won by two shots, so I threw a champagne party for the press to be like Tony Lema. I won $1200, the champagne cost me $120, and I had blisters from popping every cork myself."[22]

In 1965, Mann established herself as one of the Tour's top players with her U.S. Open win at Atlantic City Country Club in New Jersey. The Open win began a span of eleven years in which Mann would win thirty five tournaments – ten of those in 1968 and eight in 1969. Yet Mann found that success wasn't exactly what she thought it would be.

"After I won the Open, I felt let down," Mann said. "I said to Marlene Hagge, 'Is that all there is?' She was soothing, but I'd worked so hard that I couldn't imagine why I didn't feel more overwhelmed.

"In 1968, I won ten tournaments, and in 1969, I was leading money winner, having won eight tournaments," Mann continued. "I had made a tremendous effort, and it still wasn't satisfying.... I wanted to set records, to be one of the best, in the Hall of Fame, but I never thought I was worthy compared to Patty Berg, Mickey Wright, Betsy Rawls, and Kathy Whitworth."[23]

It was during this period that Mann began to look beyond golf for meaning, and she began to grow personally.

"In 1966 I started winning regularly and my confidence soared," Mann wrote in 1981. "I thought I was invulnerable and that the streak would never end. But then it dawned on me that when I was off the course and away from the golf scene, there was a world I couldn't relate to. I realized there was more to life than golf, sports and being number one. Still it came as a real shock to find out that my essence as a human being wasn't so terrific.

"For the next several years I worked on growing up emotionally as well as on my golf game," Mann continued. "I struggled to fit into the real world without losing my identity as an athlete."[24]

Mann dabbled in psychology, read *The Power of Positive Thinking*, worked with long-time friend Bob Hagge to learn self-hypnosis which she said "didn't always work" and turned to Marlene Hagge for advice on her appearance and the way she dressed.

Mann gained self-confidence and a greater awareness of the world outside golf. She developed an "image," and like other women athletes, she found that the "image" often got more publicity than the "substance." Gwilym S. Brown of *Sports Illustrated* focused his article, not on the hard-fought victory Mann put together, but on the 1965 Women's Open tradition at the Atlantic City Country Club and the absence of Mickey Wright in the field. In fact he chose to describe the new U.S. Women's Open champion as a "bumptious blonde" with the "build of a whooping crane and the personality of a puppy."[25]

Thirty years later, an "aware" Mann, quoted by Liz Kahn, is outspoken about the issue of image.

"I got extra attention, won ten tournaments, but I was more on the fashion pages than the sports pages...," Mann said. "Women golfers want people to see more of them than their bodies. They are serious and like to be treated that way. They want people to see how they relate to a golf club, a golf ball, a flag, a hole."[26]

While the press continued to write about the short, vibrantly colored skirts that showed off Mann's long legs, she continued to knock down flagsticks and sink putts. In 1968, the year she carded ten wins, she also had 23 rounds with scores in the 60's to set an LPGA record that remained unbroken until 1980 by Amy Alcott with 25 sub-70 rounds. In 1969, Mann was the Tour's leading money winner. By 1973, Mann had collected 31 victories, and she had become known as one of the "Big Three" along with Mickey Wright and Kathy Whitworth.

It was then that her years of personal consciousness-raising began to readjust her focus. Mann began to look beyond the world of range balls and tee shots toward the meetings and boardrooms that affected the over-all organizational pattern of the LPGA itself.

The Activist... and the Advocate

"My one objection to the tour is that we don't afford ourselves the opportunity to embrace enough of life," Mann said in Liz Kahn's *The LPGA*. "The lack of awareness of what is going on outside is sometimes extraordinary. Women want to include more things in their lives. It's in our nature to do so – not to be boxed in."[27]

Mann broke out of the "box" in 1973 when she was elected president of the LPGA. There is no doubt Mann loved – and had thrived under – the semi-sorority atmosphere of the mid-1970's tour.

"The real attraction of being on tour has nothing to do with money," Mann said. "It is not material; it is spiritual.... The women represent so much more than a family. They are the only people who know what you really go through; there is a kinship that cannot be replaced."[28]

But, "President" Mann was no longer the shy 19-year-old who took a survey to see if she should join the tour in 1960. She was now willing to speak out about her own beliefs, and she was convinced that the organization's continued growth depended upon increased exposure.

"The players don't realize they are leaders in women's sports," Mann said. "Upon analysis they absolutely are. They have the biggest, the most organized and best women's sports organization in the world. And they have no idea of it. Knowledge of self makes for better marketing."[29]

Mann backed up that belief with action during 1975, the key year of her three-year term as president, when she was instrumental in pulling Ray Volpe away from the National Hockey League and installing him as commissioner of the LPGA.

"When we hired Ray Volpe the number one skill requirement was marketing," Mann said. "Number 10 was a knowledge of golf."[30]

Sarah Ballard points out in her short history of the LPGA that "the expression 'servicing the media' is marketing jargon for getting the word around, making sure the newspapers and the television stations have a story, exposure whether in print or on the air. In this vein, Volpe had no peer." Ballard points out that Volpe also had the advantage of great timing. "He had been in office only two years when Nancy Lopez emerged as the LPGA's first bona fide superstar of the electronic age." Even Volpe admitted his success in bringing the LPGA out of the doldrums was helped along by Lopez.

"Nancy would make anyone look good," Volpe said.[31]

Mann's commitment to change and the marketing skill of Volpe altered the course of the LPGA. But Mann's effort had a high personal price.

"My golf seemed so secondary while I was president," Mann said. In 1975, I played 28 tournaments, won four, and was third money winner. I could barely get to the course in time to tee off; there was so much other activity. I burned myself out a bit, and by June 1976, I went down the tubes."[32]

In addition to the physical strain of playing and serving as president, at the end of her term, Mann experienced a sense of let down similar to what she had felt after her Open win in 1965.

"I had launched a ship, and then I had to let it go, which was not easy," Mann said. "I was depressed thinking that no one on tour would say thank you to me for what I had done. Some would, others never would, and ten years later, players wouldn't give a damn. When I stopped being president of the LPGA, I was depressed for eight months. I couldn't let go."[33]

In 1976 Mann's role as LPGA president ended, but shortly after she embarked on a role that was completely new and one that she approached with trepidation. At a golf school cocktail party she met golf instructor Jim Hardy. In April 1979 the two were married.

"While I was on tour, I always felt I wouldn't get married...," Mann said. "I was elusive. I couldn't settle down because I traveled so much, and I didn't know enough about close relationships. In a way it was an excuse for saying, I live this life so I can't be close to anyone."[34]

Only one year after her marriage Mann faced one of the toughest decisions of her life – retirement.

Her last win was the Lawson Open in 1975. By 1980 she had slipped to 114 on the money list. At the Mary Kay Classic in Dallas, the frustration of not playing well forced her to quit in the middle of the round.

"My skills were not up to the quality of the golf course, which wasn't all that tough," Mann said. "I reached the 12th green, had a putt for a bogey, and I didn't hole out. I whacked my ball right across the green into a hazard. My playing partners were stunned, and I said, 'Sorry ladies, I hope I didn't scare you. I just can't hack it anymore.' And, I walked in."[35]

Mann spent the winter of 1981 on the practice tee and returned to the tour in the spring, but her game just didn't return and she knew she could no longer put off the inevitable.

"I went back on tour and made $960 in eight tournaments," Mann said. "To begin with I was very nervous and excited, and I putted terribly. Then I fell back into the feeling it was the same old stuff, and that I stood to lose more being out on tour than I had to gain."[36]

Her difficulty in leaving the tour was based on feelings that most people – especially athletes – experience when they face retirement and her love of the game itself.

"I can't say enough about my love for golf, and how I love the pursuit of its mastery," Mann said. "I also did not want the next generation to replace me. It is always difficult for an athlete. All of us want it to go on forever, to put things in a time warp. It is difficult to discover you can't perform."[37]

Mann left the tour in 1981, but the self-confidence and poise remained with her. In addition, Mann had developed an understanding of the way in which sports fit into the larger world. When Mann left the tour she applied what she had learned to the business world.

She founded and is president of Carol Mann, Inc. which provides unique corporate golf programs at PGA, LPGA and Senior Tour sites. She also formed Carol Mann Golf Services, the first woman-owned and operated course design and management firm.

In 1979 Mann was named a trustee of the Women's Sports Foundation. The timing of her relationship with the organization placed her directly in the center of one of the most difficult controversies in women's sports, and Mann did not back away from the opportunity to speak out.

In 1981 Billie Jean King, embroiled in a palimony suit, admitted a lesbian affair with Marilyn Barnett. The press presented the situation as a scandal that could adversely affect the future of all women's sports. Mann writing in *Women's Sports* magazine took a stand.

"While I personally believe that the sex lives of athletes and everyone else are strictly their own business, Billie Jean's recent admission of a homosexual affair may cost women's sports plenty," Mann wrote. "For that reason we can't ignore it.... The success and celebrity status created [by the women's tennis and golf tours], to some extent, a fantasy land for women's sports. Perhaps in the long run Billie Jean's public discussion of what should have remained her private life will help create a sense of reality in sports, and show the world we're human too. That would be one very good thing to come out of all this.

"I'm especially concerned with the public reaction to King's admission," Mann continued. "In recent years it's been gratifying to see how much more acceptable it is for girls and young women to pursue sports as amateurs and professionals. It would be a terrible injustice if parents didn't continue to encourage such active lifestyles.

"Participating in sports is probably the most valuable experience girls can have while growing up. What they discover on the field, court and course spills over into the rest of their personal and professional lives. They learn how to win, how to lose, how to rely totally on themselves and how to work together with a team. They come to understand defeat without being devastated by it, and how to channel their energy and anger."[38]

> ### CAROL MANN
>
> #### Career Highlights
>
> Multiple winner in eight of her 22 years on Tour
>
> 10 tournament wins: 1968
>
> Scoring average of 72.04 stood as a record until Nancy Lopez broke it in 1978.
>
> Most rounds (23) below 70: 1968, record stood until 1980.

In the *Women's Sports* article, Mann used her own personal experience to support her position for participation in athletics.

"I've done a lot of thinking lately about the value of being an athlete and about the golf tour's success story," Mann wrote. "I wouldn't trade my experiences for anything in the world."[39]

Mann describes her work with the Women's Sports Foundation as her "non-profit making life." She was elected president of the organization in 1985. The position allowed her to continue to express her views about the place of women in sports.

"Women athletes are still not acceptable," Mann said. "I believe in freedom of physical self-expression, not only in the approved list of those sports considered feminine, such as dance, ice skating, and aerobics.... Little girls need the opportunity to use their bodies in movement, not just to please and attract, nor do I want women to be men, but they need a gamut of self-expression."[40]

In 1987, Mann faced one more challenge. She was separated from Jim Hardy and a year later the couple was divorced.

"I thought I got married forever," Mann said. "But, it seems that I married someone who had been divorced once before, and it was easier for him to give up on the marriage than it was for me.... Jim remarried, and I plunged myself into my work. It is a pattern I have followed before, and I understand it."[41]

In 1990, as Mann was concluding her term as Women's Sports Foundation president, she once again spoke out against discrimination – this time in connection with the 1990 PGA Championship when the event was taken from Shoal Creek Country Club in Birmingham, Alabama, because the club did not admit African-American members.

Interviewed in *U.S. News & World Report*, Mann related her own experiences with discrimination at golf clubs – specifically Pine Valley Golf Club, the exclusive male bastion in New Jersey.

"I've come through the rage; I'm like a recovering female," Mann said. "I was invited to play Pine Valley a couple of times, after 3 o'clock on a Sunday. I better not repeat my reply."[42]

Broadening her view, Mann commented on the impact of the Shoal Creek incident.

"Playing a game professionally is a very narrow existence," Mann said. "These players have little breadth of experience or knowledge of the real world. They live inside the ropes. Frankly, you almost have to have a narrow outlook to succeed at this. They don't see it, but golf and society have changed this week. Who you hire and who you promote, who you accept and where you socialize, are all eventually going to be different. Through humanizing straight talk, we're about to learn we have things in common. The ripple is going to be long and wide."[43]

Mann began her career plagued by insecurities and lacking self-assuredness. She used her career not only to collect the rewards of fame, but also to build her own sense of self. At the end she found the success that can come from athletic skill, a comfort with herself and the strength to speak out and pave the way for those who would come after her.

More importantly, the young U.S. Open champion, who felt let down and questioned the value of working toward and achieving a goal, found that, in fact, that is not all there is. There is more, and it lies within each person.

"I've walked on the moon," Mann said. "I enjoy being a person, and getting old and dying are fine. I never think how people will remember Carol Mann. The mark I made is an intimate satisfaction."[44]

Teeing off at the 1995 Sprint Senior Challenge.

Betsy Rawls

The swing that produced 88 Tour victories.

Kathy Whitworth

Mickey's golf swing has been compared to Ben Hogan's.
Hogan himself said, Wright had the best golf swing he
had ever seen – man or woman.

Mickey Wright

Currently, McDonald's LPGA Championship Director,
Betsy acknowledges the applause at the 1998 World Golf
Hall of Fame Dedication and Induction Ceremonies.

Betsy Rawls

"Greats" of the game share some fun at the 1995 Sprint Senior Challenge.
From left to right: Marilyn Smith (partially hidden), Jane Blalock, Mickey Wright,
Marlene Hagge (bottom center), Judy Rankin, Kathy Whitworth, Carol Mann (right front).

(Above) Driving off the tee at the
1995 Sprint Senior Challenge.

Sandra Haynie

(Left) Walking with determination while playing the
1995 Sprint Senior Challenge.

Kathy Whitworth

Mickey Wright

Mickey warms up in the early morning mist for the 1995 Sprint Senior Challenge. Dedicated to perfection, even after almost 30 years away from the tour, Wright was one of the first players to arrive at the range each day of the event – old habits seem to die hard.

Mickey Wright

Carol Mann (left) and Sandra Haynie (right) on the putting green at LPGA International Golf Club preparing for the 1995 Sprint Senior Challenge. Practice takes a second seat to "catching up."

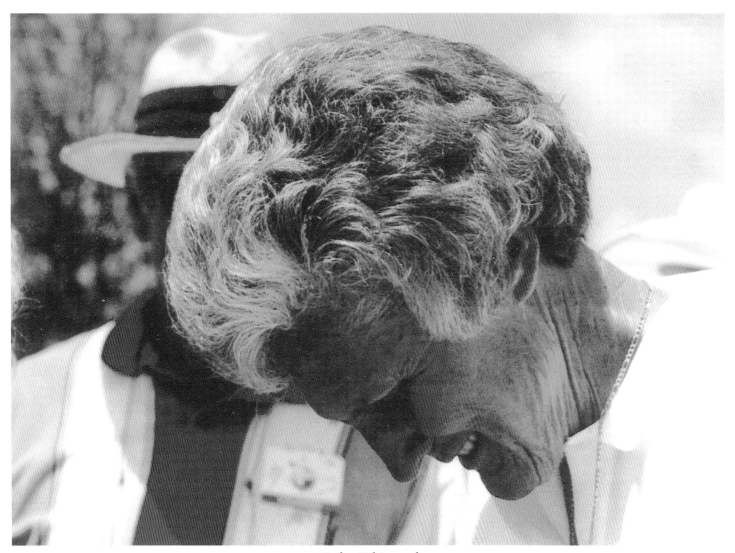

Kathy Whitworth

Kathy warms up her swing in the morning mist at the 1995 Sprint Senior Challenge. Thirty years before, as a rookie, Whitworth took the players already on Tour as role models.

Kathy Whitworth

Carol Mann (left) works on the touch that made her a great putter.

Kathy Whitworth (right) recovers from the rough.

Betsy Rawls

Sandra Haynie (left) and Carol Mann

Kathy Whitworth (left) embraces an old Tour friend at the 1995 Sprint Senior Challenge.

Sandra (center) chats with old friends, Donna Caponi
(left), Sandra Palmer (back to camera), Betsy Rawls
(behind Palmer) and Marilyn Smith (right).

Sandra Haynie

Carol Mann (left) talks with Pat Bradley.

1998 World Golf Hall of Fame
Dedication and Induction Ceremonies

Carol Mann

Two "old friends" - Kathy Whitworth
(left) and Mickey Wright - chat.
Between them, these "friends" hold
170 LPGA Tournament titles.

Part III

TRANSITIONS

1980's - 90's

Setting the Scene

Title IX legislation requiring equal access to sports for girls and women in public schools and colleges forever changed the world for all women's sports. It is the single most important factor in the history of the LPGA Tour. Because of Title IX and the resulting equality in terms of money and equipment, school athletic programs for girls and women gained sophistication. The results of these programs were better athletes and more of them.

In golf those young, talented athletes found their way to the LPGA Tour. As the Tour grew in number of players, the interest in the Tour by Corporate America increased. The "product" the

Tour had to offer began to attract the interest of corporations, and that interest was transformed into sponsorship dollars.

In the 1980's JoAnne Carner (1982) and Nancy Lopez (1987) were inducted into the Hall of Fame. Their induction was significant because it represents a "changing of the guard." Carner, born in 1939, was the last of the "pioneers" to be inducted. Lopez, born in 1956, was the first of the "Title IX Generation" to be inducted.

By the end of the 1980's the Tour had completely transformed itself into Big Business Sports. It was no longer a small "family" of players who struggled along as best they could. It was a place where young, aggressive woman athletes looked for a career. It was a place where athletes could make money – not just a living.

In the 1990's the Tour matured even more, and attracted more players, sponsors and fans. Five players were inducted into the Hall: Pat Bradley, Patty Sheehan, Betsy King and, under new Hall criteria, Amy Alcott and Beth Daniel. These players were a "whole new breed." They were high profile sports celebrities. Title IX had given sustenance to the programs through which these players honed their skills. Title IX had made sports accessible for these young women. And these young women would give something back. Through their visibility, talent and personality, they would paint an image of sports as an acceptable – almost desirable – activity for all women at every level of skill.

Lopez, Bradley, King, Sheehan, Alcott and Daniel were born into the peaceful and prosperous world of the late 1950's. They grew up in a world of civil unrest and the divisive nightmare of Vietnam. As children their world was very close to idealic. As young adults, they lived in the chaos that was the 1960's, and then in the 1970's, in a world changing at the speed of light. Like others of their generation, Lopez, Bradley, King, Sheehan, Alcott and Daniel were the product of enormous social change. In the venue of sport they would represent the impact of that change. Along with JoAnne Carner – the lone representative of another era – this generation of Tour players would demand recognition and respect for what they were – professional women athletes.

Chapter 10

Lover of the Game...

JoAnne Carner

Here comes 'Big Momma." The whispered phrase spreads from spectator to spectator like a wave. People lean forward across the ropes and crane their necks to get a glimpse of JoAnne Carner as she walks onto the practice tee at the JAL Big Apple Classic in 1979.

The 40-year-old Carner, a huge Styrofoam cup of coffee in one hand and two packs of cigarettes in the other, strolls to an open spot on the range. The tall mustached young man who is carrying her bag drops it next to a large bucket of range balls.

Carner turns to the crowd and holds up the coffee, "It's pretty early, how can you be out here without one of these?" The crowd laughs, Carner throws the cigarettes to the ground and grabs an iron from the bag. She hits three shots and asks her caddie for the driver. She hits eight shots. Each flies a long way but fades off to the right just before landing. Carner puts the club back in the bag.

"Well, that's enough of that," she says to no one in particular, and the crowd laughs again. "I guess I know where I'm going to be all day, probably in the rough."

She picks up the coffee and cigarettes and starts to walk off the practice tee. "Let's go over to the bunker," she says to her caddie.

At the bunker's edge, Carner dumps the entire bucket of balls into grass that is at least four inches high. She hits each ball from the high grass up onto the practice green. When all the balls are gone, the caddie collects the balls while Carner sips coffee and lights a cigarette.

"Put 'em in the bunker," Carner says.

The caddie drops the balls from the bucket in the sand. Carner hits every one out, brushes some loose grains of sand from her shorts and says, "Okay, let's go putt."

Ten minutes later, Carner is standing on the first tee.

"Holder of twenty-one LPGA titles, and two time U.S. Open Champion," The announcer says. "From Kirkland, Washington, JoAnne Carner."

The crowd applauds warmly. Carner smiles and waves her hand as she tees up the ball. Her drive soars over the hill 200 yards down the fairway and fades to the right landing in the rough just short of the tree line.

Carner picks up the tee and smiles at her caddie, "I told ya," she says, recreating the fade of the shot with a sweeping gesture to the right. "Lets go."

For the first nine holes of the round, Carner's drives never find a fairway, but she manages eight pars and one birdie. The practice from the four-inch high grass paid off.

JoAnne Carner

Began playing in earnest: age 14

First tournament win: 1954-55, Washington State Public Links

First LPGA victory: 1970

Most recent LPGA victory: 1985

JoAnne Carner has spent most of her life – a total to date of 44 years – competing on golf courses. She played amateur golf on the national level for fourteen years, from 1956 through 1970. She won everything there is to win. Five times in those fourteen years she won the ultimate amateur prize – the U.S. Amateur Championship. Carner has played professionally for 30 years, building a record of 42 LPGA victories. One more tour win will make her the oldest player to ever win a tour event.

As with most older players, she is constantly questioned about when she will retire. In 1982, at age 43, she answered adamantly, "I'm not going to retire. You retire. I'm never going to retire." Seventeen years later Carner is still playing. Her schedule has decreased to fifteen tournaments a season because of her husband, Don's battle against Parkinson's disease, but she is still playing competitive golf.

JoAnne grew up as the youngest of five children in the Gunderson (her maiden name) family. She has three older sisters and a brother, Bill, born 13 months before JoAnne. It was Bill who introduced JoAnne to golf.

"Bill and I were like twins growing up," JoAnne said. "He worked at the local 9-hole public course, and I tagged along.

"We played after the customers went home, with old taped up clubs, wearing gloves 'til they fell apart," Carner said. "We played in the moonlight, which is why I'm such a feel player."[3]

Carner's parents did not play golf, but they encouraged their youngest daughter to take the game as far as she could. Carner's first teacher was Gordon Jenkins. She describes him not as a golf professional, but as a "good golfer." When she was fourteen, Jenkins entered her in her first tournament. As Carner describes the event, it seems to have been a local weekly competition, and her fellow competitors quickly realized that the young golfer could play rings around them.

"Playing with a 24 handicap, I sent two balls out of bounds, three putted three times, and won with a 79," Carner said. "They screamed blue murder, and the following week when I did the same, they cut my handicap to 12."[4]

Carner's parents were not the only people who recognized her potential. She got encouragement and support from much of the Kirkland community. When she won the Washington State Public Links championship, she received an honorary membership to a private club in Seattle. In 1956, when she won the U.S. Junior Girl's Championship and was runner-up in the U.S. Amateur, the seventeen year-old became a local celebrity.

"When I won the National Junior, they gave me a ticker tape parade from Seattle to my hometown," Carner said. "It was really exciting."[5]

From the very beginning of her career, Carner's love of competition was evident, and she attributes it to the attitude of her parents.

"My parents supported me through my amateur career," Carner said. "The fact that they raised us as individuals developed my competitive instincts."[6]

The Great "Gundy"

Carner began playing world class amateur golf at age 16 when she was still JoAnne Gunderson. Her sometimes-cocky confidence, backed by outstanding skill and fierce competitiveness, soon earned her a colorful nickname – The Great Gundy.

Outstanding amateur player, Anne Quast Sander, in an interview with author and TV commentator Rhonda Glenn recalled her first meeting with Carner.

"The first time I met JoAnne, she was fourteen and I was thirteen," Sander said. "I was putting. I'll never forget it; she came up to me and said, "Whatcha practicing for? Afraid, I'm gonna beat you?"[7]

Carner would beat Sander, and almost every other amateur woman golfer. Her amateur record is unrivaled. She won five U.S. Amateur titles (1957, 1960, 1962, 1966 and 1968), only Glenna Collett Vare won more (six). She is the only player to win the U.S. Girls Junior Championship (1956), the U.S. Amateur and the U.S. Women's Open (1971 and 1976). As an amateur Carner won the 1969 Burdine's Invitational, an LPGA Tour event. No amateur has won an LPGA event since.

Amateur golf and Carner were made for each other. The head-to-head competition of match play, which is the format for most major amateur events, suited Carner's combative nature. It allowed her to use a strategy few others possessed – scout the competition, and then intimidate them.

"I just loved everything about amateur golf," Carner said. "I still do. I knew my opponents. I watched their mannerisms. I knew who I had if I killed a drive on the first hole or birdied the first two holes, and I knew the ones I couldn't give any leeway to. My theory was to get my opponents trying to make birdies, and then I knew I had them. They would go for the pin and end up in the bunker with a bogey."[8]

When Carner played amateur golf, she was a true "amateur." Although golf was a major part of her life, for most of her amateur career, she did other things in addition to playing golf. Her amateur career began while she was in her teens. She played amateur golf while at Arizona State University (Carner graduated with a degree in physical education, and her golf skill earned her one of the first college golf scholarships given to a woman.). After college Carner worked in an insurance company and an electronics company. After her marriage, she and her husband owned and operated a 9-hole golf course.

Carner's decade-plus amateur record is outstanding, but the fact that she did other things while she accumulated that record makes it unique, spectacular and quite different from most of the young women amateur players in golf today. Had she remained an amateur, "The Great Gundy" might have been able to simplify that nickname to "The Greatest."

Big Momma

"I had no desire to be a pro," Carner said. "I loved amateur golf. Then I ran out of goals. My USGA record was something around 910 victories out of 1000 matches. I was extremely confident.

The only incentive left was to win two more Amateurs and beat Glenna Collett's record. My husband, Don, said I needed more of a challenge. Pro golf was it."[9]

In 1970, at age 30, Carner joined the LPGA Tour. She started her new life with typical Carner confidence, but the difference between amateur golf and the pro tour was something Carner did not expect.

"I expected to take over the tour immediately," Carner said. "Sandra Haynie told me it would take four years, and I said baloney, but it did. I was used to match play and winning, not staying there and grinding it out for $500."[10]

The transition to professional golf took more time than Carner had anticipated because Carner needed to develop a new mind-set for the stroke play format of the Tour.

"As an amateur, I either won or lost," Carner said. "In pro golf, if you're not playing well and are in 40th place, you still have to stay in there. That was real hard to learn. Opening rounds were tough for me – and still are, because you're playing the golf course. I love it on Sunday."[11]

Carner also learned quickly to keep from watching the swings of other golfers – no matter how great the player or the swing.

"Once I became fascinated by Kathy Whitworth's swing," Carner said. "The next thing I knew, I was standing with all my weight on my left foot. After the round, I asked Don what in the world was wrong. He demonstrated. Now I don't watch at all. In fact, I've trained myself to look for four-leaf clovers, even in the desert."[12]

The other, and more difficult, obstacle Carner had to overcome was the attitude of her fellow tour players. As an amateur, Carner had played in six LPGA events. Her record in those events did not endear her to the professionals in the field – she had one victory and two-second place finishes. When Carner joined the tour, her new colleagues tried to beat her at her own game – they tried to intimate her.

"They were a tough bunch," Carner said. "They'd try to needle me on the practice tee.

"Fay Crocker stood and analyzed my swing," Carner continued. "So, I asked if I could watch her hit balls and then needled her so much she couldn't get it airborne. I was paired with Marilynn

Smith, and when I hit a shot three feet from the hole, she said, 'Why didn't you hit a seven or eight iron instead of a punched nine? I replied, 'I got it three feet from the hole. What do you want?'"[13]

All the pros accomplished was to turn up Carner's competitive drive a notch or two. One can almost imagine her thinking to herself, "Okay, the game is on." It's hard to kid a kidder, and it's almost impossible to beat an expert at intimidation. Carner took everything the pros threw at her, and then gave it right back.

"When I first came on tour, some of the lady pros didn't care for me too much, probably because of my amateur success," Carner said. "They tried some mental games on me. I thought it was poor sportsmanship. They seemed to practice all the time, and they were so serious. I liked to just play – tee it up and play. I came up with a little mental game of my own; I would practice away from the tournament site and then show up early to have my cigarette and coffee and just relax beforehand. It drove some of them crazy. They never saw me practice. We did those kinds of things in those days."[14]

> ### JoAnne Carner
>
> **Amateur Career Highlights**
>
> **U. S. Girls Junior Champion:1956**
>
> **Five U.S. Amateur Championships:**
> **1957, 1960, 1962, 1966, 1968**
>
> **Four Curtis Cup appearances:**
> **1958, 5960, 1962, 1964**

Despite having to adjust to a sibling-like rivalry situation with her fellow professionals, Carner thrived on the competition in the pro ranks, and her career took off. Although she had a few swing problems her first year on tour, she managed to get her first LPGA win as a rookie professional. Her first major victory – the U.S. Women's Open – came in her second season. She went on to win 40 more (and still counting) events.

Carner's trademark with the fans is the chatter, quips and one-liners that she throws out to the spectators who line the fairways. Her sense of humor is as legendary as her golf record, but for Carner, the chatter is a way for her to relax.

"Concentration and getting involved with the shot are important," Carner said. "But, if I get too serious I can't play. I relieve the pressure by light chatter with the gallery, although I never get into conversation."[15]

Carner is also known for her spontaneous use of "body English," and showing her emotions on the course. When you watch Carner play you are never in doubt as to whether she liked or hated a shot. Her reactions on the course give insight to just how competitive she is.

"I have never had any trouble controlling my emotions," Carner said. "My problem has been to gear up – I have to drink five cups of coffee in the morning. However, being paired with good players like Jane Blalock, Sandra Palmer, Judy Rankin, Hollis Stacy, and Sally Little is motivating since they play well and force you to do the same."[16]

Because of her on course personality, Carner has the image of an extrovert, yet she is a very private person. Off the golf course Carner can be quiet and sometimes reserved.

Golf writer Liz Kahn describes Carner as responding well in press conferences, but "difficult to interview" in a one-on-one situation.[17]

It is not so much Carner's personality that comes out in one-on-one situations as it is her expectation that everyone will be as competitive as she, and will enjoy the challenge as much as she does.

In 1996, just before the start of the season, Carner was playing in a very small charity event near her home in Palm Beach, Florida. A local golf writer – new to the newspaper business, not too much younger than Carner, and a good golfer who had played most of her golf in the "Carner era" – asked to talk with Carner as she walked to her car to put away her clubs. Carner graciously agreed, but began the conversation with a brusque, "What do ya want to know?"

A bit taken aback, the writer blurted out three questions – all in one breath – that she had prepared in her mind while she had watched Carner play the round earlier that day. Obviously anxious to get started on her drive home, Carner answered each question fully, but exactly to the point with no elaboration. The writer, sensing Carner's distraction, ended the conversation by telling Carner that of all the people she had interviewed, Carner was hardest to approach because she was one of the writer's role models as a golfer.

Carner stopped packing her golf bag into the trunk of her car turned to the writer and gave some unsolicited advice.

"That's nice for me," Carner said. "But, don't forget what your job is."[18]

And Then There is Don

There are two loves in JoAnne's life – golf and Don Carner. Don and JoAnne were married in 1964. JoAnne was 24 and Don quite a bit older.

"There are two things we don't discuss," Don said. "JoAnne's weight and my age."[19]

As a celebrity marriage, the Carner's is unique – it has lasted 34 years. It is based on an unusual concept in the world of today's relationships – mutual respect.

"I was successful before I met JoAnne," Don said. "I have taught her to be independent and to think well. We never have arguments because there is no point in being mean to someone. We depend on each other in our relationship and do everything together."[20]

"Don has been a big influence," JoAnne said. "He has handled the business side of my life. He has observed my golf, analyzed it, motivated me, and kept me sharp. Everyone thinks we're crazy to be together so much, but we thoroughly enjoy doing everything together.

"That's the reason I've played in very few pro-ams," JoAnne continued. "Don has given up everything for me to play, so when I'm off, that's his time, and we do what he wants. We used to do a lot of trout and bass fishing; now we're into ocean fishing."[21]

Although JoAnne has spent her life traveling with the tour, in the first 20 years of their marriage, the Carners were separated only 19 days. In JoAnne's early years on tour, the couple traveled the circuit in a trailer so they could be together.

"I won most of my tournaments out of that trailer," JoAnne said. "Sometimes we had to fly and stay in hotels. I never could win those times. With the trailer, we could park on a river or a lake and could look out and see water or grass. We didn't own a house for ten years. People thought we were nuts, but they were jealous, too."[22]

The Carners have one rule that they never break. It was formed when JoAnne was having a swing problem and began working on her game with the late tour player and teaching professional Gardner Dickinson.

"Don went to every lesson," JoAnne said. "Later when I worked with Sam Snead, he listened carefully. Now when we work, we're together. But we made an agreement: If I shot 78 or 80, we would postpone discussing my round for an hour. We'd cool off. If we went right to the practice tee after a bad round, we'd only start arguing because I'm hot and Don is really hot."[23]

JoAnne Carner

Professional Highlights

The only woman to have won USGA Girls Junior, U.S. Amateur and U.S. Open

Recorded 12 consecutive top-10 finishes in majors from 1980-84

The Carners never had children, and JoAnne explains why.

"Don and I talked about having children," JoAnne said. "To me you have to do one thing or the other. Some people have raised kids and stayed on tour, but I don't think I could have done that."[24]

In the mid 1990's Don was diagnosed with Parkinson's disease. JoAnne cut her tour schedule back to be with him. In 1996 she played only three tour events. With Don stabilized a bit, JoAnne played 10 events in 1997. And, in 1997, she lent her name to a charity fishing tournament in the Palm Beach area to benefit the American Parkinson Disease Association. JoAnne and Don still feel uncomfortable being separated.

What's in a Name?

Carner's nickname as an amateur – "the Great Gundy" – was a natural outgrowth of the self-assured, almost cocky, attitude that the young Carner (or at that time Gunderson) brought to the game. It was bestowed upon her by her fellow amateur players, and reflected Carner's competitive personality.

The story of "Big Momma" – invented by a fellow professional and more reflective of the mature Carner – is similar. Over the years, as JoAnne has changed, the name's meaning has changed.

"Before the Open playoff against Sandra Palmer in 1976, [Palmer] said, 'I'm going up against Big Momma,'" Carner explained. "It just came out that way; I hit the ball much farther than she did."[25]

The name then signified her ability to hit the ball long. It was perfect for Carner the professional. She loves to hit the ball long.

"In the old days, players wanted to be ball-strikers first, chippers and putters second," Carner said. "Now, it's the other way around. But, I've always been a ball-striker. I love nailing a drive. What a feeling. That is how you intimidate an opponent in my book."[26]

The name also made reference to Carner's build – controlling her weight has always been a struggle. "My husband hated the name, but the caddies kept it alive. I'd put up some birdies, and they'd say, 'Uh-oh, here comes Big Momma.'"[27]

In the ensuing years, Carner has trimmed down, and although she has not lost much distance, her length has changed much like it does for all golfers as they go through the aging process. "Big Momma" however is still applicable – the meaning has just shifted.

Carner – still confidant and occasionally showing the cockiness of her youth – is now the Tour's senior stateswoman, and the nickname reflects that status. But, more than that the name reflects Carner's relationship with the Tour's young players.

"If a young player has a problem, chances are Carner has the solution," Barry McDermott wrote in a 1982 *Sports Illustrated* article.[28]

At the 1979 JAL Big Apple Classic, Carner showed what McDermott meant. Having come off a year in which she was ranked fourth on the money list, Carner was paired in the tournament's first round with a young amateur from New Jersey. The young woman had been invited to the event by virtue of her recent victory in the New Jersey State Amateur, and she had plans to eventually join the Tour. But, even for a player of that caliber, playing in a tour event with one of the best women golfers who ever lived might lead to a good case of butterflies. From her first tee shot it was obvious that the young amateur was distracted. She was hardly able to get the ball airborne, and just managed to bogey the first hole.

As she approached the second tee, disappointment showed on her face. Her tentative, nervous swing off the second tee produced a low hook that barreled its way into the woods to the left of the fairway. Disappointment turned to despair.

As the group walked off the tee, JoAnne caught up with the young woman, put her arm around her shoulder and talked quietly as they both walked into the woods. JoAnne hunted for the ball, and spotted it quickly. The young player hit a recovery shot that landed in the trees just right of the green. JoAnne again stayed with the player, and walked the entire fairway with her. She stopped only to hit her shot to the green, then continued on into the right woods and found the player's ball again. She stood with the player while she pitched out and onto the green, and then walked with her as the two made their way to the green.

The player two-putted for a par, as did Carner. JoAnne once more set her pace to that of the young player, chatting pleasantly with her as they walked the short distance to the next tee. The player's drive off the third tee was strong and straight, and each shot after that became a bit more solid. The young face was now calm and confident. With each solid shot JoAnne, now leaving the player on her own, offered the standard "good shot." The player finished the remaining holes on the front nine with pars, and at the end of the round posted a score of 75.[29]

Nancy Lopez summed up Carner's legacy to the tour.

"JoAnne made the way easier for players like me," Lopez said. "JoAnne showed a lot of us what it meant to be a fierce competitor and a normal person. No one plays this game with more passion than JoAnne. The fact that she's still out there says that much."[30]

Carner is still out there, and she probably will be for some time to come because her passion for the game remains.

"I know I am a legend in my lifetime, and I love taking on the rookies," Carner said. "When they said I was getting too old some years ago, I worked very hard on my game, and I felt I was getting better and better. I get pleasure from playing well. I enjoy my golf more than anyone. I could go and play all by myself, without any gallery, and be in seventh heaven."[31]

Chapter 11

The Perfect Star...
Nancy Lopez

In a game that is, at its essence, a study in imperfection, the truth is Nancy Lopez is perfect. Her smile is perfect. Her hair is perfect – never, even in a 40 MPH wind, is a strand out of place. She dresses perfectly. She behaves perfectly. She has the perfect family. She even has the perfect problem – a constant struggle to control her weight – which she handles perfectly.

Lopez is the perfect image for the LPGA and women's golf. She is a humble winner. Perfect. And, she is a gracious loser. Perfect. Yet the most astounding aspect of Nancy Lopez's perfection is the fateful blend of her skill and personality with history. The timing of her arrival on the Tour was not simply perfect, it was impeccable. For the LPGA, Lopez was the right person, at the right time, in the right place. She began her career on tour when the future of the LPGA was, at best, listless and, at worst, possible failure.

In 1977, the LPGA was in trouble. The $3 million in prize money was extremely low in comparison with men's golf, but more importantly, to the LPGA players, it was not even close to their booming sister professional sport – women's tennis. Sponsorship for tournaments was a "hard sell," and although the players were skilled and competitive, there was not a singular personality on Tour with the charisma to be an "attraction." Going into its 30th year, the Tour was struggling.

NANCY LOPEZ

Began playing golf: age 8

First tournament win: 1966, Alamogordo Pee Wee Championship

First LPGA victory: 1978

Most recent victory: 1997

Then, in 1978, fate smiled on the LPGA – in the form of the smile of a 21-year-old woman with a very good golf game. In February of that year, Nancy Lopez's golf game produced her first LPGA tournament victory. By June, after her fifth consecutive victory in as many starts, Nancy Lopez's smile had won the hearts of golf fans around the world. The LPGA had what they had not had since Babe Zaharias. They had a "star."

Lopez's golf game, smile, and friendly, almost intimate relationship with the fans would take the LPGA where they had never been before. Lopez's personality resurrected the LPGA. It became the largest women's professional sports organization in the world. It expanded both its sponsor base and its television exposure. Eighteen years later in 1985 – the last year Lopez was ranked number one on the money list – the Tour would produce $9 million in prize money.

Nancy Lopez was the "star" with the "perfect image." But, what made her the "perfect star" was that it was not an image. Teams of public relations consultants and media manipulation did not create it.

The Nancy Lopez who, to this day never refuses to sign an autograph, is real. The Nancy Lopez who is respectful to everyone she meets, is real. The Nancy Lopez whose warm smile appears whether she wins or loses, is real. The Nancy Lopez that everyone sees, is real and she may very well be perfect.

On January 6, 1957 in Torrance, California, twelve years after their first child, Delma, was born, Domingo and Marina Lopez celebrated the arrival of their second daughter, Nancy Marie. Shortly after Nancy's birth, the Mexican-American couple moved their family to Roswell, New Mexico where Domingo operated an auto body repair shop.

When Nancy was four, her sister Delma married and moved back to California. Despite the twelve-year age difference, the sisters were close and young Nancy found it difficult to accept Delma's leaving home.

"I hated it when Delma left," Nancy said. "I still remember how, as she packed her clothes to go I ran over and took each thing out of her suitcase a moment after she had carefully put it in."[1]

Lopez spent the remainder of her childhood, for all intents and purposes, as an only child. Both Domingo and Marina were avid golfers. Domingo had been an outstanding pitcher as a young man. Although he had the potential to make baseball a career, the responsibilities of his family made a try at the majors almost impossible. He turned his considerable athletic skills to golf and played to a 2-handicap. Marina, focusing her energy into being a wife and mother, played only as a weekend golfer but the game was a serious passion for her.

For the couple, golf was an activity that they could do together. They spent weekends on the golf course, and after Delma's marriage, Nancy began to accompany Mom and Dad.

"Dad was real good," Nancy said. "Mom was just a week-end type golfer, but they both loved the game and each other and they played a lot together. I used to tag along and watch."[2]

One weekend afternoon on Roswell's municipal golf course, when Nancy was eight, Domingo handed Nancy her mother's 4-wood. With that simple event, the Lopez's life, and the history of women's golf changed.

"Dad pulled Mom's 4-wood out of her bag," Nancy said. "He handed it to me, and simply said, 'Hit it. You just keep on hitting until you get that ball into the hole. Now stay just back of us, little one, but keep up too, because people in back will be right close and we don't want you to get in the way or anything like that, you see?"[3]

Nancy did see – quite well in fact. Although her memory of that first round is vague, Domingo has made it part of the family history.

"Dad has told me that the whole thing immediately and unexpectedly became very complicated," Lopez said. "Right away my ball flew over my parents' heads and each time they went on ahead, and I waited to fall back of them, the same thing happened.... Apparently, I never missed, but would just step up and swing and I kept knocking that ball on the nose and down the fairway. It did slow things up for my folks and me to keep playing this sort of leapfrog pace, and my Dad was nervous about blocking the people in back of us, so once I had reached the green he would only allow me to take one putt with my mother's putter. He would say, 'I'll give you that' on any putt I had left myself, and tell me to pick up my ball and hustle off the green.

"I would score for myself whatever number of strokes I'd taken up to where I was then lying on the green, but I didn't add anything for the conceded putt," Lopez continued. "That was logical, wasn't it? I scored the actual shots I had taken. Also, I was teeing up every shot on the fairway, and I guess that's one good reason why my 4-woods soared so well and never beaned my dear parents. It was some time later that I learned the rules didn't allow that, and that you had to putt out and count every stroke. But that day I had a very gratifying score using my rules.... The big thing was that I was completely hooked on golf."[4]

Lopez may have been "hooked" on golf, but, at the age of eight, she was not necessarily "driven." Her first memories of what pleased her about golf relate more to equipment than great golf shots.

"I remember sounds," Lopez says. "I remember going out with my mom and dad and pulling a golf cart behind them. There were little pebbles in the wheels, and I loved that sound. And, I remember the sound of sticking a club back in the bag and the sound of walking on concrete with spikes. I loved the sound the cleats made, and at the beginning I wanted golf shoes for myself just to walk around in much more than I wanted golf clubs to play with."[5]

"Driven" or not, Lopez did succeed. At age nine, she won her first event. In fact, she lapped the field in the 27-hole PeeWee tournament held in Alamogordo, New Mexico – her victory margin was 110 strokes.

To reward the budding star after her first win, Domingo began a victory tradition that would continue for several years.

"Dad was so excited and pleased that as an extra prize he bought me my favorite present at the time, a Barbie doll," Lopez said. "Each time after that when I did something special in golf, Dad came through with a doll that meant more to me than any medal or cup."[6]

Fueled by the prospect of adding to her growing doll collection, Lopez continued to practice, and improve. The young player's game was honed, not by a team of specialists, but by one person – her father. He was her golf professional, coach and motivator. And, although in those early years she met a great deal of success, Domingo also helped her to deal with the inevitable – failure.

"When you're young, you cry about bad shots or scores," Lopez said. "I'd cry, and he could always calm me down. He was always very positive. He was never the type of dad to pressure me. If I was playing in a little city tournament and I lost, he'd say, 'You have to accept that. You may win some, but you are going to lose a lot more.' It made a lot of sense to me. I think it made losing a lot easier to take."[7]

Lopez may have lost occasionally, but she won more often. At age twelve, a year before she could officially be called a teenager, she won the New Mexico State Women's Amateur Championship. The win was a harbinger of the outstanding success Lopez would find as an adult in golf, but that prophetic meaning was lost to the little girl. And, at least part of the driving force behind her performance was still something other than a hardened desire to be the best.

"I may have reached the ripe old age of twelve," Lopez said. "I may have shot a course record of 75 at the University South course in Albuquerque in the run toward winning the state championship, but collecting Barbie dolls was still big stuff. Dad said, 'Nancy won. Nancy gets every doll in the shop.'"[8]

Obstacles

From that first round played with her mother's 4-wood, it was obvious that Lopez had talent. The nurturing and development of that talent presented a challenge to the Lopez family. There were two obstacles that threatened the full realization of Lopez's potential – money and her status as a minority.

The Lopez family was able to live comfortably on what Domingo made from his auto body shop. Golf, especially high level amateur golf, is an expensive activity. Giving Nancy the opportunity to take golf from "fun" to a career placed severe financial pressure on the Lopez family.

"The money Dad made from the auto body shop had supported us very pleasantly," Nancy said. "The trouble was that there wasn't much money left over for what he and Mom now considered our prime necessity – giving their child every chance to develop her golfing skills."

"My mother made the first move," Lopez continued. "Three golfers in the family added up to one too many. She used the excuse that a recent gall bladder operation she had undergone probably made it wise for her to give up the game. So that is what she did – turning over all her clubs to me. The fact is that although she was never very good at it, my mother loved golf and, seeing what she did for me in later years, it's my bet that her explanation about her gall bladder was just so I wouldn't feel guilty about her sacrifice. She always had me and my sister much more in her mind than herself."[9]

Marina Lopez's support of her daughter's quest to reach her potential extended beyond understanding the financial challenge to the family.

"When I started to do well as an amateur," Lopez said. "Mom never let me wash dishes again because she insisted that the hot water would soften my hands and so harm my swing."[10]

With Marina's sacrifice and Domingo's hard work, the family was able to put aside $100 each month that was earmarked for Nancy's travel expenses to junior golf tournaments. The "in- home" savings plan succeeded as did the young golfer.

After her phenomenal New Mexico Women's amateur win at age twelve, Lopez went on to win the Western Junior Championship three times, and in 1972 and 1974 she won the USGA Junior

Girls National title. In 1975, as an amateur she finished second in the U.S. Open. The following year she entered the University of Tulsa on a golf scholarship. She won the 1976 AIAW National Championship, and she was a member of the 1976 U.S. Curtis Cup and World Amateur teams.

At the University of Tulsa, Lopez, who had been an excellent student all her life, majored in engineering. After a short period, she realized the travel required as a member of the golf team kept her out of class too much for her to keep up with the rigorous courses. At the end of her freshman year, she changed her major. By the time Lopez finished her sophomore year at Tulsa, she had achieved most of the coveted prizes available in women's amateur golf, and the game had become the major focus of her life.

"Golf was taking up too much of my time to do a good scholastic job," Lopez said. "That is why I was ready to stop college at the end of my second year and set out for a professional golfing life."[11]

Perhaps even more important in Lopez's decision to leave college was Domingo and Marina. For Lopez, the time had come to repay the hard work and financial sacrifice that her parents had made. The only place for her to do that was on tour.

The second obstacle Lopez faced was less overt than financial sacrifice. As Mexican-Americans, the Lopez's did not fit the affluent WASP image that characterized golf up to that point in its history.

"Dad has a strong Spanish accent and flavor to his speech," Lopez said. "Although that didn't rub off on a girl who grew up so Americanized as I did, all of us Lopezes are definitely and unashamedly Mexican Americans. In Roswell that was not a social asset.

"It's a very pleasant town, and I have good memories of it," Lopez continued. "But, we had the sort of minority status that minorities invariably suffer everywhere. In my case it certainly never was any tragedy, and just about all of my friends were Anglos and good friends, but one could get snubbed when one least expected it. Being Mexican-American, I never felt I was given an opportunity I didn't have to work for. I felt doors close in my face. Some of this stuff I didn't know was discrimination at the time. But I look back at it now, and I think it was. I've felt prejudice as a woman, too. That isn't good either."[12]

The biggest hurdle that Lopez's heritage, and perhaps her sex, presented was an inability to join the Roswell's country club, a facility with a first-rate golf course. Lopez was forced to hone her game on the rocky fairways of the municipal course.

"The point is that while I could play on the municipal course, that wasn't a well-kept, regulation layout that could have challenged my developing game," Lopez said. "Its chief virtue was that you could play there for $1.25.

"Certainly the dues at the country club would have been pretty tough for Dad to manage," Lopez continued. "But the whole idea was academic anyhow. Mexican-Americans like my parents would not have been welcome members, and if they didn't join I obviously couldn't and wouldn't. I am sure I wouldn't have been happy in that atmosphere in any event. Although people were perfectly nice to me when I played at the club in a city tournament, I was just as happy to get away between rounds. There was a polite frostiness about the whole place that made me quite reconciled to going back and playing on the municipal course."[13]

Lopez is philosophical about her experience, suggesting it may have been a "disadvantage" that, in the long run, turned into an "advantage."

"I sometimes wonder what would have happened if a teaching professional from a country club had latched onto me at that stage," Lopez said. "My Dad left my natural game alone, but I don't know if a pro could have resisted taking me apart and putting me together again."[14]

To this day, Lopez plays with that "natural game." She has never worked with a teaching professional; never had any teacher other than Domingo Lopez. She emphasizes that the most technical advice he ever gave was a simple "come up on the backswing real slow and real high, extend, and hit the ball."[15]

The experience Lopez had as a Mexican-American and the way she learned to react to it may have prepared her for the interpersonal challenge her first phenomenally successful year on the LPGA Tour would produce – jealousy.

"The main thing I remember is that the players didn't really know me," Lopez said. "I was on the golf course, then I went to the pressroom for my interview, then I went back to the practice tee, and by the time I was done everyone had gone. So I was never in the locker room with other players. I think they thought I was some sort of snob. And I think the press blew it up a little.

"I remember this one girl said, 'I hope she breaks a leg,'" Lopez continued. "I read things like that, comments other girls made. It was jealousy, of course. But I've always said that I know what I stand for and how I live my life, and the only person I try to please is God. I said, 'I'm just going to talk with my golf clubs.' And, that's what I did."[16]

Meteor on Tour

There is no other way to describe Lopez's arrival on Tour except meteoric. In her first full year on tour, 1978, she won nine events including a record-setting five in a row and a major (the LPGA Championship). That year she won the LPGA's Triple Crown – Rookie of the Year, Player of the Year, and the Vare Trophy for the lowest scoring average – and was ranked number one on the money list. She followed in her sophomore year, 1979, by winning eight events, posting a second consecutive number one money list ranking, Player of the Year and Vare Trophy.

Her record start in professional golf was simply unprecedented. The feat caught the attention of the media, while Nancy's smile and personality caught the imagination of golf fans. It was magical, and Nancy was the booster rocket that sent women's golf to new, probably never imagined, heights.

Nancy Lopez became an instant star. Her life instantly changed, and the young woman who wanted to repay her parents' sacrifice, thoroughly, and without a hint of egoism, enjoyed every minute of it.

> ### NANCY LOPEZ
>
> **Amateur Career Highlights**
>
> **New Mexico Women's Amateur: 1969, age 12**
>
> **USGA Junior Girls Championship: 1972 & 1974**
>
> **Three-time Western Junior Champion**
>
> **Mexican Amateur: 1975**
>
> **AIAW Championship: 1976**
>
> **Curtis Cup and World Amateur: 1976**

"I loved it," Lopez said. "I didn't have a care in the world except to play golf. I thought the attention was great. It was like "Would you like to have a car?" and somebody would give me a car for the week of a tournament. Mercedes gave me a car for a year for free. Limos would pick me up. People would send their planes to get me. And I would make all kinds of money in one day.

"I was doing outings every Monday for $500," Lopez continued. "My manager called me one day and said, 'Well, you aren't playing for $500 anymore, you are playing for $15,000.' I said, "Are they crazy? For one day they are going to pay me $15,000?' So, I enjoyed the attention. I kind of thrived on it."[17]

Those first two years on tour justified the judgment and faith Domingo and Marina had shown in their daughter's talent and character. In those two years, the Lopez family reaped the rewards of their years of focusing on one goal. The rewards, however, did not come without sadness.

Lopez joined the tour in July 1977. Her first few tour events resulted in what is typically expected of a rookie – nothing spectacular, except for her second place finish in the U.S. Open. It was her second Open runner-up finish; in 1975 she finished in the number two spot as an amateur. By late September Lopez was beginning to make her fellow competitors take notice. Late in the season, she had two consecutive second place finishes – one in the European Colgate Championship, and then a second place finish to Debbie Austin in the Long Island Charity Classic.

It seemed Lopez's breakthrough as a tour winner was only a matter of time. Then tragedy struck. On September 29, Marina Lopez died from complications only minutes after surgery to remove her appendix.

"The saddest thing in my life has been Mom's unexpected death," Lopez said. "She had an appendix operation and everything seemed to be all right and then, only minutes later, she died. I was on tour but telephoning every day, and I had been completely reassured about her only an hour before Delma called to tell me the catastrophic news. I dropped out of the tour and flew home to be with Dad. I owed her so much, and I was just on the edge of being able to repay her to some extent for all the years she lavished on me when suddenly she was gone."[18]

Lopez did not return to the tour until February 1978 for the Bent Tree Ladies Classic in Sarasota, Florida. The event was the first of her 48 career wins.

"I've always felt that the toughening experience of such a tragedy might have been a factor in strengthening my determination," Lopez said. "In any event, I dedicated that tournament to my Mom's memory, and she's never been out of my thoughts for very long ever since. Nor will she ever be. It is some consolation that she did have the joy of seeing me emerging as a star in my rookie year as a pro, and to know that I was likely to fulfill the promise she wanted so badly for me. But, I certainly wish she were still here to share in what has happened since."[19]

Marina would certainly be proud of "what has happened since" in terms of her daughter's career in golf, but she would be overjoyed at Nancy's natural ability to handle her success graciously and in doing so, touch the hearts of golf fans.

Lopez is unique among "superstars" – she does not consider herself "super."

"I was never comfortable thinking I was better than everybody else," Lopez said. "I might have felt it or thought it once in a while. But, I was never comfortable showing it. I could never walk around saying, 'Hey, I'm better than you.' Just because you play golf better than a lot of people in the world doesn't mean you are that big a deal."[20]

Lopez is unique among athletes – she understands that an athlete's relationship to fans must be nurtured.

"Some people marvel at how I don't seem annoyed by requests, even when they come at inappropriate times such as walking to the first tee for the final round of a big tournament," Lopez said. "The fact is that I like and appreciate such attention, and it never upsets me. I feel that they are doing me a favor in asking me to sign their program, and not the other way around. I think that even when you're tired of signing, especially after a tough round, it's something you owe your fans. If they are going to come out and spend money and tramp around to see me, then I can sign autographs. People will really be on your side if you sign an autograph, or smile and say 'hello.' It's important to a golf fan, and golf fans are important to me."[21]

Lopez's achievement in her rookie season – nine wins including five in a row – was amazing. It amazed golf fans. It amazed the LPGA.

Of everything that happened in those first two amazing years on tour, one stands out as the most significant for Lopez as a golfer. It was her defeat of Mickey Wright in a play-off early in the 1979 season.

> ### NANCY LOPEZ
>
> #### Professional Highlights
>
> **Won nine events in a single year:1978, including a record setting five in a row.**
>
> **21 top-10 finishes in 25 starts:1985**

It was the only time Lopez and Wright have ever faced each other. The confrontation was more than one player against another; it was the end of one era and the beginning of another.

In a 1997 interview Lopez reflected on the significance of her first two years on tour. In that reflection Lopez referred specifically to her confrontation with Mickey Wright. By doing so, she showed she had the insight to understand that the real significance of her achievement was not in the number of wins, but in the quality of the players against whom she competed. She also demonstrated that she was personally aware that her one competitive meeting with Mickey Wright symbolized the dawn of a new era, and that the outcome would legitimize her own position along with Wright as a golf legend.

"If I could not be me, I'd look at it [the five consecutive wins] and say, 'Yeah, that's pretty amazing,'" Lopez said. "It was a big deal. But what really was a big deal to me then was to beat Mickey Wright, one of the best players to ever play golf. I thought that was a real big deal!"[22]

Priorities

Lopez, like many other successful women of her generation, "has it all" – a successful career and a wonderful family. She is married to Ray Knight, a former professional baseball player and manager. The Knight family includes their three daughters and Ray's son from his first marriage. Her success in achieving what she wanted – a career in golf and a family – is a direct result of focusing on priorities that have been part of her character since her childhood. Lopez's strong sense of family has always been the most important part of her life. In her book, *The Education of a Woman Golfer*, written in 1979 as she completed her second year on tour and had established herself as the brightest star in women's golf, Lopez talked about the importance for her of a life outside golf.

"I guess when you've seen your parents happy in a conventional marriage, you've got to believe that they had something great going for them," Lopez said. "I still value traditional roles. I was brought up very old-fashioned and I guess it stuck. I still think their ways were good ways."[23]

Ten years – and three children – later, Lopez talked again about the importance of her life outside golf in an article for *Golf Magazine*.

"All the glamour, fame, signing autographs and admiration doesn't mean anything if you don't have anything at home," Lopez said. "We have a lot of love in our family."[24]

The process of "getting it all" has not been easy for Lopez. Her golf career developed smoothly, took off immediately, and except for relatively short "slump" periods, has been consistently successful. Finding a personal life that was "old-fashioned" and "traditional" took a bit more work and got off to a rocky start.

In 1978 Lopez met sportscaster Tim Melton at the Lady Keystone Open in Hershey, Pennsylvania. Lopez had just won her record setting fifth consecutive tournament, and Melton was assigned to do an interview with her. At week's end, Lopez's win streak had ended – she finished thirteenth – but she had begun a relationship with Melton. She and Melton were married less than six months later, on Nancy's twenty-sixth birthday, in January 1979.

The marriage may have been the period in Nancy's life that was most difficult for her. It was a time in which she was forced to confront the real world as it existed for her – a world class athlete and celebrity.

Golf had always been relatively easy for Lopez. She worked hard at it – putting in the time and effort needed to be a world class player. Her success seemed to be an easy and natural result of her effort. Developing a marriage was not as easy as developing a golf swing. It was especially difficult when that golf swing was the most famous in the world, and when Nancy's model marriage was one that was "traditional."

Like other women who "wanted it all," Lopez found that "having it all" put too much stress on each part of the "all."

"When I was newly married to Tim my game really suffered," Lopez said. "That was in 1981. I wasn't practicing. I wasn't devoting as much time to my game. I really struggled. I was embarrassed to be out there. Every night I'd cry in my hotel room. I was by myself a lot. I had to work my own way out of it."[25]

To find her way out, she was forced to end her marriage. It was not an easy thing for Lopez to do. But, it was a decision that showed she had found the same maturity off the golf course that she had on the course.

"I went through my divorce in 1981," Lopez said. "When you marry you just don't think it's going to happen to you. But, I realized what kind of husband I would need to cope with my career, and unfortunately it wasn't Tim.

"It takes a very, very strong man to deal with the attention, the money you make, and all of the other things that go with it," Lopez continued. "A lot of men can't deal with it. You wouldn't think it would be that much of a problem, but it was. I remember the disappointment when I realized that what I wanted for my game wasn't important to him."[26]

One of the people who helped Lopez through that divorce in 1981 was Ray Knight. Knight had been a friend of the Melton's, and Nancy turned to Ray for advice when she began to realize that she would have to end her marriage.

"He was my only friend during that period when I was struggling the most," Lopez said.[27]

After Lopez and Melton separated, Nancy and Ray talked on the telephone almost constantly. Neither considered their relationship any more than a friendship. That all changed.

"One night about three weeks before she was divorced, we went out to dinner," Knight said. "That was really the first time I thought I might be falling in love with her. After that it was just an explosion. It was really a friendship that turned into a romance."[28]

Lopez and Knight were married in 1982. A year later their first child was born and Nancy had achieved her "off-course" goal. She had an "old-fashioned" and "traditional" family – Nancy Lopez style.

The Knight marriage works perhaps because both Nancy and Ray are professional athletes. They understand the demands made by each other's talent.

"After I married Ray, I felt that golf was second," Lopez said. "He made me happier than golf did. But Ray never pressured me not to go anywhere to play golf, and I had often felt that pressure from Tim. There were times that Tim asked me not to leave."[29]

"I've never asked her to come home, and I never would," Knight said. "Nancy is known the world over because she has such great talent, and I don't want her to waste it."[30]

Although Ray and Nancy understand the demands and needs of each other's career, a family still puts pressure on both of them as parents. The priorities that Nancy has set for herself reflect the values that she learned as a child.

"I wanted to have a family," Lopez said. "I could have just played golf and never had children at all. But then you grow old and risk ending up alone. To someday have grandchildren, being a parent, experiencing family, that's special to me. And golf won't be there forever. I mean, competitively, it won't be there forever. I'd be a very lonely person if I couldn't play golf and I didn't have a family, either."[31]

"Mid-life Opportunity"

Lopez's drive to succeed in golf has always been based on the fun she finds in the game, the kick she gets from winning and her natural desire to relate to people – even those she does not know. It has never been based on ego or a burning desire to be the best there is.

"I don't know that I ever felt I was going to become a professional and play on the women's tour," Lopez said. "I just remember loving to play and wanting to win. And playing with my dad almost every day, I'd get really mad when I got beat, and he'd say, 'Well, you've got to practice harder if you want to win.' So, I'd go out there and work harder. I know I sacrificed a lot of my young life to play, because I didn't really participate in a lot of things with my friends. I always chose to play golf instead."[32]

In 1998, Lopez was in her twentieth year on tour. The year before, in 1997, she had posted her forty-eighth victory – her first win in four years – and she finished second to Allison Nicholas at the U.S. Open – a championship she has never won. She took the young player all the way to the the last hole before losing by one shot. She had accomplished about as much as anyone could in golf and she had accomplished what she wanted in her personal life.

At age 41, Lopez was rededicating herself to golf, and her goals seem to be more definitive than when she began her career. She wants to win 50 events, and she called her renewed interest in her career a mid-life opportunity, not a mid-life crisis.

"I just never thought I'd be 40," Lopez said. "It's that simple. When I look at the young players out here now, it seems like I was just there, just 19. It seems like yesterday. Because I feel like I could go out with these girls and have a good time. Your mind tells you, 'I am still 20.' I guess you don't see yourself as being older. I just think I'm still 20."[33]

Perhaps the star that brought the LPGA to a new level of visibility twenty years ago is about to break through the twilight and light up the sky once more. That might be just perfect.

Chapter 12

Woman on a Mission...
Pat Bradley

I completed my mission." That simple statement is how Pat Bradley summed the career that, in 1991, put her into the LPGA Hall of Fame. The statement really sums up Bradley herself – very much to the point, no extra fanfare and expressing total success.

When Bradley plays golf she looks like she is on a mission. She strides purposefully down the fairway, visor pulled down over her brow. Her eyes seldom wander from the target, and her face expresses a calm, focused confidence. Her conversations are limited, hushed and related to the task at hand.

When watching Bradley play golf, one has a sense that even if she does not "win" she will not "fail." You can almost feel the force of her will. Each decision is calculated. Each shot is an attack. Each round produces as much as it can.

"I am not out here spinning my wheels," Bradley said. "I never think, 'I don't feel up to it this week.' I get out of each tournament what I possibly can. If I can't win – and no one can win every week – I'm going to do my damnedest to finish the best I can. I'll fight and scrape to finish in the top 10 or the top five."[1]

No military commander, sending a soldier on a crucial mission, could ask any more. If that soldier were Bradley, the commander could feel confident that the mission would be accomplished.

Patricia Ellen Bradley was born on March 24, 1951. She is the third oldest of Richard and Kathleen Bradley's six children. The other five are boys.

As the only sister of five brothers, Bradley understandably became an outstanding all-around athlete. In high school at Westford Academy she played field hockey, basketball and softball, captaining all three teams. In basketball, she was one of the team's leading scorers, with a career high of 39 points in one game. She was shortstop on the school's softball team, maintaining a batting average of .700. Skiing was Bradley's main sport as a youngster. She began skiing at age six and by age ten, Bradley was competing in age-group races throughout New England. When she was a junior in high school, she trained with the Olympic ski team.

More than her interest in sports and her intense competitive experience, Pat's relationship with her family played the crucial role in both defining her "mission" and developing the golf course persona that became known as the "stare" or the "gaze" by her fellow tour players. In a world dominated by five boys, Bradley quickly developed an intensity and toughness that allowed her to carve out a place in the Bradley household.

"At times it was tough being the only girl," Bradley said. "With five boys you can get set apart. I think that's where I developed the competitive edge. We are very much a sports family. The denominators in the Bradley household are golf and skiing. With five brothers, it was survival of the fittest. Even at the dinner table, it was very competitive. If you were slow, you wouldn't eat. Looking back, I wouldn't have wanted it any other way. I have great brothers, and I have enjoyed them very much."[2]

As a young athlete, Bradley was good, but she seemed to get by on raw talent alone. She never really had to work to succeed. Bradley admits that if she had showed more drive, she probably would have reached world-class level in skiing.

"When I trained with the Olympic skiers, I dreamed of the Olympics," Bradley said. "But, I didn't give it enough effort."[3]

Bradley's father changed all that. He introduced her to golf.

"I took up golf at eleven, through my dad, who was the big influence," Bradley said. "He was an average player, he caddied in his younger days, and he believed in golf as a game of ladies and gentlemen, of honesty and etiquette. He wanted all of his children to experience its greatness."[4]

Bradley had just as much natural talent in golf as she did in other sports, but developing that talent was a slow process and the game was not one of Bradley's favorites.

"I wasn't thrilled with this slow-moving game," Bradley said. "With five brothers, I was more into team sports. Although I had natural ability and talent, I did not become good very quickly. In national amateur tournaments or the U.S. Amateur, I was easily beaten by girls who played the game year round instead of seasonally, as I did. I won regional tournaments; so that locally I was a star, although nationally I was no one."[5]

Golf, for Bradley, could have gone the way of her skiing career – lots of potential, but not enough effort. Instead, Dick Bradley, without undue pressure and lovingly, focused his daughter's attention. He gave her a "mission."

"Pat was a terrific skier," Pat's mother, Kathleen said. "When she finished high school, she didn't know whether to try out for the U.S. ski team or go south and play golf. So her dad stepped in and said, 'You're going south to play golf.'"[6]

> **PAT BRADLEY**
>
> **Began Playing golf: age 11**
>
> **First tournament win:1967, New Hampshire Amateur**
>
> **First LPGA victory:1976**
>
> **Most recent victory:1995**

Bradley went south and golf became her life. She spent two years on the golf team at Miami-Dade Junior College, which boasted one of the nation's finest junior college women's golf programs. In 1973, Bradley transferred to Florida International University, a new school that had recently been founded in Miami. At FIU Bradley was the women's golf team. She was the only woman representing the school. That year she placed fifth in the AIAW Championship Tournament and was named an All-American. After graduating from FIU in 1974 with a degree in physical education, Bradley entered the LPGA Qualifying School that was held in Miami. The woman who five years earlier had been a "no one" at amateur golf's national level, finished first in the Qualifying tournament and had earned an LPGA Tour Card.

Within two years, Bradley had won her first LPGA event and had broken into the top 10 on the money list. She remained in the top 10 for all but one of the following 10 years. In 1986, Bradley had a "dream season." She won five times, collected $492,000 and for the first time in her career was ranked number one. Bradley certainly was a success, but it was not enough. There was still the "mission."

"My dad's goal was for me to reach the Hall of Fame, and I had a fear of failing him," Bradley said. "For many years I felt in my heart I was Hall of Fame material but not in my mind. I was not completing the mission."[7]

The Mission: Part I

Bradley's rise to golf stardom was not the meteoric ride of Nancy Lopez. Instead, Bradley's was more characteristic of her New England background – steady, conservative and solid.

"I was very silent in my moves up the ladder," Bradley said. "My first principal goal was winning Player of the Year, and it took me thirteen years to do that. I think I've been driven more by the fear of failure than the joy of success.... You look at a Beth Daniel, a Holis Stacy, a Nancy Lopez – I couldn't hold a candle to them as amateurs."[8]

Bradley may not have been able to defeat Daniel, Stacy and Lopez as amateurs, but as a professional she has more than held her own. She has beaten those players and others in her thirty-one LPGA Tournament wins, finished in the top twenty-five on the money list twenty out of twenty-four years, and has six major tournament victories. She was the only player to have won all four modern major events – the U.S. Open, LPGA Championship, the Dinah Shore and the Du Maurier Championship – until Julie Inkster matched that record in 1999. Bradley is the only player to come close to "golf's grand slam." In 1986, she won three of the four major titles – the Dinah Shore, the LPGA Championship and the DuMaurier.

Professional golf seemed to suit Bradley. It was serious, and for keeps. And, she had experience playing for money. When Bradley played amateur golf, although she seldom won trophies, she was good at winning money. Her first teacher, John Wirbel of Nashua (New Hampshire) Country Club encouraged her to play pick-up games with the "guys" at Nashua. The matches were usually for $10, and the "guys" could get a bit rough.

"There was a lot of swearing and what we call 'color' out there." Bradley said.[9]

Pat was the only women who was part of the group known as the Hatreds – part of the fun was, within the bounds of good clean competition, to make things on the course as "unfriendly" as possible, hence the name.

Former *New York Daily News* sportswriter, Mike Lupica, was part of the group and he recalled that Bradley was forced on the group.

"John Wirbel made us do it," Lucia said. "She was always practicing, a foreign concept to us. I'm sure she's still walking around with my allowance."[10]

If the tour made Bradley feel at home because of the rough and tumble competition, it also exposed her to people whom she could use as role models, and learning from them helped her over the rough spots.

"I felt very comfortable on tour," Bradley said. "I gravitated to the older players, learning from Judy Rankin, Sandra Haynie, Donna Caponi, Marlene Hagge and Sandra Post. It didn't come easily, but I strived mentally and physically, learning course management, patience, and realizing that working on my game around the greens was the most important part."[11]

What Bradley learned was not always limited to what might improve her game.

"I played with Marlene Hagge for the first time in England," Bradley said. "I remember being told she was the fastest player on tour. 'Don't hold up Marlene,' I was told. On the first hole, I took a 9 but I was in the hole before Marlene made her 4. I didn't want to hold her up."[12]

PAT BRADLEY

Amateur Career Highlights

New Hampshire Amateur: 1967 & 1969

All-American at Florida International University: 1970

New England Amateur: 1972 & 1973

Bradley succeeded because, again like the ancestors of her New England heritage, she was a "grinder." She worked hard both on the practice tee and during a round. She took the good days when they came, and tried to create the best she could out of the not so-good-days.

"I would give myself pep talks," Bradley said. "I would tell myself, 'Relax, be patient, things will turn around. You're being tested; they're trying to make you strong by giving you little challenges. It's up to you to meet them and succeed.'"[13]

Bradley succeeded but it seemed that no one really noticed. Her non-glamorous "grinder" image and quiet, reserved personality did not make for great media copy.

As Jan Stephanson, who finished second to Bradley ten years earlier in the 1974 LPGA Qualifying School, said in 1984, "Pat Bradley is a great player, but what can you say about Pat Bradley but what she shot? All she does is practice and play."[14]

Bradley and Stephanson were not the best of friends either on the course or off, and the comment did not do much to relieve the tension between the two players. It does point out that the media was not all that interested in a player who just sort of plugged along, no matter how successful.

The reputation as a reserved, non-charismatic, and leaning toward loner personality has followed Bradley throughout her career. Bradley took Stephanson's 1984 comment in stride without rancor and at every juncture during her career has met the criticism by giving her own "take" on Pat Bradley.

"I'm not extremely colorful in the way I play," Bradley said in 1986. "But, I'm a very smart player. I'm solid and consistent: flares don't start firing when I get to the tee as they might for others. But, the bottom line is that I get the job done. I'm also shy. Nancy Lopez is kind of our Arnold Palmer, and JoAnne Carner is our Lee Trevino. I admire them both. But, I have to be myself, and I hope people admire me for the way I am."[15]

"Disciplined is probably a [good word for me]," Bradley said in 1992. "I do enjoy people, but I have a job that needs to be done, and that comes first."[16]

The other problem for Bradley was that, despite her ability to stay at the top end of the money list, she gained a reputation as a great second place finisher, and not a player you could count on to win. In a sense, what should have been an admirable quality, her consistency, became a detriment.

"Hers is a very strange case," Fellow Hall of Famer, JoAnne Carner said in 1985. "A lot of things have covered up Pat Bradley's success. Lopez came on the scene, Stephenson turned into our own little soap opera, and now younger players like Juli Inkster and Patty Sheehan are getting in on the action. But to win so much money and not be well known, it is tough to tolerate."[17]

For Bradley who had been the first LPGA player to reach the $2 million, $3 million and $4 million mark, it was hard to tolerate. But, with typical patience, Bradley has explained it, defended it and accepted it throughout her career.

"When you are in the hunt in 19 out of 28 tournaments, it takes it out of you," Bradley said in 1984. "It's depressing, but who wants to listen to my bellyaching when I make $220,000 in a year without a win?"[18]

"Probably the thing that kept me back was I expected so much out of myself," Bradley said in a 1986 interview. "I have a hard time dealing with being mediocre. I've probably been my own worst enemy. That's hindered me, but if I wasn't like that I probably wouldn't be where I am today. Sure I'd like to have turned some of those seconds into firsts, but Pat Bradley is Pat Bradley.

"I have a lot of seconds, and some would say only 19 wins," Bradley continued. "But, 19 wins, with five majors, is terrific on this tour."[19]

"By 1986, I had paid a lot of dues and put in my time," Bradley said in 1993. "Finishing first is easy – there are no questions to be answered. Finishing third is no problem, since there are two ahead of you. Finishing second leaves all the questions to be answered. Finishing second over the years helped me build character."[20]

In 1985, Bradley was very close to breaking away from being an "also ran." She finished just behind Nancy Lopez on the money list – second again, but it was a horse race until the end. She was so close, and Bradley was so pleased with her performance in 1985, that she gave herself what she called her "own Player of the Year award." For Christmas, she bought herself a $7000 Rolex watch – a duplicate of what the LPGA awarded Lopez.

The gesture told two things about Bradley. First, that she was very comfortable with herself and her accomplishments. The gesture pointed out her self-motivation and realistic self-appreciation. Second, Bradley may have known something about herself that no one else suspected. She was about to put an end to the criticism and questions about her status as the tour's perennial bridesmaid. The self -awarded Rolex was a harbinger of things to come.

Bradley's 1986 season was record setting. She dominated the tour. That year, Bradley won five times; three of those were majors. After 13 years on tour she was ranked number one on the money list for the first time, and won the Vare Trophy for the lowest scoring average for the first time. But, more important, she got a second Rolex watch – this time awarded by the LPGA. In 1986, Bradley reached the first goal of the mission that began in 1974 – she was Player of the Year.

"It was frustrating in past years, because deep down I knew I had the talent to win," Bradley said. "I've gotten raked over the coals for what I haven't done. Now maybe I'll get praised for what I have done. After 13 years my number has come up. People have become aware of what Pat Bradley has done."[21]

Even the guy who originated the mission seemed pleased and proud. Perhaps Pat's father was more proud of the way his daughter demonstrated her character than of the accomplishments she achieved.

"For all her aggressiveness in athletics, she's kind of a sensitive person," Bradley's father said. "She might have had doubts about whether she could win. But she kept plugging away just the same."[22]

By the opening of the 1987 season, Bradley had reached the top. She had accumulated twenty victories. She was well over half way to the Hall of Fame. She seemed right on track to the ultimate goal. The mission was going well.

The Ultimate Test

Bradley went into the 1987 season with her confidence high and her sights firmly set on beginning the final push for the ten wins that would get her into the Hall of Fame. The 1987 season ended for Bradley in disappointment. She had slipped from first on the money list to fifteenth, and she was only one win closer to the Hall. The 1988 campaign was even worse. She won no events, and finished 109th on the money list with $15,000. Her scoring average had soared from 71.10 in 1986 to 75.19 at the end of 1988.

"Eighty six was wonderful," Bradley said. "I was accomplishing so much, it was hell. I mean hell. Nothing comes easy to me and to do well I have to put more than 110 percent of myself into it, and that is very taxing. I am always driving."[23]

Bradley believed that her performance decline was a combination of a let-down after the 1986 season and fatigue. After taking a week off during the middle of 1987, she began to think that the problem was in her swing.

"The first thing I said to myself was, 'There's something wrong with my swing,'" Bradley said. "There can't be anything wrong with me! I just had the greatest year of my life."[24]

Bradley's poor performance continued even after she had seen Gail Davis, an ex-tour player and teaching pro who had taken over where Bradley's first teacher, John Wirbel, had left off. The time spent with Davis made no difference.

"In May of 1987, I started hitting the ball short," Bradley said. "I usually hit my eight iron 130 yards, and suddenly I couldn't hit it 115. Then I started getting the jitters. I thought I was putting too much pressure on myself. Everytime a symptom came up, I put it off to something else."[25]

Like so many other athletes, Bradley never considered the possibility of a physical problem. She constantly related the poor quality of her performance to swing mechanics, the pressure of competition, lack of mental toughness, or other mental problems.

"I have always thought of myself as a strong person," Bradley said. "I kept thinking that if I didn't feel really sick, there must not be anything wrong with me. But I was getting to be a mess. My heart rate was 150 at rest. I was extremely tired but I couldn't sleep soundly. After a while, I thought I must have been having a nervous breakdown. I was frightened because the feelings I was having were so strange."[26]

By 1988, even Bradley's fellow tour players were noticing a change. Val Skinner was shocked one day when she attempted to help Bradley with her swing. While on the practice tee she saw Bradley's hands shake so badly that she could not tee up the balls.

"We all knew, inside the tour, that this was one of the greatest players of all time," Val Skinner said. "Pat wasn't as calm and as comfortable with herself and her game. I noticed an unsettled air about her. Her golf swing suffered. She started questioning her skills, something Pat never had done. She wasn't sure about even wanting to play anymore. I asked, 'How about the Hall of Fame?' and she said, 'Oh, I don't know.'"[27]

Interestingly no one connected with the tour mentioned their concern to Bradley.

"Everyone was concerned but expected Bradley to pull through on her own – she always had," Barbara Matson wrote in a 1989 article for *Golf Magazine*.[28]

Bradley believes the silence was partially due to the way she responded to the problem.

"No one came up and asked what was wrong," Bradley said. "But, I don't hold that against anybody. We all have our own problems to deal with on the tour. I just hid in the privacy of my own room. I didn't want to go to a doctor because I was afraid of what he might find. I found myself slipping in and out of the locker room avoiding people. I became very embarrassed by the way I performed. I'd have a flight in the morning and would be up at 5:30 so I could be out of the hotel before anybody else woke up."[29]

Finally in April 1988, Bradley's brother Tom attended the Dinah Shore to watch Pat play. He was dumbstruck by his sister's condition. He could see there was something seriously wrong. Tom called Pat's mother. Kathleen Bradley finally convinced her daughter to see a doctor.

"Tommy called my mother, and it was she who finally made me listen," Bradley said. "She had questioned me before about something being wrong, but I was so adamant about saying I would deal with it. This time, she was adamant. She said I was not helping myself by saying all I needed was one good week of golf. If I wasn't going to do something, she was going to take me and get some help."[30]

Bradley saw a doctor friend in Dallas. Within days she was diagnosed with the thyroid condition known as Graves' disease. She immediately received treatment with radioactive iodine to render the thyroid gland non-functioning. Relief from the symptoms was almost immediate. Once the iodine therapy was completed, Bradley was put on a synthetic thyroid medication. Like all Graves' disease patients, Bradley will continue to take the medication for the rest of her life.

"I could have kept running away from the problem, or quit, but eventually I dealt with it," Bradley said. "I went through the embarrassment and the humiliation."[31]

By the summer of 1988 Bradley had recovered enough to rejoin the tour. With renewed strength and no tremors, Bradley's game began to improve. She played her first event after her treatment in August and the difference was obvious. She was on her way back, but almost immediately there would be another tragic hurdle.

PAT BRADLEY

Professional Highlights

Since 1974 participated in 648 tournaments, claims 312 top-10 finishes with 208 of those in the top five.

One of two players to win all four of the modern majors.

Led Tour in five statistical categories:1991

Solheim Cup team: 1990, 1992, 1996

Within a week after Bradley's return to the tour, her father died suddenly of a heart attack.

"I played great at the Planters Pat Bradley Invitational in August," Bradley said. "And then, just when I was feeling encouraged, I had the tragedy of my dad's death. He died four days after the Planters tournament.

"My illness had taken a lot out of my dad," Bradley continued. "He lived and died with every shot I made. He'd had a heart attack on the Monday before my tournament started, but he didn't want me to know. I wish I had known, but it was his wish. I spent a month at home with my family after his death, but I didn't pick up the tour after that. I just didn't have anything left."[32]

The Mission: Part II

Graves' disease had left Bradley – the "mission commando" – weak and struggling to right herself. Richard Bradley's death left his daughter without a "mission commander." The strong, quiet New Englander needed time to heal physically and mentally. She joined the tour again for the 1989 season. In early spring she got what she needed – a win.

"It was so satisfying winning the Al Star Centinela in Los Angeles in April," Bradley said. "It was my first win in two years. My mom was there. She had gone through the whole thing with me, and at that moment, it was all behind us. I had won 22 tournaments before that, but this was the sweetest. I not only won it for me but for my family. I felt my dad was close to me during that last round."[33]

In 1990, Bradley and her "stare" were back in full force. She won three times that year. In 1991, through August she had won three events, and was one short of the thirty she needed for qualification into the Hall of Fame. In September, it happened. The 30th Bradley win came at the MSB LPGA Classic.

Seventeen years earlier Kathleen Bradley, out of uncontrolled excitement for her daughter's first win, had begun a "Bradley victory tradition." She went out on the porch of the Bradley house in Westford and rang a cowbell that the family had used when the children were young to call them to dinner. Kathleen received the news of that first win at 3:00 AM, and that's when the cowbell rang. For the next 17 years, the Bradley's neighbors could expect that bell to ring any time, night or day, when Pat won. On that day in September 1991, the bell rang its loudest.

"I knew she'd do well," Kathleen Bradley said. "Never in my wildest dreams did I think she'd be in the Hall of Fame. She doesn't crave the spotlight, and she doesn't get it because she's so low-key."[34]

The woman on a mission had overcome a lot to accomplish the goal. First there was the "image" problem – too reserved. Then there was the "winning" problem – always came in second. Illness almost ended not only her career, but also her life. Finally, the loss of her inspiration – her father. But, through it all Bradley never lost her sense of self.

"I feel I am one of the greats – the statistics and the victories speak for themselves," Bradley said. "I may not be up there attracting publicity or may not be a household name; I may be far behind in superstar quality, not as acceptable as some others, but in facts and figures I'm up with the greats.

"I enjoy communicating, doing my job, answering questions directly and to the point, but I'm not in for a popularity contest," Bradley continued. "I grew up with five brothers not showing their emotions – I'm sure if you got into the psychology of siblings and emotions, it would explain a lot. I didn't see a lot of emotion, so I hold mine in and don't let down my guard, which is not so appealing to people."[35]

The unemotional New Englander did show emotion when she finally knew she had captured her 30th victory and made it into the Hall. When she finished the 1991 MSB LPGA Classic event with a bogie on the 18th hole, she was unaware that she had won the event.

"When I was told, I broke down and cried in the scorer's tent because I realized my mission was finally over and complete," Bradley said. "It was a tremendous relief. Commitment was the key, and I had made it. Nothing came easy to me. You can have success, failure, setback, and defeat, and rise above it."[36]

Chapter 13

Born to Win...

Patty Sheehan

The small serene New England community of Middlebury, Vermont is home to one of the most prestigious institutions in academia – Middlebury College. The college is the focal point of the town's life. Consequently, although the college is known in academic circles for its outstanding programs in foreign languages and several other areas, for those that work at the school and live in the town, Middlebury is also a hot bed of athletics.

In the late 1960's Middlebury fielded one of the strongest hockey teams in their NCAA division. The rink portion of the field house was unheated to maintain the ice. Despite the unpleasant cold of the building, every home game was filled to standing room only with fans – all bundled against the frigid interior and more than ready, at the end of each period, to spend a few minutes in the warmth of the heated lobby.

The Middlebury College Football team was by no means a powerhouse. In fact, their record in 1968 was 0-6. Yet, the town shut down every Saturday afternoon when the team played at home. The stands were packed. Although the very sporadic cheering was only for very occasional first downs, it was as enthusiastic as if the team were scoring at will.

The crowning jewel of this "closet" sports-obsessed town and college was the Middlebury College Snow Bowl – a tiny gem among Vermont ski areas. The Snow Bowl was both the arena of Middlebury's greatest athletic triumphs – those of its ski team – and the social meeting place of the entire community for the winter months. The Snow Bowl boasted the only ski jump in Vermont, and its majestic presence dominated the landscape at the Snow Bowl. It was one of the best 50-meter ski jumps in the east, often producing jumps of 200 feet. It looks imposing and scary.

On a bitter, yet invigoratingly cold, Vermont mid-winter day in 1965, the college ski coach's tiny 9-year-old daughter climbed to the top of the Snow Bowl's ski jump. Standing among the college men of the jumping team, Patty Sheehan matter-of-factly announced she was about to make a jump. Former Middlebury Ski Team member, John Morton was there. The following is an abbreviated version of his account of Sheehan's first jump.

"Why don't you ride the landing hill first," suggested Patty's father, BoBo Sheehan.

The little girl's eyes were questioning – as though she were thinking, "what does he know?" Of course, BoBo Sheehan knew a lot. He had been the Middlebury ski coach for almost 20 years, and the 1956 U.S. Olympic Team Ski Coach.

Patty looked up at her father, and smiling said, "Naw, I wanna take it from the top."

Patty waited while each skier, understanding the terror that the hill could yield, nervously checked and re-checked his bindings before starting down the inrun. Finally, Patty's patience dissolved as the jumper just ahead of her checked his equipment for the sixth time.

"Cheez, are you gonna check your bindings all afternoon, or are you gonna jump?" Patty asked. The jumper stepped to the side, and turning to the young upstart, said, "Well, if you're in such a big rush, be my guest."

Patty shuffled her skies so that the tips hung over the edge of the inrun's trestle. She grabbed the railings and pushed. Her small body sped down the inrun. She was hurled into space, and seconds later, she landed softly on her skies. As the outrun gradually slowed her momentum, she turned back toward the hill and smiled happily.[1]

Five years later, Patty Sheehan would trade the flat boards of alpine skies for the flat blade of a putter. But, the confidence and almost naive courage that she showed as a nine-year-old would remain part of her personality for the rest of her life. Just as it took her to the top of the Snow Bowl's ski jump, it would take her to the top of women's golf – the LPGA Hall of Fame.

Patty Sheehan managed, through fate, to do what Kathy Whitworth said was necessary for success – she was born into a small town.

> ### PATTY SHEEHAN
>
> **Began playing golf: age 4**
>
> **First tournament win: 1968, Hidden Valley "All Teens"**
>
> **First LPGA victory: 1981**
>
> **Most recent LPGA victory: 1996**

Sheehan was born on October 27, 1956 in Middlebury, Vermont. Sheehan's father, Robert "BoBo" Sheehan, a graduate of Middlebury College, was a superior athlete who returned to his alma mater as athletic director. At one time or another BoBo coached every intercollegiate sport the college offered. Nine months before Patty's birth, BoBo served as coach for the U.S. Ski Team at the 1956 Winter Olympics.

On the Saturday Patty was born, BoBo was coaching the Middlebury football team at the school's football stadium. Middlebury's hospital is no more than 500 yards from the college's athletic fields. As BoBo called out defensive plays, the stadium's loudspeaker announced, "Here's a final: Patricia Leslie Sheehan, seven pounds, fifteen ounces." The crowd went wild. You simply can't get much more small town than that.

Sheehan added two more elements to Whitworth's formula for success. First, Sheehan had the good fortune to inherit her parent's genes. Patty's mother, Leslie equaled her husband in athletic skill and was a fine skier. Second, her parents created an environment that encouraged and rewarded athletic participation and success. In Patty Sheehan's destiny there was no "nature vs. nurture" controversy. For her, "nature" and "nurture" worked harmoniously to produce an athletic body and an athletic personality.

Sheehan was the youngest of four children. Her three siblings were all boys. With the college's athletic facilities at her disposal, the young Sheehan did not shy away from participation in the rough and tumble play of her brothers. In fact, she was stimulated and challenged by it.

"I knew she was an athlete when she was four," BoBo Sheehan said. "I watched her keep up with her older brothers. She was a better football player than any of the boys."

All three boys skied. Butch, Patty's oldest brother, was a member of the Junior National Ski Team, and Jack, second oldest of the Sheehan boys, held a United States Junior Championship. Butch played football and golf. Jack was a pole-vaulter. Steve, the youngest of the boys, played football, skied and won interscholastic golf championships in Nevada and California.

If you were a Sheehan, you were an athlete, and Patty did not deviate from the norm. She began to ski almost as soon as she could walk, and by the age of four she was racing in age group competitions. By age 13 she was ranked number one in her age group among junior skiers in the nation. Sheehan did not restrict her sports activities to skiing. She was an outstanding basketball player, and is adept at almost every sport.

Sheehan admits that she understood early that pleasing a crowd pleased her, and that her early experiences made the stress of her career choice more familiar and easier to handle.

As a youngster Sheehan played in a Middlebury College half-time exhibition football game. She was the only girl on the field, and it was her first glimpse of fame.

"I caught a pass and ran it in for a touchdown, fighting off would-be tacklers all the way," Sheehan said. "How that crowd cheered. I loved it. I'd never been in front of a bunch of people and heard them applaud – especially applaud me. The cheers sent little chills up and down my spine. My throat got lumpy. Swallowing was hard. Thirty years later I still like doing things that make people cheer – like knocking irons stiff, getting up and down from bunkers, and draining forty-footers."

Sheehan's introduction to golf came at the same time that she began competing as a skier – at age four. BoBo and Leslie both played golf, and often brought Patty along. She would ride on her mother's pull cart, and occasionally knock a ball down the fairway with a cut-off 2-iron.

By the time Sheehan was six, she had graduated to the caddie ranks. Patty made 25 cents a round by pulling Leslie's pull cart. At age 10, the young Sheehan hit the big time for caddies. She carried her mother's bag in the 1966 Vermont State Women's Amateur Championship. Leslie, never lower than an 18 handicap, did not win, but did have a career low nine hole score – 42. Unfortunately, her back nine score was 57. Leslie Sheehan remembers the event, and her daughter's reaction.

"I shot 42-57-99," Leslie said. "I can still see her face on the front nine, as it was my lowest nine-hole score ever. She was so proud of me."

Sheehan "dabbled" in golf, a game she really did not like all that much, during this part of her life. She took part in the junior program run by Dud Phinney at Middlebury Golf Club.

"Dud taught us how not to kill each other in junior class," Sheehan said. "And he made us responsible for the balls we hit. Dud made a game of picking up our practice balls. That was really more fun than hitting them. He also taught us to be responsible for paying for our lessons."

The lessons with Dud Phinney cost twenty-five cents.

In 1967, after over twenty years on the Middlebury athletic staff, BoBo wanted a new challenge. He took a job as vice-president and general manager at Alpine Meadows Ski Resort in California. The Sheehan family, who had lived a lifetime in the nurturing atmosphere of rural New England headed west.

Moving the most prominent sports family of a small state like Vermont created major fallout. *The Vermont Sunday News* called the event "A Major Blow to the State of Vermont." For years the colleges ski teams and football teams were compared to BoBo-coached teams. BoBo and his family were the town's lamented heroes.

The move west, however, was the catalyst that brought Patty to golf. In 1968, the family settled in Reno, Nevada. Patty continued to ski at the junior national level, but the organizational pattern of the western associations was different from the highly organized programs in New England, and the joy of the sport for Sheehan, who had been competing since age four, was beginning to wear thin.

"The meets were unorganized compared to those in the east," Sheehan said. "The races weren't run on time. The snow was not as hard packed as in Vermont.... Even though I was number one in the country in my age group by the time I was thirteen I felt quittin' time coming on."

Quit, she did. Sheehan turned to the sport that she had half-heartedly participated in during the summer months when skiing was impossible – golf. Patty joined the junior program directed by Ed Jones, the golf professional at Hidden Valley Country Club in Reno.

"I hated golf," Sheehan said. "Golf is an extremely difficult game to learn, especially for kids with their short attention spans. But my family all played. So it was either play or be left home alone. I played. I think if we had stayed in Vermont, I would have stuck with skiing. But I stumbled into something pretty big for myself in golf."

Sheehan's golf career began at age eleven. Ed Jones was her first and only instructor.

"As a young golfer I was not a pretty sight," Sheehan said. "I had only one club – the 2-iron I'd used for every shot since I was four. I had a serious problem with my swing. [Ed] was on the practice tee giving little kids lessons when I met him. I decided I'd better get into Ed's junior program. I am still in it. That is, I'm still working on my game with Ed."

The event that changed Sheehan from "golf hater" to golfer was a small "all-teens" tournament played at Hidden Valley sponsored by a local optometrist, Dr. Don Zunini. At age eleven, Sheehan was not eligible for the event. But, the scarcity of girl participants forced tournament organizers to bend the age eligibility rules to include Patty. That "rule bending" may have been the major factor in creating the thirteenth member of the LPGA Hall of Fame. The future hall of famers debut was less than auspicious. She finished at the bottom of the field.

"Boy, did I love that competition," Sheehan said. "Playing in a tournament gave me a really, really good feeling. Dr. Zunini's tournament was the real beginning of my relationship with the game of golf. It gave me the push I needed, because I hated losing."

The following year, at age twelve – still not of legitimate entry age – Sheehan began what would become her Hall of Fame quest with her first ever tournament win – the Hidden Valley "All-Teens."

From the Perfect Childhood to the Realities of "Life"

There is no doubt that Sheehan's childhood was as close to idyllic as one can get. Her pre-teen years were spent living in a small town where the entire community both nurtured her, and encouraged a sense of self-esteem by rewarding, through their approval, Sheehan's talent and interest in sports. Her family provided a structure that was ever supportive and a model for her own beliefs and values. While in her teens, Sheehan identified what would be her life-engaging work, and met almost immediate success.

By the time Sheehan was ready for college, she was a perfect example of the "new breed, 1970's" young women – self-confident, self-assured, talented and goal-directed. Except, for one thing. Sheehan did not want to leave the security of home.

"I was not grown up enough to leave," Sheehan said. "I was not ready. Besides, the price was right at home: love, room, board – no charge. Also I was extremely shy. I didn't want to leave Mommy and Daddy."

Perhaps all that support and encouragement was simply too good to give up. Sheehan attributes her shyness to her birth position as youngest and only girl among three brothers.

"They were the leaders," Sheehan said. "I just tagged along with them, hanging back. They took care of me."

For three years Sheehan lived at home and attended the University of Nevada at Reno. Although the school did not field a women's golf team, Sheehan did play in intercollegiate events as an individual. UNR would arrange for a coach from another school to act as Sheehan's chaperone.

"I had to have a chaperone," Sheehan said. "It was not because I was naughty. It was the law."

Although Title IX legislation had been in effect for two years, Sheehan finally realized that golf at UNR would not meet her needs, or allow her to find the level of competition she needed.

"I started looking around for another school," Sheehan said. "I just wasn't getting to play enough at the University of Nevada."

Sheehan was offered a scholarship at the University of Tulsa. At that time, Tulsa fielded one of the strongest women golf programs in the nation. In 1976, the All-American Women's Golf Squad included one of Tulsa's players – a young woman from New Mexico, Nancy Lopez.

Sheehan was within one day of signing with Tulsa in 1979 when she backed away.

"I decided Tulsa wasn't right for me," Sheehan said. "For one thing the golf team was away from school for weeks at a time.... I didn't figure I'd get much of an education there."

Perhaps, although Sheehan had gained some maturity, Tulsa was just too big. At a family meeting Patty's mother suggested that San Jose State University was only a five-hour drive from home. BoBo commented that San Jose is close to skiing. And, Patty added that she had a lot of friends – including future LPGA great Juli Inkster (then Simpson) – in the San Jose area.

San Jose State seemed to offer a middle ground for Sheehan who still seemed uncomfortable with straying too far from home – a place to play "major league" college golf in an organized program, yet a place that was more like home than Tulsa.

San Jose it was, and it was San Jose that gave Patty the opportunity to hone the game that would take her to the Tour.

Sheehan won back-to-back California Amateur Championships in 1977 and 1978. She was runner-up in the U.S. Amateur in 1979, and in 1980 she won the National Intercollegiate

Championship. She also played on the 1980 Curtis Cup Team, winning four matches. Sheehan took her game to Tour qualifying that year, and finished first by six shots.

The decision to play professionally was not automatic. Sheehan had been considering it for months. Sheehan's mentor, Ed Jones told her she was not ready; that she lacked maturity. Then just before the 1980 National Intercollegiate Championship, Sheehan discussed it with Juli Simpson. Because of an administrative slip-up, Sheehan found herself fifteen credits short of graduation from San Jose State. When Sheehan talked with Simpson about becoming a professional, Simpson considered her student status as well as her golf talent.

"What else are you going to do with your life?" Simpson answered.

The day after she won the intercollegiate championship, Sheehan declared herself a professional.

Sheehan met immediate success on Tour. She was named Rookie of the Year in 1981 and finished the year ranked number 11 on the money list with $118,000 in prize money. Her first year on tour was punctuated with her first Tour victory – the Mazda Classic. Yet that first year also took a toll on Sheehan personally. The small town girl who had learned to like applause at age ten at the football exhibition in Middlebury, Vermont seemed overwhelmed by the demands and pressures placed on a world class woman athlete.

PATTY SHEEHAN

Amateur Career Highlights

Nevada State Amateur:1975 through 1978

California Amateur1978 & 1979

AIAW Championship:1978 & 1979
Curtis Cup Team:1980

"I had lost the definition of what my life is supposed to be about," Sheehan said. "I had to get away – just had to – get away from the tour. Golf had ceased being fun for me. I was unhappy and frustrated. Everything I worked so hard for wasn't fun anymore. I felt a lot of pressure to be the best player in the world and to be the best representative possible for the LPGA. Everyone wanted a piece of me. I couldn't just be myself anymore. I guess it was a classic case of burnout."

Summing up her feelings to her then manager, Margaret Leonard, Sheehan said, "I'm the best in the world. There is nowhere for me to go but down."

Sheehan did not go down; she went home. She spent five weeks of the 1982 season at her condominium in Los Gatos without touching a golf club. She gave herself time to reflect.

"My LPGA ranking didn't mean diddly unless I had my self-worth," Sheehan said. "My self-worth had eroded on the tour."

In these five weeks, Sheehan found for herself the strength of character that her life to that point had developed. For after those five weeks, Sheehan was able to meet the challenge of the "cold cruel world" as an adult.

Sheehan won three times in 1982 and finished an astounding fourth on the money list. In 1983, just her third year on tour, Sheehan won Player of the Year honors and won her first major championship – the LPGA Championship. The 1984 season saw Sheehan successfully defend her 1983 LPGA Championship title and win the Vare Trophy for the Tour's lowest scoring average (71.40). By 1985, after only five years on tour, Sheehan had earned over $1million in prize money, and with fourteen victories had played her way to the halfway point in the criteria for the Hall of Fame.

The "Thrill of Victory and the Agony of Defeat"

Through the rest of the 1980's Sheehan was never ranked lower than seventh on the money list. At the end of the 1989 season, she had accumulated 20 LPGA victories. Then in October 1989 Sheehan's world began to shake at its foundations – both literally and figuratively.

Sheehan was at the World Series game in Candlestick Park on October 17, 1989. A little after 5:00 PM, the stadium trembled from the effect of an earthquake that measured 7.1 on the Richter scale. The devastation that is now a part of California's history left Sheehan a victim. Her home, which was uninsured, was destroyed. Sheehan was able to recover financially, and eventually built a new home in Reno. The personal disaster, however, was closely followed by an equally traumatic quake in her career.

For all her success, Sheehan had never won a U.S. Open Championship. An Open Championship, for most players, represents the epitome of success. The Open is probably the one championship that every player wants most to win. It is the National Championship. Sheehan had that desire.

"It's the one I've most wanted to win," Sheehan said. "I've spent most of my life preparing to win it, but so many different happenings have gotten in the way."

Sheehan had come close twice. In 1983 she finished second to Jan Stephenson, and in 1988 second to Liselotte Neumann. Players who fail to win major championships, especially the Open, often gain a reputation for "choking." In 1990, Sheehan became one of those players.

The 1990 U.S. Open was played at the Atlanta Athletic Club. The weather was simply atrocious. Several rain delays forced suspension of play on the first day. Twenty-seven players were unable to finish and had to complete first round play on the morning of the second day. Sheehan, although caught in the delays, managed to complete her round, and was tied with Jane Geddes at six-under par for the lead. The second day was another disaster. Severe weather forced a six-hour delay. Sheehan hit her first shot off the first tee at 6:15 PM. A second six-hour delay on Saturday created a unique situation. It had taken three days to complete two rounds of the championship, and the final two rounds – 36 holes – would be played on one day, Sunday.

At the end of the second round, Sheehan was at 10-under par, and held a six-shot lead over the rest of the field. On Sunday, Sheehan birdied two of the first three holes to go to 12-under par. Then with thirty-three holes left to play, Sheehan's game began to come apart. After a first round 66 and a second round 68, Sheehan finished the morning round on Sunday with a 75. She now held a five shot lead over Betsy King.

"I didn't feel well that Sunday," Sheehan said. "Doctors told me later that I not only probably had low blood sugar, but was also dehydrated. There were two times I almost passed out. My legs would simply not move."

By the final nine holes, Sheehan had lost the lead and trailed King by two shots. On the fourteenth and fifteenth holes, Sheehan made birdies to bring her back into a tie with King. But, at the par three seventeenth, Sheehan drove into a bunker and missed a 25-foot putt for par. King, who had finished her round, now had a one shot lead. Sheehan needed birdie on the eighteenth hole for a tie, and it did not happen. Sheehan had not only lost, but she had "blown" what was at one point an eleven-shot lead.

PATTY SHEEHAN

Solheim Cup Team: 1990, 1992, 1994, 1996

Crossed $5 million mark in earnings:1996

To add to the calamity, TV commentator, Judy Rankin, asked Sheehan for an interview as she walked off the eighteenth green. Sheehan, in what many have suggested was poor judgment, granted the interview. Responding to the pressure of the previous four days and the emotional impact of the moment, Sheehan wept as the live interview was shown to viewers across the nation.

The result was that Sheehan was not only criticized for losing an almost insurmountable lead, but she was ridiculed for the emotional outburst. As Betty Hicks points out in her biography of Sheehan, the incident was perfect for some to affirm the statement made by TV commentator Bob Rosburg that "women are too emotional [to play the game]."

Sheehan understood, after the fact, that the interview was not one of her better decisions. The media played the loss as an albatross that would haunt Sheehan, but she saw it more philosophically.

"The Open of '90 taught me how to win, how not to put so much pressure on myself," Sheehan said. "I know now that all the nightmares after that Open – and I literally had nightmares – were not suffered for nothing. Because now I can relax, knowing that I can never again be as disappointed as I was at Atlanta Athletic Club in July of 1990."

In the short span of ten months, the woman with the "charmed" life had been forced to face adversity twice – the personal devastation of the earthquake, and the professional challenge of the Open loss. Although painful, both were lessons well-learned.

Poetic Justice

Often a loss like Sheehan experienced in the Open can destroy a player's career. For some players the experience devastates them – shaking their confidence that in turn adversely affects their game. Their minds begin to focus on how they lost the huge lead, and they become "gun shy." Usually that attitude results in defensive play that more often than not keeps the player from attacking the course. In addition, players who have lost major events after leading as Sheehan did, face pressure from the media. Sportswriters love to ask the question, "Will they win again?"

Sheehan faced both of those challenges after the 1990 Open. Her response was that of a trained skier – when you fall, get up and go down the hill as fast as you can. She played the LPGA event the week following the Open and finished a close second to Beth Daniel. From her comments about the reception that she received by the players at the event, it was obvious that Sheehan had gained the maturity she needed to put the Open behind her.

"When I walked out onto the practice tee, there was an awful hush," Sheehan said. "Like walking into a church for a funeral. None of the players would speak to me, because they didn't know what to say. There'd been a death in the family, almost. But my spirit hadn't died."

Sheehan finished the 1990 season with five victories and the lowest scoring average of her career (70.62). She had lost the Open – again – but she had survived.

Sheehan struggled with an injury to her left hand throughout the 1991 season. She won only once. By 1992, her hand had healed and she again played well. In June she won back-to-back events at Rochester and Toledo. Her confidence level going into the 1992 Open, which was played at Oakmont Country Club in Pennsylvania, was high. She would need every ounce of that confidence.

After the opening two rounds Sheehan trailed Juli Inkster by one shot. In the third round Inkster shot 71 and Sheehan shot 70. The two players were in a dead heat going into the final round on Sunday. On the fifteenth hole, a birdie brought Sheehan to within one stroke of Inkster, but Sheehan bogeyed sixteen and was two shots back with two holes to play. Then, as both players strode to their second shot on the seventeenth, it looked like history was about to repeat itself. A storm forced a rain delay of almost two hours.

As Sheehan sat in the locker room, memories of Atlanta flooded her mind, but this time her mind talked back.

"I told myself I'd lost several Opens with cave-ins," Sheehan said. "It was time I showed some guts."

Sheehan birdies the 17th and 18th while Inkster parred both. At the end of regulation play, the former San Jose State teammates were tied, and would play an 18-hole playoff on Monday.

On Monday, Sheehan's 35 on the front nine gave her a one-shot lead over Inkster. A birdie by Sheehan on thirteen and a bogey by Inkster on fourteen gave Sheehan a four shot lead as the players stood on the fifteenth tee.

"After Atlanta, I'm not sure how much lead I would need to feel comfortable," Sheehan said. "Maybe fifteen or twenty?"

On sixteen, Sheehan birdied again to take a five shot lead into the last two holes. She would need almost every one of those five shots. Inkster birdied seventeen and Sheehan bogeyed – the lead was now three. On eighteen Inkster parred, and Sheehan bogeyed one more time. But, the match had run out of holes before Sheehan ran out of strokes.

Twelve years after her entry into the professional ranks and two years after a devastating defeat in the event that can make or break a player's career, Sheehan had played her way back. She had won the U.S. Open. Sheehan would not stop at one Open victory. She would win the Open for a second time in 1994.

"The Hall Calls"

By the start of the 1993 season, Sheehan had accumulated 29 victories – two of them majors, the LPGA Championship and the U.S. Open. She was one victory short of the criteria for the LPGA Hall of Fame. Sheehan's manager, Rebecca Gaston, supplied Patty's fans with buttons that read, "The Hall Calls."

It took less than three months for Sheehan to answer that call. On March 22, 1993, Sheehan won the Standard Register Ping Classic. It was her 30th victory, and it made Sheehan the thirteenth member of the LPGA Hall of Fame.

Thirteen seemed a charmed number for Sheehan. Her qualification for the Hall of Fame occurred in her thirteenth season on tour. Sheehan had reached the Hall of Fame standards faster than anyone else.

On the green at tournament's end Sheehan was showered with champagne by her fellow competitors, and received a bouquet of 30 red roses from then LPGA Commissioner, Charles Meachem. Then it was time to face the press.

"I'm happy to get it over with, happy to be in the Hall of Fame," Sheehan said. "I'm glad not to have to think about it anymore. It's been quite a burden."

Sheehan's feat was an announcement to the world that the new breed of women athletes had arrived. Yet, this "new woman athlete" who had won millions more in prize money than any of her LPGA founding ancestors, seemed to understand intuitively the relationship between her opportunity to succeed at what she did best and the LPGA founders' early sacrifices. She paid them perhaps the highest compliment possible by expressing how much she would have liked to compete with them.

"I feel a little misplaced and out of my era, because I have great empathy with the women who started the tour and where they are today," Sheehan said. "The majority of players have forgotten where we came from. I appreciate the history, the grand old women of golf who played their hearts out and sometimes hardly got paid for what they did. I would have loved to have played in that era."[2]

Like those women who had come before, "the burden" of the Hall of Fame was meant for Sheehan to carry. The Tomboy from the athletic family, nurtured in the bosom of a small New England town had lived up to her potential and reached her destiny.

Having achieved her destiny in sports, Sheehan at age 41 began a new challenge – that of a parent. In July of 1997, Sheehan adopted a baby girl.

"I've accomplished just about everything I set out to do in my career," Sheehan said in 1998. "But the hard work and focus that it took to fulfill those goals required that I make sacrifices in my personal and social life. I finally decided it was time to do something about that. Eight months ago, Rebecca Gaston, my partner and manager of 12 years, and I adopted a little girl, Bryce.

"Becoming a parent has removed what was always my one greatest worry – what would I do after my golf career ended," Sheehan continued. "Winning tournaments is great fun, but after the last putt has dropped and the ecstasy of receiving the trophy has passed, all that's left is the rest of the evening. Many times I've won a tournament and gone to dinner that evening by myself.

"Completing the adoption felt better than any U.S. Open victory. The happiness is more permanent. I see this precious little person every day.... I travel with Rebecca, our two dogs, Quincey and Sherlock, and Bryce every week. My life has never been so complete. I've never been more content or happy."[3]

Chapter 14

Ice...
Betsy King

I n 1985, Betsy King was in her ninth season on the LPGA Tour. The year before she had not only earned her first LPGA victory, after a long seven-year wait, but added two more wins to make her the tour's leading money winner in 1984.

By the fall of 1985, King had notched two more wins, and was ranked a respectable sixth on the money list. As the 1985 season wound down, King used a free week in the tour schedule to visit with a friend and relax in South Florida.

The friend, a male teaching pro, was determined to make the week a real "vacation" for King by arranging several non-golf recreational activities – not an especially easy task for a young man whose life was built around golf. With the help of the other two golf professionals from the club at which the young pro worked, he was able to put together an afternoon boat trip on the North Fork of Florida's St. Lucie River.

Since the golf professional's experience with boats was nil, the boat's owner – a young woman who knew about as much about golf as she did about nuclear physics – agreed to act as "captain" and "tour guide." King, the golf pro and the boat owner were joined by three other women teaching pros from the area, one of whom was a childhood friend of King.

It is important to understand that, as a celebrity, Betsy King has never been considered one of the most gregarious. She is often described as the tour's "invisible woman." Writing in *Golf Magazine*, James Dodson relates a comment by a television talk-show host who described King as "so dull she needed a new personality."[1] That may be a bit extreme, but King is definitely quiet and reticent – especially in a group.

On the boat trip, so carefully planned by her friend, King was pretty much the Betsy King known by the media. She spoke little, was a bit standoffish and basically just watched the water go by as the group cruised to a restaurant on the river for dinner. At dinner and during the ride back to the owner's home, conversation was strained and King remained quiet while the rest of the group attempted to make things "fun."

After the rather bumbling "crew" got the boat docked and ship-shape, the boat's owner invited the entire group into her home for a game of charades. Immediately King's deep blue eyes began to sparkle. King came alive. Her "fellow passengers" were now her "team" members. She was outgoing and made every attempt to find the strength – in terms of charades – for each person on her team. The King who, only hours ago, had been quiet and reserved was now a cheerleader who offered encouragement and "high five's" to each member of her team. King chatted happily with everyone, laughed and concentrated those sparkling blue eyes fiercely on each person as they wildly gestured to convey "book, song or movie." The group had finally found a way to make King comfortable enough to relate – the game was on and the competition had begun.[2]

It has always been competition that brings out King's personality. It has always been competition that brings out the best in King. She began to play golf at age ten, but as a youngster in her hometown of Reading, Pennsylvania, she also played basketball, softball and field hockey. In fact, she liked those three sports better than golf. Her competition then was her older brother.

"I always wanted to beat my brother at everything," King said. "In basketball I would make him play 20 times until I beat him."[3]

It was King's drive to compete that may have kept her from focusing on golf during her teens. Her high school had no girls' golf team, so King focused on team sports, and her amateur golf experience was limited.

"I didn't play much amateur golf," King said. "Except I did play in the U.S. Juniors twice."[4]

If lack of competition kept King from golf in high school, the desire to compete brought her to serious golf while she was at Furman University. An injury left her with only one competitive avenue – golf – and it quickly became her career.

"In my junior year at Furman, where I was a P.E. major, I injured my knee playing basketball," King said. "Afterward, I concentrated on golf. Since I didn't want to teach P.E., I turned professional at 22."[5]

> **BETSY KING**
>
> **Began serious golf as a student at Furman University: age 18**
>
> **First LPGA victory:1984**
>
> **Most recent victory:1997**

From the start, King's competitive drive was reflected in her work habits and her approach to the game.

"I work pretty hard," King said. "I'm self-motivated, and would be the same in any job I did, since I'm so competitive."[6]

King had to be self-motivated because for her first seven years on tour, she experienced little in the way of external gratification. Although she was able to win enough in prize money to support her career, King and her game seemed stalled in no-man's land. She was good – except for the 1980 season, King never finished below 30th on the money list those first seven years. But, she did not have the one thing that every competitor wants – a win.

"For a lot of reasons, it's hard for me to remember my first few years on Tour," King said. "But I do recall that I reached a point where I thought I might never win a tournament. I'd even begun to come to terms with that. I thought well, I'm going to be the best non-winner who's ever been out here."[7]

BETSY KING

Amateur Career Highlights

Furman University National Collegiate Championship Team:1976

U.S. Open, Low amateur:1976

Those first seven years were not easy for King. She felt deeply the frustration of not realizing the potential she believed was in her. If competition brought out the best in King, the frustration of those first years on tour highlighted emotions that King was not pleased to find.

"Early in my career I was jealous of other people's achievements," King said. "[That] is not right. [It] is not a correct emotion."[8]

By the beginning of the 1980 season, King's game had reached a low point. It was then that two things happened. One changed her game and the path that King's career would take. The other changed her life.

At the Ping Team Championship in Portland, Oregon, King teamed with Donna White. While the two hit balls on the practice tee before the event, King struggled to get the ball airborne. On the range, working with some of the other players was respected teaching professional Ed Oldfield. White saw Oldfield and "introduced" him to King.

"Oldfield, get over here," White said. "My partner can't get the ball off the ground."[9]

The introduction began a teacher-student relationship that would bring King out of the Tour's no-man's land into its top echelon of players. But, the relationship began tentatively, and it would be years before anyone but King and Oldfield noticed the difference.

"She had serious problems," Oldfield said. "Her divots were going way right, and the ball was going way left. I watched her play, and on one par-5 she couldn't carry a fairway wood 100 yards over water. She had to lay up with a wedge."[10]

Despite the problems, Oldfield saw King's potential. He also saw a young woman with determination and perseverance.

"Most pros probably couldn't handle changing their swing altogether – it takes an exceptional person," Oldfield said. "I quickly realized Betsy King was that person. She was so patient, so trusting, so sincere. And, ironically, beneath that calm exterior, I'd never seen anyone who wanted to be the best player in the world more than Betsy King. She was willing to do whatever it took."[11]

King may have appeared calm to Oldfield, but in reality, she was a basket case. Oldfield spends the winter months teaching in Phoenix, and on the morning of her first lesson, King and her father, Weir, scoured the city for a spot to practice before meeting with Oldfield.

"We found a deserted playground," Weir said. "She was hitting balls, and I was chasing them – and a cop came and chased us. I think that was the low point in her career. But, that afternoon Ed told me that she was going to be one of the five best players in the world."[12]

King's friend and fellow tour player, Donna White, was also the catalyst for another introduction that year. In January, White, an active member of the Fellowship of Christian Athletes, invited King to the organization's annual Tee-Off Conference. It was an invitation that would change King's life.

"To be honest, my game was at rock-bottom and I went to the conference mainly because there would be a chance to get in some extra practice time," King said. "But something happened. The speaker talked about making difficult choices, choosing the narrow path, having a personal relationship with God. Around me were these people like Donna White and I saw how well they handled the pressure of life on the Tour. I suddenly knew I'd discovered truth. Truth with a capital T."[13]

"Truth" with a capital "T"

Betsy King is defined by her strong faith. She has declared herself a Christian. King sees her faith as the force that guides her entire life.

"Sometimes the tour is lonely," King said. "So when you are with people who care for one another, the social aspect helps. People say joining the Fellowship (Fellowship of Christian Athletes) is a crutch, but I believe the Bible is the inspired word of God and He can do things through me. My faith is important to me and carries into my golf.

"My faith gives me perspective," King said. "Scripture tells you to forget what is behind and press toward what is ahead, toward the goal to win the prize. The hardest thing is to forget what is behind. I use my faith as my sports psychologist. Why not get it from the guy who knows everything?"[14]

For King, faith helps to bring a sense of calm to the intensely competitive world she faces every day.

"Before the first tournament in 1989, I remember praying, 'Lord, I want to be where you want me to be, whether it's out here or somewhere else.' On the first hole of the year, a par-3, I hit an eight- or nine- iron to forty feet and made the putt for birdie. I shot 64 and went on to win the tournament. Not that playing well is an indication that you're in the right place. But, I felt I was seeing what He desired for me and not just what I wanted. There's a sense of peace and relief about that."[15]

King's commitment to her faith carries beyond the golf course as well. One of her many volunteer charity projects is with Habitat for Humanity, an organization which uses volunteers to construct homes for the poor. Every year King schedules a week off the tour to work with the group.

"You're basically somebody's servant for a week," King said, describing the Habitat for Humanity experience. "Whatever they want you to do, you do – tile a floor, drive to the hardware store, work on the roof, you name it. I'm not too good at the building part."[16]

Ever the competitor, King makes the Habitat work fun by adding a bit of competition.

"We make up games," King said. "Like who can hammer the most nails, or who can hammer a nail in the fewest strokes."[17]

At the conclusion of the 1993 LPGA season, King – who had won the last event of the year – traveled to Romania as part of Alternative Ministries, a group offering relief in the form of food and clothing to orphans in that nation. The experience affected King deeply.

"We were standing in snow, freezing, dealing with young children who live under a train station," King said. "It gave me a perspective that has changed my life. I went from celebrating an incredible win and season to extreme sadness. I was so happy, and then it all became very, very clear. I said to myself, 'How important is golf, anyway.'"[18]

The Misunderstood Ms. King

Scattered among Betsy King's 31 LPGA victories are six major championships – two U.S. Opens (back-to-back, 1989 and 1990), three Dinah Shores (1987, 1990, 1997), and one LPGA Championship (1992). She has won Player of the Year honors three times, and the Vare Trophy for low scoring average twice. Yet she remains the "star" nobody knows.

> ### BETSY KING
>
> **Professional Highlights**
>
> **Winless her 1st seven years, King won 20 times: 1984 and 1989**
>
> **14 top-ten finishes: 1992**
>
> **Solheim Cup Team: 1992, 1994, 1996, 1998**

The problem for King is image. Her naturally shy, soft-spoken and reticent personality makes King a player who is simply not "public relations" oriented. King's intense work ethic and relentless pursuit of perfection in her golf game makes the practice range a more important place for her to be than the interview room. King has never been a media "darling." She is often labeled as dull, bland, and invisible.

"Betsy is maybe the most misunderstood person out here," fellow tour player, Meg Mallon said. "People say she is nice, as though that were a fault. But beneath that calm exterior is a remarkable person who has the courage of her convictions. For what it's worth, she might be the most competitive person out here. She's only invisible to the press because she doesn't fit the model of what they think a champion should be."[19]

Although King is usually stoic, she does admit that her "media image" is sometimes painful, even to her.

"At one point a few years ago I felt the press basically ignored me," King said. "I was finally winning tournaments and no one seemed particularly interested. Then when they did begin to write about me, I got burned. They seemed to know the story before they asked the question. If you're controversial or flamboyant, that seems to be news. But if you're somebody who has a nice demeanor, goes out, wins graciously, and loses graciously – who works hard and does her job – they say you have no fire or you're a mystery. Or worse yet that you're dull or invisible. I confess those labels hurt. How do they know what's going on inside my head?"[20]

Still, King is unwilling to change.

"I probably don't come across that well to the public," King said. "But, I don't want to change. I want to be honest, and the only emotion I sometimes show is anger, which I know is wrong. Golf is a way to make a living; it can't be more than that, because you can't base your self-worth on something which is just another day at the office. It is impossible to get psyched up every day and live and die by what you do, but I care about it."[21]

In a sport that requires maintaining an even temperament, it is King's lack of emotion that is most often commented on. Yet King insists that she does "feel" the highs and lows as much as any other player.

"I'm a private person," King said. "People misread me. I'm very emotional. People probably won't believe that, but it's true."[22]

To prove that "it's true," King talked about her reaction as she walked to the 18th green at Five Farms Golf Club in 1989 as she won her first U.S. Open Championship.

"Did I feel much emotion when I won at Five Farms?" King said. "Yes, the fans were hollering like a baseball game, and I thought for a second I was going to cry when I reached the last green. I was slightly scared, but enjoying it, and trying to respond the best way I could. When I go to a play or a concert, I get choked up when someone receives a standing ovation, and I cry. It's funny to get a standing ovation yourself."[23]

Not quite ten years later, in 1997, when she won the Dinah Shore for the third time, King's reaction was much more open. She ran along the walkway leading to the 18th green at Mission

Hills in Palm Springs grinning and giving "high five's" to the spectators in the stands. It was as close as "dull, bland" Betsy King comes to a victory lap.

The Invisible Star Gives Visibility to the Tour

The progress of King's career was a lot like the academic career of some youngsters – they struggle in elementary and high school, and then blossom into fine college students, perhaps taking education all the way to a Ph.D.

King's early career gave no indication that it would lead to entry into the Hall of Fame. King went winless for seven long years before she won an LPGA event. When she finally did win in 1984, she almost literally won "everything in sight." Had anyone noticed, it would have been clear that King was the process of putting together a career to match the great players of any era. In the five-year period between 1984 and 1989, King collected twenty wins. She was the winningest professional golfer during that period. In the ten-year period between 1984 and 1994, King did not go winless in any one of those years. Since 1984, King has had only three seasons in which she did not have a win.

By 1993 King had 29 wins. Suddenly, the "invisible woman" began to attract attention. One more win would put her in the Hall of Fame. The question on every media person's lips when they talked with King was, "When will you get number 30?"

Every time it was asked, King answered. But by June of 1994, she was tiring of it.

"I'm not worried about it at all," King said in an interview with Joe Juliano. "I feel fine. I'm playing fine. I don't think it's an issue per se. It's like anything else. When you get asked the same thing over and over again, it gets a little tiring."[24]

Tiring or not, King was asked the question for the next year. Her thirtieth win would not come until June 25, 1995 – 41 tournaments and the better part of two years after win number 29. Like she did at the beginning of her career, King endured a long wait before meeting success.

The wait was hard on King. It required patience and perseverance – two qualities King had already shown to be part of her character. But, it also made her something she had never been before – the center of attention.

"One of the things about being unknown," King said. "You can get all the practice time you desire."[25]

Ironically King – the player with the lowest media profile – through her long struggle for the win that would put her in the Hall of Fame, would do something that other more visible players had not been able to do. King's drive for the Hall focused the golf world's attention on the LPGA Hall of Fame itself. Golf fans who did not know there was an LPGA Hall of Fame became caught up in the "will she, or won't she" hype put out by the media. Of all the Hall of Famers, it is perhaps the publicity shy King who brought the institution to public attention.

As each of those 41 tournaments passed without King in the top spot, she created for the Tour and the Hall the one thing she could never create for herself – drama.

King qualified for the Hall of Fame by winning the Shop-Rite LPGA Classic in Atlantic City. The drama had ended. Like the plays and concerts at which the unemotional King cries when the performers get a standing ovation, that time had come for her. Her response was typical of King the golfer, not King the theatergoer. But, it also may go a long way in bringing understanding about King the person.

"It was gratifying to have my peers come out and support me and congratulate me," King said. "Towards the end of your career you appreciate it more, knowing that you must have been a good player. It all adds to the concept that we're a family from generation-to-generation. It must have been God's timing, because my parents were there and the next day I had a Pro-Am in my hometown nearby. There were thirty people waiting in the lane to my parents' house to meet me. It was very touching.

"I always felt I would do it," King continued. "Although the longer time goes by, the harder it gets. My faith helped, and I am a grinder – a perfectionist – who battles for my own satisfaction."[26]

Chapter 15

A New Breed...
Amy Alcott

The television screen was alive with the antics of Saturday morning cartoons. Eight-year-old Amy munched cereal and smiled as she watched the cavorting characters. But then the scene changed. The brash, vivid colors of the cartoons were replaced by the sophisticated muted tones of lush fairways, obsessively immaculate greens and conservatively dressed golfers. The loud banter of Daffy and The RoadRunner faded into the almost whispering voices of golf announcers.

Amy didn't turn the TV off. In fact, her attention became more acute. This is what she had been waiting for.

"The 'Wide World of Golf' came on after the cartoons," Alcott said. "And I thought 'what a fascinating game.' It wasn't push or pull or bang into people.[1] After I had seen a number of tournaments, I was convinced of three things: Every golfer had a Texas drawl. Everyone was named Byron or Labron. And their conversation consisted of one phrase, 'Good shot, Pards.'"[2]

Young Amy, living in Southern California, did not speak with a Texas drawl. She did not even know anyone who was named Byron, and she had no idea of who "Pards" was. What she did know is that she wanted to try the game she saw every Saturday morning on TV.

"To me it was like a beautiful ballet," Alcott said. "That people could swing so smoothly and hit a stationary object so far. I began to wonder what the challenge was in the game. How do you hit the ball perfectly every time?"[3]

That question would become the driving force for the rest of her life.

Amy Alcott was born on February 22, 1956 in Kansas City, Missouri. The youngest of three children, Amy and her family moved to Santa Monica, California when Amy was six months old.

Alcott's childhood centered around sports, and a strong desire to compete has always been part of her personality.

"I was a tomboy, athletic, and the best girl in school at sports," Amy said. "I had tremendous desire from within to do well. I was born to be a fighter and to be competitive, which I don't think you learn – it is born in people who are successful."[4]

Alcott's father did not play golf nor did her mother, but after Amy's exposure to the game via TV, both her parents supported young Amy in her new interest. Since Alcott was only eight years old when she first started hitting balls, she was too young to play on any of the local golf courses. For the future Hall of Famer, this was only a minor problem. She developed "Alcott Golf and Country Club" – better known as the Alcott front yard. Soup cans were buried in the grass to simulate holes, and her father brought in some sand to make a miniature bunker. The proximity of the "course" to the house, and Alcott's not-yet-developed skill necessitated one other modification. Amy kept hitting balls into the windows of the Alcott home. The Alcott's solved the problem by installing a net – which operated like window drapes – covering the entire front of the house.

"When I pulled it closed to practice, it looked like the house was being fumigated," Alcott said.[5]

Amy took the country club idea one step further by trying to issue membership cards to the other families in the neighborhood.

"Whenever my folks invited friends over to go swimming, I'd make them sign for their soft drinks," Alcott said. "Then I'd send them bills at the end of the month."[6]

Eventually - if only to get rid of the netting on the house - Amy got involved in taking lessons. Her first, and only teacher was Walter Keller, the professional, owner and operator of an indoor driving range in West Los Angeles. Within minutes of meeting Amy, Keller knew her potential was unlimited. His only comment to Amy's mother was "Mrs. Alcott you're a blessed woman."[7]

From that point on Amy spent most of her free time at Walter Keller's Golf School, and at age ten played her first tournament. As a junior golfer, Alcott won 115 championships including the Junior World Championship in the 13-14 age group, the U.S. Girls Junior Championship in 1973, and three Los Angeles Junior Championships. At age 17, Alcott set a course record at Pebble Beach. Her round of 70 beat, by two strokes, the old record set by Babe Zaharias.

> ### AMY ALCOTT
>
> **Began to play golf - age 8**
>
> **First LPGA victory: 1975,**
>
> **Most recent victory: 1991,**

Alcott's success as a junior made her a "star." Like most child stars her intensity and focus made her different.

"Growing up, I never had a lot of friends," Alcott said. "I felt like an outcast and not like all the girls at school, who made fun of me. I was a loner, very much misunderstood. I had a seriousness about me that people considered strange. Because my parents didn't play golf, all the motivation and drive came from me."[8]

As her junior golf career peaked at age 16, Alcott was faced with a lifestyle change. Her parents separated and eventually divorced. The adjustment was not easy for her.

"I stayed with my mother when my parents split up, and although I'd sensed that it was coming and felt it was right for both parents, it did affect me. I was always family-oriented, and often I would go somewhere and wish I had my dad with me."[9]

The adjustment to her parent's separation was made a bit easier when Alcott joined Riviera Country Club in Los Angeles. The famous old traditional club had everything a sixteen -year-old golf prodigy could want. It was one of the best golf courses in the world, had tons of golf history involving the greatest who played the game, and boasted a membership that included several well known celebrities. Pamela Wallace writing in 1975 points out that at Riviera, Alcott had found a place to fit in.

"Famous members like Dean Martin, Glen Campbell and Peter Falk found the talented youngster immensely appealing and she quickly became their unofficial mascot. Later some of them, including Martin, became her sponsors on the tour .... It is obvious that Amy likes the club and feels comfortable with all its inhabitants. There her dedication to golf is admired."[10]

With the new feeling of comfort she had developed at Riviera, and the desire to test herself against the best, Alcott passed up several college scholarship offers. Not long after she graduated from high school, the eighteen-year-old Alcott was ready to take her game on tour.

Young, Cocky, and Most important, Good

Alcott joined the LPGA Tour in 1975. Although it could have been a risky decision, Alcott seems to have made it easily, with firm resolve that it was right, and with no regret at all.

"Nowadays, most of the girls go through college first," Alcott said. "But I felt I was ready then to play on the tour. I wanted to prove myself against the best. I thought, 'Do I want to be in some classroom, or out playing golf?'"[11]

"My mother put me on a plane to Miami to the qualifying school," Alcott said. "And, with a tear in her eye said, 'I've taught you everything I can teach you. Off you go.'"[12]

Off she went, indeed. Alcott's first LPGA event was on January 18, 1975. Less than a month later, on February 9, she won her first professional tournament. It was the third event she had entered. The win made her an instant celebrity, and caused the media to set high expectations for the not yet twenty-year-old Alcott.

At the close of the 1975 season, Pamela Wallace wrote in the *Saturday Evening Post*, "After only six professional tournaments people were calling Amy: an almost certain choice for LPGA rookie of the Year, the most promising golfer, male or female, to come along in years; and the girl who will finally bring women's golf up to the status of women's tennis."[13]

In an interview for *Sports Illustrated* in July 1975, Alcott gave her reaction to her phenomenal start on tour.

"I'm not surprised I won so early," Alcott said. "I won because I played the best. It was super – I had the confidence and determination to rip it up, and I did. People knew I was a contender the minute I teed it up."[14]

The comment was open and honest – two traits that characterize Alcott. They are also two traits that earned her a reputation for being cocky, and made her acceptance on tour difficult. For the first few years of her career, veteran players showed at least a bit of resentment of the 19-year-old's success. Alcott believes the reaction of others to her attitude may have been a knee-jerk response based on the milieu of the mid-1970's.

"When I first turned pro, they called me cocky, but mostly I was good," Alcott said in a 1991 interview. "I think I was just ahead of my time. Nowadays, if you're cocky and good, they call you confident."[15]

If Alcott believes the difference between cocky and confident might be defined by the time in which you live, she also takes personal responsibility for her reputation of being brash.

"There's a certain amount of bullshit involved in being a celebrity," Alcott said. "You have to say the right thing at the right time. I have a little trouble with that."[16]

During her first years on tour, Alcott found that she faced the same social problems she had while she was in high school – her seriousness and tendency to be a loner kept her from making friends.

"When I first came out on tour, people teased me about being 18 going on 30," Alcott said. "I didn't have any friends my own age. It bothered me. I didn't know how to be the kind of person to have friends. I was too selfish. I don't think I saw that then. I wondered why I'd never had friends.[17]

"I felt I was different and lived on another planet," Alcott said. "Even now I don't have a lot of friends on tour. I'm wrapped up in being me, and I find it hard to open up and make friends; so people give up on me before I feel comfortable with them. I feel a part of the tour only in the sense that everyone plays golf, but I don't feel a sense of belonging."[18]

Alcott not only admits her difficulty in making friends, but also seems to intuitively know it may be the part of her personality that makes her so successful.

"I have my share of insecurities," Alcott said. "A lot of it was that I never fit in as a kid, growing up being a tomboy. Entertainers by nature tend to be very insecure, but it's their insecurity that makes them get out there and prove to others and to themselves that they are worthy and that they are great."[19]

During Alcott's early years on tour, the most important relationship in her life was with her mother, Lea. For several years, when not on tour, Alcott continued to live with her mother in an apartment in Santa Monica.

"We're best friends," Alcott said in a 1975 interview. "[We're] not just mother and daughter. She's the best friend I'll ever have. She drove me all over California to tournaments when I was growing up."[20]

AMY ALCOTT

Amateur Career Highlights

Won 115 championships including Junior World Championship (13-14 age group)

U.S. Girls Junior Championship: 1973

Despite Alcott's difficulty with tour friendships and her feelings of not belonging, she continued to succeed. By her fifth year on tour Alcott had accumulated nine victories. She won four times in 1979 and 1980, and again in 1984. Although she has never been ranked number one on the money list, between 1975 and 1988 she finished each season ranked in the top twenty. Between 1975 and 1986, Alcott won at least one event every year. But the real defining moment of Alcott's career came at the U.S. Open in 1980. It would bring her center stage as a major player in the LPGA drama, and it would serve as the way in which she would from then on define herself.

In July 1980 in Nashville it was hot. Temperatures at Richland Country Club were above 100 degrees each day that players teed it up for the Women's U. S. Open. Media stories focused more on how each player kept from passing out than on how they controlled their driver off the tee.

Alcott's opening round 70 tied her for the lead with Barbara Moxness. According to *Sports Illustrated's* Barry McDermott, "the heat caused her hands to become swollen and she had to keep putting ice on them."[21] In all four rounds Alcott fought the heat by wearing a kerchief around her neck, a painter's cap pulled down close to her eyes and munching potassium caplets. She shot 70 again on Friday to be the sole leader. Her 68 on Saturday widened the gap, and a 72 on Sunday gave her the wire-to-wire victory. It made her only the ninth player to ever lead an Open for the entire event. Her 280 four-round total set a 72-hole tournament record.

The event was televised, and since Alcott lead each round, she had maximum TV exposure. Viewers saw the young woman with the kerchief defy the outrageous conditions and just keep determinedly striding down fairway-after-fairway, never giving in to the heat – both environmental and emotional - and yet still smiling and having a good time. For the public, the image set Alcott apart. After that Open she was no longer just one of the good young players who were changing the face of the LPGA. She was a tough, determined golfer who maintained a sense of humor while fighting adversity. She had been a prodigy in 1975. In 1980, Alcott became a recognizable celebrity.

For Alcott, the Open was even more important. It allowed her to reach her own definition of her potential.

"The highlight of my golfing career was winning the 1980 U.S. Open...," Alcott said. "Ever since I was little, I wanted that title, and it became a fixation.... After that, when people announced me as U.S. Open Champion on the first tee, my drive would automatically go 10 yards further. No one can ever take it away, and what I did in winning was greatness. That gives me pride because it is one thing to want it and another to do it. That one achievement is worth a lifetime of working for it."[22]

No One "Finah" at the Dinah

The tournament with which Alcott is most associated is the Dinah Shore. She and Betsy King are the only player to win the event three times.

Alcott's dominance at the Dinah Shore began in 1983. Beth Daniel, who led for most of the first two rounds, began to stumble late in the third round. Into the opening slipped Kathy Whitworth, at age 43 looking for her 85th victory, and Alcott, who had kept herself within striking distance all week. On the final day, Daniel double-bogeyed two holes and bogeyed one hole on the front nine to lose the lead for good. Whitworth made bogeys when she needed pars, and her final round 72 was only good enough to tie with Daniel for second.

Alcott took the lead with a birdie on the 12th hole and never let it go. At the tournament's end, Alcott had won her third major – she had won the Peter Jackson in 1979 and the Open in 1980. She had also beaten the best of the old guard, Whitworth, and one of her own generation of new players, Daniel.

The win was typical of Alcott's ability to always keep herself in contention, and a tribute to her understanding of what it takes to win.

"I think there is a common denominator for the Rankins, the Carners, and so on," Alcott said in 1980. "I can't pick out the little details of the style of each, but they all share determination, desire and guts. Determination is the fight in each one; desire means each wants to play super golf in every shot; and guts are what you need to play the big shot when it's called for."[23]

It would be five years before Alcott won another Dinah Shore. In 1988 Alcott was suffering through a slump. She had accumulated 26 LPGA victories, but for the first time in 13 years, during the 1987 season, had gone winless.

Alcott played well at Phoenix the week before the Dinah Shore. She led after the second round and eventually finished fourth. Her comment at a pre-tournament press conference should have made everyone wary. "I have the same feeling I had when I won the U.S. Open in 1980," Alcott said.[24]

Alcott shot 71 in the first round and then followed with a blistering 66 to take the lead. In the post-round interview she was the ever-cocky Alcott.

"I love walking up the 18th fairway knowing all those people in the gallery appreciate what an artist I am with a golf club," Alcott said. "I love knowing I am one of the best."[25]

Alcott made history on Saturday with a second consecutive 66 - creating the best back-to-back rounds in Dinah Shore history. But, the real history was made on Sunday and it would not be related to what she did with her golf clubs.

By the 11th hole in the last round, Colleen Walker, who had trailed by four shots, had worked her way back to only a one shot deficit. On the 14th hole, Alcott made birdie to increase her lead to two shots. Pars on the final four holes kept Walker at bay and gave Alcott her second Dinah Shore crown.

After the final putt dropped into the cup, Alcott did something that had not been seen on the LPGA Tour. She grabbed Bill Kurre, her caddie, and the two jumped into the lake that guards the 18th green at Mission Hills Country Club. Like the TV shots of Alcott, the stoic battler in the 1980 U.S. Open, the "diving" Alcott was beamed to millions of homes, immediately building a new image for the 32 year old star – one of bravado and a bit irreverent.

At the time, the LPGA was lagging far behind both the PGA Tour and the relatively young Senior PGA Tour in TV ratings. Even Alcott admitted the antic was perhaps a little "unladylike."

"I think sometimes people think that I have too much class to do something like that," Alcott said.[26]

Yet what Alcott had done was to give the LPGA some desperately needed pizzazz. The image she had created with her reaction to the win was something she had been thinking about since her first year on tour.

"It used to be a group of women traveling on a circuit, leading a tough existence, trying to grind out a livelihood," Alcott said about the LPGA in 1975. "Now it's changed and it's a fresher, younger approach. Now it's girls who can play well and provide an entertainment because they're attractive. You're on stage when you're out there, just like in show business."[27]

Thirteen years later, as she came out of the lake dripping wet, she had shown the world exactly what she had meant.

Alcott's third Dinah Shore win in 1991 came at a time when Alcott faced one of her greatest personal challenges. Meeting and living through that challenge changed both Alcott's view of life and the importance of golf.

The 1990 season was another slump year for Alcott. It was the first season in her career that she did not finish among the top 20 money winners. It was one of only two years in which she had not won at least one event. It was also the year that Alcott's mother died.

Early in 1990, Lea was diagnosed with cancer, and she died in August. Alcott had faced the death of her father, with whom she had remained close, ten years earlier. The death of her mother left Alcott alone, searching for meaning. After 15 years of the grind on tour, she found it harder to find that meaning in golf.

"We used to finish each other's sentences; she was my best friend," Alcott said. "Golf didn't seem very important for a while.[28] Losing both parents is very hard. You have to make adjustments in your life and face your own mortality. It is also a slight letdown when you realize that the emphasis in your career has shifted from being totally centered on golf, to one in which golf is merely an important part of your life. It may seem fractional, but it is a big difference when you no longer are eating it, breathing it and sleeping it."[29]

During the winter of 1991, Alcott turned back to golf. She spent hours on the practice tee.

"I worked very hard this winter," Alcott said in a 1991 interview for the *New York Times*. "I think it was almost a solace for me after the death of my mom to throw myself into golf."[30]

The work and solace resulted in Alcott not just "coming back," but making the biggest "splash" that she could in March at the Dinah Shore. Her birdie on the 72nd hole gave her an eight shot victory over Dottie Mochrie, and her play all week had been close to perfect. In 72 holes she had missed only nine greens, and carded eighteen birdies against only three bogeys. Her 15-under-par total of 273 set a new scoring record for the event. And then there was the lake.

Alcott had been working on a book – *Amy Alcott's Guide to Women's Golf* – which was published two years later in 1993. The book's Forward had already been written by none other than tournament host Dinah Shore. In that Forward, Shore wrote that if Alcott ever won the event for a third time, she would join her in a swim.

Only seconds after her 12-foot birdie putt disappeared into the cup on the final hole, Alcott looked to Shore who ever so slightly nodded her head at the golfer. Holding hands, Alcott, Shore and ever-present caddie, Bill Kurre, ran into the lake. After a break for commercial in the TV coverage, viewers returned to watch as Shore, hair wrapped in a towel, presented the check and graciously hugged the once again soaking wet Alcott.

> ### Amy Alcott
>
> #### Professional Highlights
>
> **Has had three seasons with four victories - 1979, 1989, 1984**
>
> **Won at least once each year between 1975 and 1986: this 12 year consecutive win streak ties the LPGA record.**
>
> **Surpassed $3 million in career earnings:1994**

"I wasn't going to jump in this time but Dinah was game," Alcott said. "I thought at this point in my life, I just wanted to accept the trophy with some dignity. I guess that's just not my style."[31]

Adjusted to life without her "best friend," and with the renewed confidence furnished by the win, Alcott was again cocky. But now the cockiness contained an element of the philosophical.

"I never thought that my playing days were over because I know I'm too good," Alcott said. "But whether you are Greg Norman or Amy Alcott, nobody but nobody is at the top all the time in golf. It's a sport that goes in cycles. To be a champion in golf is to be consistent. It's one of the few sports where you can say consistency is where it's at."[32]

The victory at the Dinah Shore was Alcott's twenty-ninth LPGA win. She needed only one more victory for induction into the Hall of Fame. In the next few years she would need whatever strength she had gained from her challenges of 1990 and 1991. For she was about to face the biggest challenge of her life - winning one more time.

The Hall of Fame

In 1991, the criteria for the Hall of Fame required thirty LPGA tournament wins and two major championships. Alcott's win at the Dinah Shore that year added a fifth major championship to her resume and brought her to twenty-nine victories. Alcott's game was sharp, and it seemed only a matter of time until she would achieve the magic number of thirty. In fact only three months after the Dinah Shore, Alcott's chances looked promising. At the Atlantic City Classic in June, Alcott was just two holes away from an opportunity to qualify for the Hall. After 70 holes, Alcott was tied for the lead with Jane Geddes. Then, on the 17th hole of the final round, Alcott missed a short par putt giving Geddes a one-stroke lead. Both players parred the 18th, leaving Alcott in second place. Although disappointed and under pressure from the media, Alcott took the loss in stride.

"All anyone wants to talk about is my next win," Alcott said. "I know from experience that whenever I try to win, I don't.... I'm not a real egomaniac and I never have been. I know that I could very easily be getting on a 5:45 train with my can of tuna fish and punching a typewriter five days a week. I'm real lucky to do what I do."[33]

But, there was still time. At least that is what everyone including Alcott thought. In 1992, Alcott finished the season ranked 55th on the money list. It was the worst finish of her career, and the best finish in a tournament that she could manage was tied for eighth. In 1993, things got worse. She dropped to 76th on the money list. Alcott had been in slumps before, and in 1994, it looked like she was about to pull out of this most recent one. She finished 35th on the money list, but there was no win. The best tournament finish she could come up with was a fourth. But, there was still time. In 1995, she slipped to 75th on the money list. Time was running out.

In 1996 Alcott turned forty, and the media began to ask the question all players dread – will she win again? The fact that the next win would put her in the Hall of Fame made the question a constant albatross at every event she played.

Alcott remained calm. Whenever asked – and she was asked in almost every interview – she would patiently explain the reality of a twenty-one year career in golf.

"For about the first 17 years of my career I was pretty much a steamroller," Alcott said in 1996. "I was extremely consistent. I'd win at least one tournament every year. But the last couple of years have probably been a combination of not enough practice, plus, since I was 8 years old, all I've done is play golf. There's a burnout factor."

"It becomes more complicated," Alcott continued. "There's the question of traveling and how much dedication you have left. At times I've had trouble motivating the fire. But the fire comes back when you shoot a good round. It's like a long and winding road that leads you back to your door. Paul McCartney was right."[34]

In August the road lead Alcott very close to home. She finished second to sophomore tour player, Emilee Klein, in the Weetabix Women's British Open. But second was not good enough.

The 1997 season saw Alcott cut back her playing schedule to the least number of events she had ever played - sixteen. She had broken her kneecap in December 1996 and was sidelined until March 1997. Her return was a disaster. She made only $18,000 and was ranked 150 on the money list. The 1998 season was not much better. Another short season with only 16 events left Alcott at 101 on the money list. By December, frustration replaced the calm Alcott had shown two years earlier. She made that frustration public in an article she wrote for *Sports Illustrated*.

"Another year has passed, and I'm still not in the LPGA Hall of Fame," Alcott wrote. "For seven years now, I've heard fans call out, 'Amy, we're rooting for you to get your 30th!' But I'm stuck on 29 career wins, and according to LPGA rules, I need one more to get into the Hall.

"Don't misunderstand me – I want to win again. At 42, I have more fight in me than ever. However, this quest of mine has gotten tiring. After 23 years on tour, I'm starting to think that my biggest opponent may be the grind of traveling. Still, it's important that I get into the Hall. I think I belong there, and I'm not the only one. How the hell can you exclude players like Hollis Stacy, with her three U.S. Open titles and 15 other wins, and Beth Daniel, with her 32 victories? Fans want to see excellence rewarded. Right now, though, the Hall has only 14 players in it. Is that enough reward to cover the long history of women's golf?"[35]

There was hardly any time left. Alcott was 42. Some of her fellow competitors were literally half her age. And, each year there were more and more young, aggressive, good players.

Alcott's tone in the *Sports Illustrated* article was one of anger, and perhaps it was justified. She had 29 wins including five major championships and her career earnings were over $3 million.

It seemed as though fate had designated Alcott to "almost" status. Except... since 1985, the LPGA had been looking at the Hall of Fame criteria. In late 1998, the Hall of Fame Committee published a report that outlined new criteria for qualification based on a point system. Under the new criteria, Alcott was in - easily. In early 1999, the new criteria were presented to the LPGA membership for a vote. On February 5, 1999, the LPGA membership voted to approve the new criteria for the Hall of Fame. Once the Hall of Fame Committee presented the proposal, it was almost certain the players would ratify it.

Although it was not official, Alcott was told in January that her dream of getting into the Hall had a very good chance of coming true. And, the way she was told held special meaning for her.

Seventeen years before, Alcott was paired with JoAnne Carner in the final round of the Chevrolet World Championship of Women's Golf. Carner won the event. It was her 30th win and put her in the Hall.

"That got her into the Hall of Fame," Alcott said. "I cried. It was such a wonderful moment. I thought, 'This is where I want to be someday.'"[36]

On January 11, 1999, Alcott was at home in Santa Monica. She got a phone call from fellow tour player, Meg Mallon who had just come out of the Hall of Fame Committee meeting.

According to *Sports Illustrated* the conversation went like this:

" 'Has the commissioner called you?' Mallon asked. No, said Alcott. 'Well, hang on then,' Mallon said. 'there's someone here who wants to talk to you.'

The next thing Alcott heard was Carner's unmistakable, raspy voice. 'I've got something to tell you, if you haven't heard,' Carner began.

'I knew right then and there it was about the Hall of Fame,' Alcott says."[37]

Alcott was inducted into the Hall of Fame under criteria that requires a player to win one major championship, the Vare Trophy or the Rolex Player of the Year award and accumulate 27 points. Points are awarded by the following system: one point for each tournament win, each Vare Trophy award and each Player of the Year award; two points for each major championship. Alcott qualified well above the required 27 points with 39.

While she was on the plane traveling to the first event of the 1999 season, Alcott made a list of all the people she had met and come to know during her career. It filled six pages in her notebook.

"I'm going to have a hell of a Hall of Fame party," Alcott said. "Maybe several."[38]

Alcott continues to play a shortened LPGA schedule. She has begun to turn her intensity in other directions. She is co-partnering with American Golf Corporation on the redevelopment of Westchester Golf Course and Driving Range in Los Angeles, which will include an Amy Alcott Golf Academy. She is a playing editor for *Golf Digest*, but her new major interest takes her back to her roots as a golfer - TV. Alcott would like to start a second career in sports and lifestyle broadcasting.

Alcott has also become a major spokesperson for developing equal access and more opportunities for women and young people in golf. The concepts of access and freedom have been important to Alcott for her entire life.

"I believe in strong, independent women who know themselves and their own minds," Alcott said. "I believe in equal pay, equal opportunities, and I don't like discrimination. My freedom to do what I want means everything to me."[39]

Chapter 16

Fire...

Beth Daniel

The 22-year-old Beth Daniel wasted no time in establishing her image when she arrived on the LPGA Tour in 1979. She threw some clubs. She got fined. She showed impatience with both herself (on the golf course) and the media (in the interview room). If there was a "Peck's Bad Girl Award" on the tour, Beth would have been the front runner to receive it.

The media played up the image. Almost all articles written about Daniel during her first few years on tour include some reference to her "temper." It was good copy. Her fiery outbursts were different than the normally calm – almost to the point of bland – approach that characterized other players. Along with accolades for her long drives and towering iron shots, Daniel, in those early years, was described as "volatile," "emotional," and "snappish."

Despite the volatility, emotionality and snappishness, Daniel could play. In 1979 she won an event as a rookie and eventually took Rookie of the Year honors. In her sophomore year, 1980, Daniel won four times. She was number one on the money list again in 1981, and by 1983 – at the end of her fourth year on tour – Daniel had won thirteen LPGA tournaments.

The media was fair. They never allowed Daniel's personality to overshadow her ability. They talked about her great play, but somewhere in the stories or interviews there was always a mention of the "T" word – temper. And often, the "T" word was used as a lead in to the "P" word – potential. Daniel, it was often said, was not reaching her potential, and it was at least partially due to her emotionalism on the course.

With all this emphasis on temper and unrealized potential, the defining element of Daniel's personality was missed. No one ever described Daniel as patient. Yet the volatile, emotional, snappish Daniel would become, over the next twenty years, a study in patience.

Elizabeth Ann Daniel was born in Charleston, South Carolina on October 14, 1956. She was the youngest of Lucia and Bob Daniel's three children.

The elder Daniels were both golfers. Lucia at one time played to a 13-handicap, and Bob, an executive with Coca-Cola, played regularly. Beth was introduced to the game when she was seven years old.

"My parents didn't want to pay for a baby-sitter," Daniel said. "So, I went with them to the golf course."[1]

Daniel spent her childhood participating in all sports, but golf was the activity that got the most time. When her golf education began at age eight, Daniel's first teacher was Al Esposito, head pro at the Country Club of Charleston.

"If I told her to stand on her head and grip the club with her feet, well, by golly, she'd do it," Esposito said in a 1981 interview with *Sports Illustrated*. "When I first saw her, she was so little that you would've thought she was least likely to succeed. But she was determined. She'd pull her bag over her shoulder, and off she'd go. She just played and practiced and practiced every opportunity she got.

"I remember an early pee wee tournament," Esposito continued. "She beat several of the boys and one of them said to me, 'Beth can sure play golf, but I'm going to beat her tomorrow.' Beth was standing there and said, 'We'll see.' But you should have seen the expression in her eyes. They got so cold. It reminded me of Ben Hogan. And the next day she beat the boy again."[2]

When Daniel was fifteen, Esposito left the Country Club of Charleston and was replaced by Derek Hardy. The little girl became a tall, well-coordinated teenager, and her golf game began to improve rapidly. By 1973, Daniel, now one of Hardy's star pupils, was winning state junior events. In 1975, just a few months before her nineteenth birthday, Daniel won the first of two U.S. Women's Amateur titles (the second came at the 1977 U.S. Amateur). Daniel moved her amateur golf career to the international stage in 1976 as a member of the Curtis Cup team. She was also a Curtis Cup Team member in 1978.

BETH DANIEL
Began playing golf: age 7
First LPGA victory: 1979
Most recent LPGA victory: 1995

Daniel's competitive experience was enhanced when she attended Furman University. She was a member of the women's golf team that included fellow Hall of Famer-to-be Betsy King and future LPGA player Sherri Turner. In 1976, the Furman team won the Association of Intercollegiate Athletics for Women (AIAW) national championship by defeating the University of Tulsa whose star player was none other than Nancy Lopez.

Daniel and King shared Furman's Athlete of the Year Award in 1977, but the two could not have been more different in terms of their personality.

"Betsy studied and played golf," Daniel said. "I played golf, partied and studied a little."[3]

Daniel also created controversy on the quiet Furman campus when in her senior year she had a disagreement with her coach and left the women's team.

"I think Beth felt, not strait-jacketed, but maybe it was more discipline than she wanted," King said.[4]

Daniel was not about to end her college golf career, so she took her golf skill to the Furman men's team. She played two matches with the men and beat three quarters of the field in each event.

Playing successfully against men was not a new experience for Daniel. As a teen she often played – from the back tees – with her father's weekend golf group.

"She could always hit the ball as far as any man out there," Bob Daniel said.[5]

In 1978 Daniel graduated from Furman with a degree in physical education, but there was little doubt that her career choice would be professional golf. In 1979 she attended the LPGA Qualifying School, finished first and joined the tour. By August Daniel had won her first LPGA event. She finished her rookie season with $97,000, and easily won Rookie of the Year honors. It seemed obvious to everyone in golf that the talented Daniel was on her way to becoming the next superstar in women's golf. Daniel's future success became a given for everyone – except Beth. For her, it became a problem.

The Beth and Nancy Show

The problem for freshman LPGA tour player Daniel began almost immediately, and it came in the form of comparison. The media began to describe Daniel as the "next Nancy Lopez." Lopez had stormed on tour the year before and was Daniel's predecessor as Rookie of the Year. Lopez's charm and easy friendliness had made her the darling of the media and the instant favorite of the fans. There is no doubt that there could be a logical comparison of Daniel and Lopez in terms of golf skill. In fact, in Daniel's first LPGA tournament, she finished tied for seventh, one stroke in front of Lopez.

But Beth was not Nancy. On the course, Lopez displayed a workmanlike calm. Daniel was intense. Nancy naturally related easily to people. It took Beth some time to warm to people. They were different people with different approaches and personalities.

The media already wanted to play them against one another. They were further encouraged to compare the two young players by the LPGA Commissioner himself, Ray Volpe. In 1979, Volpe could see the marketing potential of a Lopez-Daniel rivalry, and the LPGA began to market Daniel as a worthy opponent for Lopez. At one point in early 1980, Volpe said, "Beth Daniel may be the greatest woman player in history, greater even than Mickey Wright."[6]

In 1983 and again in 1991, Daniel talked about the way the pressure of the comparison affected her.

"I had just come out on the Tour and all of a sudden I was being compared to Lopez," Daniel said in 1983. "It was like walking around with a 500-pound weight on my shoulders. I didn't like it. I didn't like it at all. As a matter of fact, I had a long talk with Ray Volpe because I wanted to find out what he really said.

"That [Volpe's comment] hurt me," Daniel said in 1991. "I felt pressure. Think about it: The commissioner was expecting me to be better than Nancy Lopez. Today, I would take that as a compliment. But I always tried to live up to everyone's expectations. I know now that's impossible."[7]

With Volpe's encouragement, the media began getting comments from other players about Daniel as the next women's golf Goliath.

Judy Rankin, who was the tour's leading money winner in 1979, is quoted as saying, "Someday that girl is going to beat all of us. She's the closest thing to Mickey Wright I've seen."[8]

Even Wright had something to say.

"In three years people will be saying, 'Nancy who?'" Wright said, then commented on her take on Daniel's intense desire. "They [the new players on tour] start earlier and burn out earlier. Plus, once you get the money sack full, the motivation fades. But Beth strikes me as one that will maintain her drive for a long time. She struck me that way three or four years ago. She really seems to want to be the best."[9]

Volpe. Rankin. Wright. In 1979, that was pressure from some of the heaviest hitters in the game. And, Daniel responded. She had a great rookie year. In her second season, 1980, she won four events, took Player of the Year and set a new record for single season earnings with over

$200,000. She also finished first on the money list. Then in her third year on tour, 1981, she finished number one on the money list again and won two events.

It should have been enough, but it wasn't. Typical of Daniel's "problem" during this period was the headline on a story that appeared in Golf Magazine early in 1980 – "Will Beth catch Nancy?" The sub-heading read, "Even if she outplays Lopez, Beth Daniel may have trouble matching Nancy's gallery-appeal."[10]

If a published story didn't compare Daniel to Lopez, it talked about her "potential," and if she would reach it. Unfulfilled potential? In her first three years on tour she had finished on top of the money list two consecutive years, won the Rookie of the Year award and Player of the Year, accumulated seven victories, and set a new record for earnings in a season. Exactly what potential hadn't she reached?

"I often wonder what it would have been like if I had come before Nancy," Daniel said in 1980. "After all, the closest any other rookie has come to my mark is winning around $40,000. What Nancy has done is phenomenal, but I don't think it's fair to compare me to her. We are different people with different games. I feel I haven't even reached my peak yet. In two or three years I should really be at my best. I still have to work on my short game."[11]

At the time, it was popular in the media to talk about the Lopez-Daniel rivalry as a replay of the Palmer-Nicklaus relationship on the PGA Tour. When asked about that comparison, the normally intense Daniel was able to show a sense of humor.

"Well, she can be Palmer because she was there first," Daniel said. "And I don't mind being Nicklaus at all."[12]

Daniel was well aware of the personality difference between herself and Lopez. She did not attempt to apologize for her own tendency to be a private person.

" People pry so much, they're so intrusive; I respect my privacy," Daniel said. "Nancy enjoys the attention, but I don't particularly thrive on it; I like to turn down appearances, which doesn't make me popular, but I don't enjoy doing them. I'm very shy, and I dislike people latching on to me because I'm Beth Daniel the golfer.

"Everyone wants to be popular, and everyone wants to be wanted," Daniel continued. "But, Lopez is in the limelight so much that she gave up something precious: her time. I treasure mine too much for that."[13]

In 1980 Daniel's play did a great deal to take the "comparison issue" out of the press. In nine out of fourteen tournaments during the second half of the tour's 1980 season, Daniel finished in better position than Lopez. During that period she had back-to-back wins on August 17 and 24 (the Patty Berg Golf Classic and the Columbia Savings LPGA Classic), and then won again less than a month later at the prestigious World Series of Women's Golf. It was time for the media to see Beth Daniel as her own person. They did. But, they also found another "problem."

Temper, Temper, Temper

Daniel's intensity and the resulting behavior on the golf course were, and to a certain extent, still are legendary. She simply is not afraid to show her emotions, and usually her anger is expressed in behavior that shows her volatile temper. Yes, she has thrown clubs. Yes, she has berated her caddie. And yes, the LPGA has fined her for that behavior. Much like tennis great Jimmy Connors, Daniel's temper has always been part of her game, and it had little if anything to do with the pressure of living up to everyone else's expectations.

"She gets discouraged easily," Daniel's mother, Lucia, said in 1980. "And she'll get down on herself if she has a bad hole. She has such a good disposition, and it's just because she cares so much about golf that she gets angry.

"I understand her feelings," Lucia continued, "But, I think she has to get over it. I cringe when I see it myself."[14]

Daniel pretty much explains her volatility almost exactly the way Connors might.

"My temper is frustration with myself," Daniel said. "When I hit a bad shot, I know I can do better, and maybe I've put a bad swing on it, or I should have changed my club. So, I'm frustrated.

I need to feel like that to push myself and work harder at the game....

"I don't necessarily call mine a temper," Daniel continued. "I'm an ultimate perfectionist, who can throw a club or a little fit after a shot and then come back to the next shot without being affected. If it was a true temper, it would affect the next shot and the next hole."[15]

Daniel had proved her equality with Lopez. But it didn't help, for according to the pundits, her "potential" was threatened by her temper.

"Insiders knew there might be a hole in [her] game: her temperament," Rhonda Glenn wrote in 1983. "Her angry reactions on the course – club slamming – were already notorious, but it was just a symptom of a perfectionism so intense observers wondered how she could stand up to the competition, week after week."[16]

Sue Hoover, writing for *Women's Sports* in a 1980 article, first refers to the Lopez comparison.

"The problem with (Daniel) gaining Rookie of the Year honors in 1979 was her instant comparison with the 1978 winner, Nancy Lopez, who won nine tournaments and $189,000 in her first year on the tour."[17]

"She cuts an elegant figure on the golf course," Hoover continued. "But when she gets angry, stand clear."[18]

Finally, Hoover quotes Hall of Famer Carol Mann.

"Beth Daniel is a dynamite golfer with tremendous potential," Mann said. "She still has to learn to reconcile her ability and her expectations, and to use her sensitivity in her favor."[19]

In a 1981 *Sports Illustrated* piece, Barry McDermott makes Daniel sound almost paranoid.

"They [LPGA officials] were after me," McDermott quotes Daniel as saying. "Every time I had a bad hole they would show up in a golf cart and start writing in their notebooks."[20]

McDermott then adds his own thoughts.

"It should be recorded that at the Women's Open – a tournament not administered by the LPGA – Daniel got hot under the collar more than once and had her worst showing of the last half of 1980."[21] Daniel finished in 10th place in the U.S. Open that year – only her third Open as a professional.

Perhaps the reason the media placed two "monkeys" on Daniel's back – a personal competition with Lopez and her own volatile behavior – may have more to do with what Daniel represented than Daniel's personality or character. Daniel was a threat to the tour's "perfect star" – Lopez.

Lopez was friendly, soft, and feminine. She was the image the Tour wanted, and she was the type of woman athlete the media would accept – womanly. Daniel was the opposite. She was intense, emotional. She even had the audacity to play on the men's golf team in college. Daniel was attractive, neat in her appearance, but she had one flaw – she played with the intensity and sometimes behaved the way a male athlete would. Her perfectionism did not fit with society's view of women – males strove to reach perfection, not women. The media was not quite ready to accept the same traits in a woman athlete that they would accept in male athletes. It would take almost another 20 years before they were ready. In the early 1980's Daniel represented, because of her skill, a threat to the world of sport. She played, thought and acted like an "athlete." The world wanted her to be a "woman" athlete.

> ## BETH DANIEL
>
> ### Amateur Career Highlights
>
> ### U.S. Amateur:1975 & 1977
>
> ### Curtis Cup Team:1976 & 1978
>
> ### World Cup Team:1978

To control the threat, she was first compared to the player who was the perfect representation of "woman" athlete – Nancy Lopez. When she showed she was equal to Lopez, another way of controlling the threat to the image was needed. There was a way to minimize the new image represented by Daniel – by creating a scenario in which Daniel's behavior might cause her to self-destruct. If Daniel did not "reach her potential" then the image of the "woman" athlete would be preserved.

In just three years on tour, Daniel had carved out a record that most players would not come close to in an entire career. The problem for Daniel was that she did not fit the image of women athletes for that time. It created almost unbearable pressure for the talented young player and it would haunt her for the rest of her career.

The Bad Times

Looking at Beth Daniel as the Jimmy Connors of women's golf is an effective analogy. She arrived on tour and immediately became the "Wonderkid." Like Connors she was also "Wonderbrat."

"We all wondered," tour player, and Daniel friend, Vicki Fergon said. "Who is this girl coming out here being such a brat?"[22]

Also, like Connors, Daniel admitted to her "immature" behavior as she matured.

"I had the attitude that I'm Beth Daniel and I belong out here, and I'm going to prove it," the 34-year-old Daniel said in 1990. "Golf was a matter of life and death."[23]

Daniel expressed the same thought though a bit stronger, in 1991.

"When I first came out here I was a brat," Daniel said. "I didn't need anybody and I was going to prove it."[24]

Prove it she did. Her first three years on tour were outstanding, ending in 1981 with a second consecutive first place finish on the money list. But, 1981 was also the beginning of a long, almost 10-year stretch, of hard-learned lessons and several soul-searching sessions that almost lead Daniel to quit the tour. Daniel's education at the "school of hard knocks" began at the 1981 U.S. Open.

The Open was played at La Grange Country Club in La Grange, Ill. Daniel played magnificently. Her final round 68 left her 8-under par for the tournament – an outstanding Open score. Unfortunately for Daniel, Pat Bradley also played outstanding golf. Her final round 66 gave her a one-shot victory over Daniel.

"I remember sitting in front of my locker thinking, 'I just played the best golf I can possibly play and I was beaten,'" Daniel said in 1991. "My deduction from that was, 'Therefore, I am not the best, and I will never be the best.' And from there I took it to, 'Well, if I can't be the best, why am I playing this game?'

"It took me probably four years to get over that," Daniel continued. "I looked at it from the total wrong point of view, but it took me awhile to get that out of my system."[25]

Daniel's recovery from her Open loss was not enhanced in 1982. That year she led the U.S. Open after the third round. In the final round, Daniel held her one stroke lead through seven holes. On the eighth hole her integrity brought on disaster.

Daniel had a ten-foot birdie putt. She addressed the ball, then looked up and told playing partner JoAnne Carner that the ball had moved – two-stroke penalty. Daniel assessed herself the penalty although none of her playing partners nor the USGA officials had seen the ball move.

"I was positive it moved," Daniel said in a 1983 interview. "I always set my putter down with a certain amount of space between the blade and the ball and that space wasn't there. I knew it had rolled. My first thought was that it was the first time it had ever happened to me. Why did it have to happen in the Open?"[26]

Daniel, concentration broken, could not recover. Janet Alex, who had been trailing, went on to win. Daniel finished 10th.

Frustration turned to anger when Daniel's fellow tour players began to ask her what happened.

"I couldn't believe it," Daniel said. "Not 'Good tournament,' but 'What happened?' And these are players talking."[27]

If Daniel was having trouble recovering mentally from the two heartbreaking Open losses, it did not show up in her game. She won five events in 1982, and in 1983 she picked up another victory. But there were signs that things might not be as good as they seemed. Her scoring average was beginning to rise. For a golfer, bigger numbers are never a sign that good things are happening.

Daniel was forced to take a five-week break in 1983 as the result of severe back spasms – the first of several injuries that would affect her career. The back problem caused Daniel to make some physical compensations which began to affect her swing. In 1984 Daniel won only once and she slipped for the first time out of the top ten on the money list. Daniel rebounded in 1985, winning once. By the end of the 1985 season – her seventh on tour – Daniel had accumulated 14 victories. It would be another four years before she would win again.

The period between 1985 and 1989 was awful for Daniel. Back problems hampered her natural swing and her confidence dropped. As she lost confidence, her putting became worse and worse.

"I probably became the worst putter on tour," Daniel said. "I lost all my confidence.... By the time I was thirty, I was thinking about quitting. I'm the kind of person who always knows she is capable of doing better even when I'm doing well. I just couldn't stand playing that poorly."[28]

Daniel's poor play affected more than her game. It also affected the way she looked at life.

"I got very depressed," Daniel said during that four-year period. "It is stupid that everything is based on what you shoot, and it's tough going through the despair... When I was 22, I thought, 'It's a party. You just go out and play golf.' I didn't care if I hit it out of bounds because I could make a couple of birdies, and I had the ability to let myself win. I know I'm still capable of winning if I'll allow myself to do it, but whereas it was once so easy now it's so hard.

"I tell myself it's a cycle," Daniel continued. "Eventually a cycle has to end, but it's hard to ride it out, and that's what I've got to do."[29]

By 1988, the Beth Daniel who struggled through tournament after tournament was a different person than the "brat" who proved to the world how good she was in the early 1980's. As it often happens, Daniel was able to turn her game around when, in 1988, adversity turned into opportunity.

No Quitter

The low point came for Daniel during 1986 and 1987. Knowing she had to do something, Daniel turned to the late Davis Love II, the well-known teaching professional and father of PGA Tour player, Davis Love III, for help with her swing and a much needed boost of confidence. She

---

BETH DANIEL

Professional Highlights

**Third LPGA player to break
$5 million mark in
career earnings: 1996**

**Solheim Cup Team: 1990, 1992,
1994, 1996**

---

also worked with Dave Pelz to improve her short game. Improvement began to become evident in 1988. Daniel jumped from 29th on the money list in 1987 to 17th at the end of 1988. More importantly, her scoring average went from 73.12 in 1987 to 71.80 in 1988.

Things were looking up for Daniel. She played well in her first three tour events in early 1988, and then in mid-March she was diagnosed with mononucleosis. Recovery demanded that she leave the tour for three months. With her game coming around and her confidence renewed, Daniel was forced to sit on the sidelines through April, May and June of the 1988 season.

The illness could have made Daniel think once more about quitting as she had after the Open setbacks in 1981 and 1982. But the 32-year-old Daniel looked at life differently than she had six years earlier.

"I had a lot of time to think about what I wanted to do," Daniel said. "I told myself I can't be as hard on myself, can't stress myself out like I used to because my body won't take it.

"I also decided I didn't want to leave the sport on a sour note," Daniel continued. "I was going to give an honest shot to finding out if I could still be the player I wanted to be. That fueled my fire. I had something to prove, which has always been a real motivating force for me."[30]

Daniel returned to the tour in July. She told sportswriter Liz Kahn that she "almost felt like a rookie."[31] Daniel began to perform just like the Daniel who was Rookie of the Year almost ten years before. She was able to play in fourteen tournaments after she returned to the tour, and finished 1988 – having played only seventeen events, nine of which she finished in the top ten – with $140,635 in prize money, and that wonderfully low number of 71.80 for a scoring average.

The first half of the 1989 season saw Daniel continue to play well. There still were no wins, but she finished second four times. Finally, in August, the four-year ordeal of wondering if she could win again ended. At the Greater Washington Open Daniel went into the final round with a four-shot lead. But the mature Daniel – although she was playing like the rookie she had been – was a bit gun-shy. She told Vicki Fergon of her fear that she would not be able to hold the lead and once more fall short of victory.

"Second's not so bad; you still make a lot of money," Fergon joked. "Just go out there and play."[32]

Daniel held the four-stroke lead and won. It was as though the floodgates had opened. In the next seven tournaments she entered, she won three. By season's end she had twenty top-ten finishes, four wins, won the Vare Trophy with a record setting scoring average of 70.38, and finished second to Betsy King on both the money list and in the Player of the Year race.

Beth was back and she didn't stop there. In 1990 she almost literally won everything. She won seven tournaments and finished in the top ten eighteen times. Daniel became Player of the Year for the second time, and for the second consecutive year she won the Vare Trophy – her scoring average was 70.54. She was the leading money winner for the third time in her career.

All of that was wonderful, but the most important event of the year for Daniel came in July when she won the Mazda LPGA Championship. After eleven years on tour, Daniel had her first victory in a major. It was a "dream" year and no one appreciated it more than Daniel.

"Although 1990 will go down in my career history as the best, it was a real watershed," Daniel said. "It meant a lot, because I had gone through such a low period when most people thought I was probably washed up.

"To be consistent enough to win the Vare Trophy in 1989 and again the following year meant a lot to me, and it was very satisfying to win the 1990 LPGA Championship playing against the best," Daniel continued. "To have, in 1990, one of the greatest years of anyone in LPGA history, also gave me real satisfaction knowing I had won the week before and three weeks previously and that I could do it again. I had reached a maturity where I knew that the feeling didn't happen often, and I cherished it rather than taking it for granted, as I did when I was younger."[33]

Daniel had battled back from illness. She had redesigned a failing golf swing and built a stronger game. She had established herself as Beth Daniel – not the next Nancy Lopez. She had matured and learned that she could use frustration and anger as a positive motivator. She was a prime example of "potential realized." She had won all the battles, but the war wasn't over. There was one more battle to suffer through.

Getting to the Hall

Daniel continued to play well through 1991 and 1992. Although she did not win in 1992, she finished second five times. Daniel faltered a bit in 1993 when she went winless and finished 40th on the money list. But she came back strong in 1994, winning four times. In June, Daniel won the JAL Big Apple Classic. It was her 30th career victory. It was then that her next battle began.

In 1994, the criteria for the LPGA Hall of Fame was 30 wins with two majors, 35 wins with one major championship, or 40 wins with no majors. In June of 1994, Daniel, 38 years old and in her 15th year on tour, had a problem. She had just won for the 30th time in her career, but she had only one major tournament victory. Daniel was again in the headlines for something other than her play on the golf course. The big question everyone asked was "Can she make the Hall of Fame?" Daniel would have to win another major, or five more non-major events. There is no doubt it was a formidable task for a 38-year-old veteran.

Yet Daniel seemed to have a new approach. For all intents and purposes she didn't take up the gauntlet. She remained quiet about her chances to make the Hall. She was demonstrating a new facet of her character – patience. She would play the waiting game. She would wait until she won – either one more major, or five more tournaments. Or, she would wait until the LPGA revised the criteria. Daniel chose to remain silent on the "Hall thing."

In 1995 she collected her 32 tournament win. Although she hit a mini-slump in 1996, her twenty-fourth place finish at the Standard Register PING made her only the third player in the tour's history to surpass $5 million in career earnings. She only played nine events in 1997 when a shoulder injury forced her to the sidelines, and in 1998 she had a decent year, but was no closer to Hall of Fame induction.

It was strange for the fiery, emotional Daniel to be so quiet about the Hall. But, perhaps a comment she made in the mid-1990's gives insight into the attitude that the 42-year-old Daniel has developed.

"I came on tour and said I would quit when I was 30, but now I look forward to the next year," Daniel said. "As a professional athlete I have certain motivations that keep me in the game.

I have tournaments I want to win, private goals to achieve. I am now comfortable with my image...."[34]

A "comfortable" Daniel did not have to fight this battle. The club-throwing, turf-thrashing rookie had learned – over the course of her 20-year career – to take things as they came.

Then in 1999, the Hall came to Daniel. When the LPGA Tour membership voted to accept revised criteria for Hall of Fame membership, Daniel was in with room to spare. Under the new criteria, Daniel had 39 points when only 27 were needed. In fact, if the new criteria had been in effect all along, Daniel would have qualified ten years earlier in 1990.

Daniel's initial reaction to her qualification for the Hall was low key. "It's a pretty cool thing." she said. But, then she added, "One of the things that means the most to me is the fact that the current Hall of Famers all agree with this criteria. Had even one Hall of Famer not agreed with it, it wouldn't have meant quite as much to me."[35]

Daniel wasted little time in living up to the image of a Hall of Famer. In May 1999, less than six months after qualifying for the Hall, Daniel set a new LPGA record. At the LPGA Corning Classic, Daniel was in contention for the first time in almost a year. She shot 62 in the tournament's second round, carding nine consecutive birdies – a new tour record.

At the press conference after the third round, Daniel was asked if she now felt that the weight of the pressure to qualify for the Hall of Fame had been lifted.

"I can honestly tell you I didn't feel a weight lifted off my shoulders. I wasn't playing golf to get in the Hall of Fame. I am honored and proud to be part of it. The reason I played golf was to see how good I could be and to win tournaments. It's an unbelievable honor. All the pressure I ever put on myself was to win. I will always put that pressure on myself. When I feel like I can no longer win, that's the day I quit."[36]

What will Daniel do when the time for her to quit does come, if ever?

"We need to give junior golfers more opportunity to play golf," Daniel said. "The LPGA has an Urban Youth program that goes into the inner city programs.... I'd like to see more programs like that. It's something I'd like to work on when I retire."[37]

A career working with juniors would give Daniel an opportunity to pass along what she learned during a career that started easy, got hard and required patience.

"Suffering makes you tougher and more appreciative," Daniel said. "I would never want to live through it again, but those hard times made me a better person and a better golfer. You can't be on top all the time. I arrived cocky, wanting to prove myself as one of the great players, and ultimately I humbled myself."[38]

Determined not to "retire",
JoAnne at age 60 still plays the Tour.

JoAnne Carner

A fan favorite, Nancy never refuses to sign an autograph.

Nancy Lopez

JoAnne Carner

Betsy makes each swing the focus of competing.

Betsy King

Pat combines natural ability, hard work and
perseverance in each swing.

Pat Bradley

Nancy Lopez

Pat Bradley

Pat Bradley at the 1998 World Golf Hall of Fame Dedication and Induction ceremonies. (left)

Pat with her caddy.

Patty and her naturally athletic swing.

Patty Sheehan

Amy's fluid and graceful swing epitimizes her concept
of the game – a beautiful ballet.

Amy Alcott

"The Great Gundy" becomes "Big Momma"...
But always remains

JoAnne Carner

Patty Sheehan and "fan".

Betsy King

The swing that gave Amy three
Dinah Shore wins.

Amy Alcott

COURTESY LPGA. CREDIT: JACK STOHLMAN

Beth "stalks" her way
to the putting green.

Beth Daniel

The "Perfect Star"

Nancy Lopez

Concentrating on lining up a putt for a birdie.

Patty Sheehan

Beth (standing left) relaxes during
a delay in play.

Beth Daniel

Beth Daniel

Patty Sheehan

Betsy King

1998 World Golf Hall of Fame
Dedication and Induction Ceremonies

Beth Daniel

Part IV

PERSPECTIVES

Ties to the past… paths ahead

"Heroes meet life's perils head on moving forward where most of us would shrink backward. When they break through seemingly impenetrable barriers to change our perceptions or point of view, they open a new world for us."[1]

The women who are members of the LPGA Hall of Fame are heroes. Through their life stories we learn how each unshrinkingly met and conquered their own perils to keep moving forward in the life path they chose. As individuals, and as a group, they broke through, and broke down, barriers – barriers that were the most impenetrable because they were the ones that defined who we are. In the end, their actions changed our perceptions. Through the way they lived their lives, we saw that it was possible to redefine who we were and what we could be.

These women challenged the fortress of sport. They made us understand that sport holds a fascination and importance in the lives of "people," not just in the lives of males. They would not accept that there was a contradiction between "woman" and "athlete." Through their example they showed us that "athlete" had no gender. They opened up a new world.

Amy Alcott

Born: February 2, 1956
Joined LPGA Tour: 1975
29 Victories
Major Championship History: U.S. Women's Open (1980); Peter Jackson Classic (1979); Nabisco Dinah Shore (1983, 1988 and 1991) Inducted into Hall of Fame: 1999

Why would these women choose a career in golf knowing it would set them apart from the normal definition of woman? The complicated answer is that they "needed" to play. For some, playing golf integrated their life and made them happy. For some, the game gave them a feeling a self-worth. For some, success in golf brought the approval they sought.

The simple answer is – they wanted to play. For all, golf was an opportunity to do what they wanted most – compete. These women did not allow others to shape their lives. They made their own choice, accepted the risk and did what they wanted to do. That core action made them heroes. It was the first barrier they broke through to change perceptions. To break that barrier, it took the characteristics that all share – independence, the competitive desire for excellence and courage. Each Hall of Famer is an individual. They each have their own personalities, eccentricities and strength. Yet there remains important commonality.

Independence

These women share a spirit of independence. It is very easy to make an analogy between the early tour and the old west. The players of the 1950's were faced with a frontier. Like our nation's early 19th century settlers who carved out farms from wilderness, these players made something from nothing.

There were no tournaments. There was no staff. The players had to find sponsor money, talk golf facility managers into letting them use the course, and do the public relations work that would bring out the spectators. Then they had to play the game. It wasn't like baseball or football where teams had a well-defined division of labor – owners who administered the sport and players who played. The LPGA Tour of 1950 was made up of independent contractors – and there were only eleven of them.

In those early years, although they did not ride in covered wagon, the players traveled in caravans. Some players shared cars or trailers while others drove alone. They were responsible for and accountable only to themselves. But, like the early frontier settlers, their independence was based on a sense of community. The early tour players were just as quick to "circle the wagons" as were the early settlers of the west. It was not unusual – in fact almost the norm – for a tournament winner in those early days to "spring" for dinner, or anonymously pay the tournament entry fee for players who were not winning.

What is amazing is that Zaharias, Jameson, Berg and Suggs were able to combine cooperation and competition. They worked together to build the organizational base of the Tour, but then were able to go on the golf course and try as hard as possible to "beat each other's brains out." The fact that they were capable of that transition is the key to understanding how independent they were, and how much they saw themselves as being self-contained. They were able to compartmentalize their

Beth Daniel

Born: October 14, 1956
Joined LPGA Tour: 1979
32 Victories
Vare Trophy Winner: 1989, 1990, and 1994
Player of the Year: 1980, 1990 and 1994
Major Championship History: LPGA
Championship (1990)
Inducted into Hall of Fame: 2000
(Qualified: 1999)

Betsy King

Born: August 13, 1955
Joined LPGA Tour: 1977
31 Victories
Vare Trophy Winner: 1987 and 1993
Player of the Year: 1984, 1989 and 1993
Major Championship History: U.S. Women's Open (1989, 1990);
LPGA Championship (1992); Nabisco Dinah Shore (1987, 1990 and 1997)
Inducted into Hall of Fame: 1995

lives. They could move between the roles of "competitor," "promoter" and "administrator" without confusing the ultimate goals of each.

As the Tour grew, like the frontier, it became more and more tame. With the increase in stability came an increase in visibility and tasks. In the 1960's and 1970's the Tour's administration slowly turned from the players to a staff, and the Tour took on a full-time commissioner. The players were still independent contractors, but their sphere of operation became bigger. There were more tournaments which meant covering more miles. Players were in demand for other types of activities – personal appearances, business relationships, and product endorsements. In this period, the Tour was still the major focus of the player's lives, but they were being drawn into dealing with other issues. They needed to make business decisions. They were making more money, and it became their responsibility to control it and organize it.

Patty Sheehan

Born: October 27, 1956
Joined LPGA Tour: 1980
35 Victories
Vare Trophy Winner: 1984
Player of the Year: 1983
Major Championship History: U.S. Women's
Open (1992, 1994); LPGA Championship
(1983, 1984 and 1993); Nabisco Dinah
Shore (1996)
Inducted into Hall of Fame: 1993

Still relatively small, the Tour maintained an atmosphere of a community based on common goals. But, the players more and more were engaged in the larger community. It meant that they had to make judgments involving people outside the circle of "trusted" friends.

Rawls, Wright, Whitworth, Haynie, and Mann were a second generation. They were not pioneers, but the independent spirit they shared with the founding generation was their criteria in making the new types of decisions that were asked of them. They were confident and strong enough to give up some control in terms of the organization, but they were able to understand the importance of maintaining the independent character of each player.

In the 1980's and 1990's the Tour leaped into the modern world of sport. The LPGA was no longer small. It was the biggest women's professional sports organization in the world. Money became important. Tournaments were economic boons for the cities in which they were played. Players could become millionaires. Life on Tour was literally a world unto itself.

Carner, Lopez, Bradley, Sheehan, King, Daniel and Alcott are stars. Their stage is a traveling extravaganza moving from one city to another. The player's world centers around the course and the hotel. There is little time for anything else. It is an existence that is far removed from the real world. Every week the player rides in a new car – they are rented, not owned. Beds don't have to be made because "home" – the hotel – has maid service. Connections to others are fleeting. Friendships are week-long connections ending when the Tour moved to the next city. Tour life now demands more than just being independent. It requires the ability to be alone.

Within this "cocoon" which is the Tour, the concept of independence takes on another, new dimension. Carner, Lopez, Bradley, Sheehan, King, Daniel and Alcott are still independent contractors. But, they make decisions that will affect the lives of several "sub-contractors" – agents, caddies, the Tour itself. Like a corporate executive, the modern Tour player's independence is control and power oriented. It comes with an expensive personal price tag that demands sensitivity and restraint. It involves the power to control the lives of others.

Betty Jameson's spirit of independence allowed her to join this new organization – the Tour – which offered no guarantees, and whose chances of failure were much higher than those for success. Mickey Wright's independent character formed the base of her life-long quest for perfection. Nancy Lopez's independence served as the strength she

Pat Bradley

Born: March 24, 1951
Joined LPGA Tour: 1974
31 Victories
Vare Trophy Winner: 1986, 1991
Player of the Year: 1986, 1991
Major Championship History: U.S. Women's Open (1981); Peter Jackson Classic (1980); duMaurier Classic (1985, 1986); Nabisco Dinah Shore (1986); LPGA Championship (1986)
Inducted into Hall of Fame: 1991

Nancy Lopez

Born: January 6, 1957
Joined LPGA Tour: 1977
48 Victories
Vare Trophy Winner: 1978, 1979 and 1985
Player of the Year: 1978, 1979, 1985 and 1988
Major Championship History: LPGA Championship (1978, 1985 and 1989)
Inducted into Hall of Fame: 1987

needed to end one marriage that would not stand the pressure of her life choice, and yet remain open to another relationship and marriage that would.

Because each of these Hall of Famers had a strong sense of independence, they were able to transcend the concept of "woman" that each of the generations embraced and see themselves as "people." Except for an interest in and talent for golf, it is easy to see each one of these women succeeding in some other field. Suggs might easily have been an early woman graduate of Harvard Law School. It is not inconceivable to think of Rawls as an astronaut. Betsy King might have succeeded extremely well as a corporate raider.

Their spirit of independence gave them the strength to challenge the system, take risks, and acknowledge their vision. It just so happened their talent drew them to the golf course.

JoAnne Carner

Born: April 4, 1939
Joined LPGA Tour: 1970
42 Victories
Vare Trophy Winner: 1974, 1975, 1981, 1982 and 1983
Player of the Year: 1974, 1981 and 1982
Major Championship History: U.S. Women's Open (1971 and 1976)
Inducted into Hall of Fame: 1982

Competitive Excellence

Babe Zaharias won her first LPGA event on March 19, 1950. Her prize money was $700. Forty-five years later, on August 20, 1995, Beth Daniel won her most recent LPGA event. Her prize money was $67,500. Even factoring in inflation, the difference is almost unbelievable.

The difference between the generations of Hall of Famers is obvious – especially when you look at the money. But the key, and the tie between the players of each generation, is the fact that they all played for money. Because they played for money, all hold that common, hard-won title – "professional."

"Today I look at the money they play for with amazement, but not envy or bitterness," Betsy Rawls said. "In the beginning, we played for so little that money wasn't the motivating factor. But when I won, it seemed like it was a lot of money at the time. I enjoyed winning when I did."[2]

There is also the image and management of the Tour itself. The early Tour was a sideshow. Today's Tour is the main event. Today's players focus on playing golf – period. The original players ran the whole show – they did everything.

The player's attitude has changed over the fifty-year history of the LPGA. Zaharias was an expert at making herself appear to be whatever the public wanted. She worked hard at making an image that would conform. Daniel expects people to accept her "as is." She makes no excuses, and gives no explanations.

But, the importance of the Hall of Fame is not finding differences. The Hall's importance is in continuity – in finding commonality.

The strongest common thread in the personality characteristics in the LPGA Hall of Famers is their desire to compete. It is not the game of golf that ties each generation of Hall of Famers together, but the love of competition. Every player from Zaharias to Daniel needed to compete. Every player from Zaharias to Daniel had an unquenchable desire to win – to be the best. Every player from Zaharias to Daniel was interested only in the classical meaning of competition – testing one's self and striving for personal excellence. It is the essence of their "sameness."

LPGA Hall of Famers have dedicated themselves and their lives to the concept of competitive excellence. They have also given back to the game they play, and to the communities in which they live.

Sandra Haynie

Born: June 4, 1943
Joined LPGA Tour: 1961
42 Victories
Player of the Year: 1970
Major Championship History: U.S. Women's Open (1974); Peter Jackson Classic (1982); LPGA Championship (1965 and 1974)
Inducted into Hall of Fame: 1977

Carol Mann

Born: February 3, 1941
Joined LPGA Tour: 1961
38 Victories
Vare Trophy Winner: 1968
Major Championship History: U.S. Women's Open (1965); Western Open (1964)
Inducted into Hall of Fame: 1977
Retired from the LPGA Tour: 1981

PLAYING FROM THE ROUGH

Amy Alcott has created a $50,000 endowment for the UCLA Children's Hospital and its Neonatal Intensive Care Unit. She is a recipient of the LPGA Good Samaritan Award and the National Multiple Sclerosis Achievement Award. Alcott also serves as a playing editor for Golf Digest magazine.

Among the numerous awards received by Patty Berg are the prestigious annual hororee at the Jack Nicklaus Memorial Tournament, and the USGA's Bob Jones Award. The University of Minnesota has established the Patty Berg Development Fund, and the Southwest Florida Regional Medical Center dedicated the Patty Berg Cancer Center in 1993. In 1978, the LPGA established the Patty Berg Award to be granted to a person for outstanding contributions to women's golf.

Pat Bradley is an Honorary Director of the Thyroid Foundation of America at Massachusetts General Hospital in Boston. She is the recipient of the National Golf Foundation's Jack Nicklaus Family of the Year Award.

JoAnne Carner is a *Golf Digest* playing editor. She has been awarded the USGA's Bob Jones Award, and supports several charities in her local area in South Florida including Martin County Special Olympics.

Sandra Haynie annually heads the celebrity pro-am "Swing against Arthritis" which benefits the N-E-C Texas Chapter of the National Arthritis Foundation.

Beth Daniel is an advocate, working for equality for all, especially women.

Betty Jameson, in 1952, founded and donated the LPGA's Vare Trophy that recognizes the player with the lowest scoring average each year.

Betsy King organized Habitat for Humanity house building projects in Phoenix, Arizona, and has traveled to Romania to work with an orphan relief organization. She is a recipient of the LPGA's Good Samaritan Award.

Kathy Whitworth

Born: September 27, 1939
Joined LPGA Tour: 1958
88 Victories
Vare Trophy Winner: 1965, 1966, 1967, 1969, 1970, 1971, 1972
Player of the Year: 1966, 1967, 1968, 1969, 1971, 1972, 1973
Major Championship History: Western Open (1967); Titleholders Championship (1965, 1966); LPGA Championship (1967, 1971, 1975)
Inducted into Hall of Fame: 1975
Retired from the LPGA Tour: 1991

Nancy Lopez has received the USGA's Bob Jones Award and the Women's Sports Foundation's Flo Hyman Award. She is a playing editor for *Golf Digest*. Her hometown, Roswell, New Mexico has honored her with the Nancy Lopez Elementary School.

Carol Mann is the author of *The 19th Hole: Favorite Golf Stories*, and is a professional advisor for *Senior Golfer Magazine*. She is a member of the Board of Stewards for the Women's Sports Foundation, and has received a presidential appointment to The White House Conference for a drug free America.

Betsy Rawls has been awarded the USGA's Bob Jones Award and the Sprint Lifetime Achievement Award.

Patty Sheehan has received the LPGA's Good Samaritan Award and the Women's Sports Foundation's Flo Hyman Award. She is a playing editor for *Golf For Women Magazine*.

Louise Suggs was the first woman ever elected to the Georgia Athletic Hall of Fame. In 1995, the McDonald's LPGA Championship was dedicated to her.

Kathy Whitworth has received the William Richardson Award from the Golf Writers Association of America for consistent outstanding contributions to golf. She writes for and represents *Golf for Women Magazine*.

Mickey Wright was named "Golfer of the Decade" by *Golf Magazine* for the years 1958-67.

Babe Didrikson Zaharias received the USGA's Bob Jones Award in 1957. A Babe Zaharias Foundation exists to raise funds

Mickey Wright

Born February 14, 1935
Joined LPGA Tour: 1955
82 Victories
Vare Trophy Winner: 1960, 1961, 1962, 1963 and 1964
Major Championship History: U.S. Women's Open (1958, 1959, 1961, 1964); Western Open (1962, 1963); Titleholders Championship (1961, 1962); LPGA Championship (1958, 1960, 1961, 1963)
Inducted into Hall of Fame: 1964
Retired from the LPGA Tour: 1969

Betsy Rawls

Born: May 4, 1928
Joined LPGA Tour: 1951
55 Victories
Vare Trophy Winner: 1959
Major Championship History: U.S. Women's Open (1951, 1953, 1957, 1960); Western Open (1952, 1959); LPGA Championship (1959, 1960)
Inducted into Hall of Fame: 1960
Retired from the LPGA Tour: 1975

253

for cancer research, and she is the focus of the Babe Didrikson Zaharias Memorial Center, a museum in Beaumont, Texas, Zaharias' hometown.

Patty Berg

Born: February 13, 1918
LPGA Founder
57 Victories
Vare Trophy Winner:1953, 1955, 1956
Major Championship History: U.S. Women's Open (1946); Western Open (1941, 1943, 1948, 1951, 1955, 1957, 1958); Titleholders (1948, 1953, 1955, 1957) Those won as an amateur: 1937, 1938 and 1939 Titleholders
Inducted into Hall of Fame: 1951
Retired from the LPGA Tour: 1969

Courage

Anyone who breaks new ground personifies courage. These women are no different. They all demonstrated courage in their dedication to their skill. It is hard to remain focused on one goal – to put in the time and effort that achieving that goal demands. It is hard and it takes courage.

Each, at some point, found the courage to override the desire to quit. Every player at some point in their career thought about quitting. Some had to deal with problems connected with their game. Carol Mann and Beth Daniel had to reconstruct their golf swing and their game in mid-career. Some had to deal with health or physical problems. Pat Bradley and Sandra Haynie fought back from illnesses. Some expressed emotional difficulties that seemed to make the quest meaningless for a period of time.. Nancy Lopez and Amy Alcott both lost their mother – the most significant person in each of their lives – at key points in their career.

None quit. All had the courage to continue.

The Tour and the Hall

In 1950, the LPGA Tour had a handful of players, a handful of tournaments and prize money that was meager at best. Today's tour boosts over 400 players who compete in over 40 events for over $36 million in prize money. The growth of the Tour has attracted players from around the world. Along with players who list their hometowns as Greenville, South Carolina and Hamilton, Montana, the LPGA Tour Media guide includes players who hail from Cheshire, England; Daejeon, Korea; Queensland, Australia; Ciboure, France; and Lima, Peru. Certainly, the not too distant future will find another "first" for the Tour and the Hall of Fame – the first foreign-born inductee.

The international characteristic of today's Tour gives it an aspect of the Tour's diversity. That diversity does not, at the present time, include Afro-Americans or other ethnic minorities. Two Afro-American women – Althea Gibson and Renee Powell – played on the Tour during the 1960's. An "integrated" Tour caused the loss of several tournaments. The Tour's organizational director at that time, Lennie Wirtz, was not intimidated and held firm. When two sponsors made their events "invitationals" as opposed to "opens" in an effort to keep Gibson and Powell from the field, Wirtz responded by saying, "We all play, or we all stay away."[3]

The LPGA continues to take a leadership role in bringing diverse populations to golf and eventually to the Tour. The LPGA Urban Youth Golf Program is a year-long community-based risk prevention program geared specifically to boys and girls ages 7-17 who reside in urban communities and who may not otherwise be exposed to golf. In addition, the LPGA has joined other golf organizations as part of another junior golf

Louise Suggs

Born: September 7, 1923
LPGA Founder
50 Victories
Vare Trophy Winner: 1957
Major Championship History: U.S. Women's Open (1949); Western Open (1949, 1953); Titleholders (1954, 1956, 1959); Those won as an amateur: 1946 Titleholders; 1946 and 1947 Western Open
Inducted into Hall of Fame: 1951
Retired from the LPGA Tour: 1965

Betty Jameson

Born: May 19, 1919
LPGA Founder
10 Victories
Conceived the idea for and donated the Vare Trophy honoring the player with the best scoring average each year.
Major Championship History: U.S. Women's Open (1947); Western Open (1954)
Inducted into Hall of Fame: 1951
Retired from the LPGA Tour: 1956

initiative – The First Tee Program. Its purpose is to create facilities and programs that make golf more affordable and accessible, with a strong emphasis on introducing children of all races and economic backgrounds to golf.

The LPGA fought another battle for diversity in 1995 when golf commentator Ben Wright chose to make uncomplimentary remarks about lesbians in golf, in general, and on the LPGA Tour specifically. The official LPGA response to the situation was to express disappointment that the affair took attention away from the major concern of the Tour and its players – golf. Through a press release, the LPGA stated that a player's sexuality should be neither the concern of the LPGA nor the press.

> ## Babe Didrikson Zaharias
>
> Born: June 26, 1914
> LPGA Founder
> 31 Victories
> Vare Trophy Winner: 1954
> Major Championship History: U.S. Women's Open (1948, 1950, 1954); Titleholders (1950 and 1952); Western Open (1950)
> Inducted into Hall of Fame: 1951
> Died: September 27, 1956 (Age 45)

The LPGA Hall of Fame is a unique sports institution. Members are not voted in or selected. They must meet a performance criterion. By establishing a performance criterion, the LPGA Hall of Fame is something that no other sports Hall of Fame is. Membership in the Hall of Fame is not an "award" or an "honor." It is a "reward." It reflects an understanding of "fame" that is more classical than modern. It sees "fame" as a reward for deeds, not being well-known or gaining celebrity.

Even the one honorary member of the Hall of Fame, Dinah Shore, was inducted for her "deeds" and not her "fame." In 1972, Shore was instrumental in bringing visibility to women's golf through the Colgate-Dinah Shore Invitational – now the Nabisco Dinah Shore, one of the LPGA's four "major" tournaments. Shore, a singer and actress, agreed to host and lend her name to the event Colgate-Palmolive planned to sponsor. An avid golfer, Shore committed herself to increasing the prize money at the event each year until it became the richest tournament on the Tour. Because of the prize money and Shore's celebrity, the Dinah Shore brought recognition to women's golf that it had not enjoyed in the past. The event, thanks to

Shore's commitment to it and the players, changed the entire image of the LPGA – from a small band of talented golfers to whom no one paid much attention, to a professional women's sports organization with a marketable product that could attract top level sponsors.

Shore's dedication to "growing" women's golf represents the same independence of spirit, competitive excellence and courage that personifies all the Hall of Famers. Her inclusion in the Hall of Fame is a reward for belief in, and unwavering support of, the LPGA and the players who were part of it.

For the players of the LPGA Tour, the Hall of Fame is almost like striving for a grade at the conclusion of an academic course. On the first day of class they tell you what the rules are for getting an "A." Then they tell you, "Oh, by the way, it's independent study. You're on your own. Go to it." In the end it does not matter if the other students liked you, or if the teachers thought you were bright. All that counts is that you organized yourself, did what you had to do, and either made the "A" or fell short.

The LPGA Hall of Fame is an interesting, and perhaps refreshing, concept in today's world of "celebrity sports." It reflects exactly what sport is about. Sport is a test – a test of what a person can do by competing against others who are equal in talent and skill.

Society may still see "woman" and "athlete" as a contradiction, but for the women who now make up the LPGA Hall of Fame, and for those women who will be inducted in the future, the distinction is lost. They are all "people" who challenged perception and changed points of view. They are heroes.

Epilogue

The criteria change for the Hall of Fame that was made in 1999 created a situation in which several players found themselves within striking distance of qualifying for the Hall.

Juli Inkster is closest to qualifying with twenty-six points. Inkster's story is interesting because at the beginning of the 1999 season, even as the new criteria was being debated and voted on,

Inkster believed she would not have a chance for the Hall. In January 1999, Inkster was seven points from qualifying with only twenty points.

"To be so close to the Hall of Fame is pretty hard to comprehend," Inkster said. "When they said they were going to change the criteria, I was slowly adding up my points, and I thought, God, I'm still seven away. I don't know if I can do that. Now six months later, I'm only a point away. It's unbelievable." [4]

What happened in that six months to the 39-year-old Inkster is unbelievable. It began in March when she won the Welch's/Circle K Championship – Hall point 21. Then, less than a month later, Inkster captured the Longs Drug Challenge title – Hall point 22.

On June 3, Inkster stood on the first tee at Old Waverly Country Club in West Point, Mississippi waiting to tee off in the 54th U.S. Women's Open. As an amateur, Inkster won three consecutive U.S. Women's Amateur titles (1980-82). She was the first person, male or female to accomplish that feat, but in her 16 years on Tour, the U.S. Women's Open was an event she had never won. Four days later, Inkster walked off the 18th green at Old Waverly holding, for the first time, the Open trophy. Since major victories are worth two points under the new Hall criteria, Inkster not only had her first Open victory, but twenty-four Hall of Fame points – just three short of qualifying.

Twenty-one days later, Inkster won again. This time it was the McDonald's LPGA Championship. The win, in conjunction with her U.S. Open victory gave Inkster the distinction of being only the second player (the first was Pat Bradley) to win all four of the modern majors. She won the Nabisco Dinah Shore and the duMaurier in 1984, her first full year on tour. The victory in the 1999 McDonaldís LPGA Championship also gave Inkster two more Hall of Fame points. Total Hall of Fame points for Inkster in the six months from January through July – an unbelievable six, leaving just one for qualification.

"It's do-able," Inkster said after her McDonald's LPGA Championship win. [5]

Juli Inkster, rookie year 1983-84, is not the only player for which the Hall of Fame is "do-able." The following chart consists of an overview of selected players who may make a run at the Hall in the next few years.

Players Close to Making the LPGA Hall of Fame

PLAYER	YEAR JOINED LPGA	WINS & AWARDS	HALL OF FAME POINTS
Annika Sorenstam	1993	16 wins (two majors) 3 Player of the Year Awards 3 Vare Trophy's	24
Hollis Stacy	1974	18 wins (four majors)	22
Laura Davies	1987	17 wins (four majors) 1 Player of the Year Awards	22
Jan Stephenson	1974	16 wins (three majors)	19
Sally Little	1971	15 wins (two majors)	17
Dottie Pepper	1987	14 wins (one major) 1 Player of the Year 1 Vare Trophy	17
Jane Geddes	1983	11 wins (two majors)	13
Liselotte Neumann	1988	12 wins (one major)	13
Meg Mallon	1987	10 wins (two majors)	12
Karrie Webb	1996	11 wins 1 Vare Trophy	12

Possible Selection to Hall of Fame by Veteran Committee

PLAYER	YEAR JOINED LPGA	WINS & AWARDS
Marilyn Smith	1950-77	21 wins (two majors)
Judy Rankin	1962-83	26 wins 2 Player of the Year Awards 3 Vare Trophies
Sandra Palmer	1964-96	19 wins (two majors) 1 Player of the Year Award
Donna Caponi	1965-88	24 wins (four majors)
Jane Blalock	1969-86	27 wins
Ayako Okamoto	1981-93	17 wins 1 Player of the Year Award

* Induction criteria for players considered under veteran category is not based on twenty-seven points, but rather on the impact the player has had on the LPGA Tour. Players nominated by the Veterans committee must be an inactive Tour member for at least five years.

At the 1995 Sprint Senior Challenge, Mickey Wright graciously agreed to this photograph when these three LPGA Tour hopefuls who had followed Wright for 18 holes that day, asked if she would pose with them.

Kathy Whitworth, at the 1996 US Women's Open, with a group of junior golfers from the Atlanta area.

Old friends – Kathy Whitworth, Patty Berg and Peggy Kirk Bell – meet at the 1996 Women's Open at Pine Needles Resort in Southern Pines, North Carolina. Berg (center) was one of the LPGA Founders, Bell (right) was one of the first women to join the tour after it was founded in 1950, and Whitworth (left), with eighty eight wins, holds the record for most wins for both the men's and women's tour.

Patty Sheehan (left) and Pat Bradley (below) sign autographs after a round. Each LPGA Tour player understands the importance of "fans". The LPGA Tour is characterized by the player's friendliness, and their willingness to relate to those "outside the ropes."

The 1995 Sprint Senior Challenge field.
Standing left to right: Donna Caponi, Sandra Haynie, Betsy Rawls, Marilyn Smith,
Kathy Whitworth, Mickey Wright, Judy Rankin, Louise Suggs
Kneeling left to right: Sandra Palmer, Jane Blalock, Marlene Hagge, Carol Mann

Kathy Whitworth

Betsy King

Patty Sheehan

At the dedication of the World Golf Hall of Fame in May 1998, there was a "competition across generations."

Louise Suggs (right) sunk a 30-foot putt to defeat Nancy Lopez (left).

Generations of LPGA Hall of Famers celebrate Pat Bradley's acheivements:
(Standing, left to right) Betsy Rawls, Pat Bradley, Nancy Lopez, Carol Mann
(Seated, left to right) Louise Suggs, Patty Berg, Betty Jameson

Notes

Chapter 1
Babe Didrikson Zaharias

1. David Roberts, "The Babe is here," Women's *Sports and Fitness* Nov-Dec 1990: 42.
2. Pete Martin, "Babe Didrikson Takes Off Her Mask," *Saturday Evening Post* 20 September 1947: 26.
3. Roberts 26
4. Susan E. Cayleff, *Babe: The Life and Legend of Babe* Didrikson Zaharias (Chicago: University of Illinois Press, 1996) 39.
5. Cayleff 39.
6. Cayleff 30.
7. Cayleff 30.
8. Babe Didrikson Zaharias, *This Life I've Led* (New York: Dell Publishing Co., 1975) 40-41.
9. Zaharias 41-42.
10. Cayleff 51.
11. Zaharias 39-40.
12. William Oscar Johnson and Nancy Williamson, "Babe," part 1, *Sports Illustrated* 6 Oct. 1975.
13. Cayleff 65.
14. Cayleff 67.
15. Cayleff 66.
16. Zaharias 72-73.
17. Zaharias 75-76.
18. Cayleff 99.
19. Zaharias 76.
20. Cayleff 100.
21. Cayleff 100.
22. Cayleff 100.
23. Cayleff 101.
24. Zaharias 77.
25. Zaharias 77.
26. Zaharias 79.
27. Zaharias 84.
28. Zaharias 84.
29. Zaharias 85.
30. Zaharias 90.
31. Zaharias 91.
32. Zaharias 92.
33. Cayleff 124.
34. Cayleff 124.
35. Zaharias 100.
36. Zaharias 101.
37. Zaharias 107.
38. Zaharias 108.
39. Zaharias 113.
40. Cayleff 137.
41. Cayleff 138.
42. Zaharias 115.
43. Johnson and Williamson.
44. Zaharias 120.
45. Zaharias 131.
46. Zaharias 137.
47. Zaharias 138.
48. Betty Hicks, *Travels with a Golf Tour Gourmet*, (Palo Alto, Ca.: Group Four, 1986) 117.
49. Zaharias 172-173.
50. Zaharias 173.
51. Zaharias 174.
52. Zaharias 174-175.
53. Zaharias 176-177.
54. Zaharias 178.
55. Hicks 61.
56. Cayleff 189.
57. Cayleff 190.
58. Cayleff.
59. Cayleff.
60. Cayleff 194.
61. Cayleff.
62. Cayleff 192.
63. Cayleff 190.
64. Cayleff 198.
65. Cayleff.
66. Cayleff 201.
67. Cayleff 203.
68. Cayleff.
69. Cayleff 208.
70. Cayleff 201.
71. Cayleff 234.

Chapter 2
Betty Jameson

1. Betty Jameson, personal interview, May 1998.
2. Jameson.
3. Jameson.
4. Jameson.
5. Liz Kahn, *The LPGA: The Unauthorized Version* (Menlo Park, CA.: Group Fore Productions, 1996) 31-33.
6. Kahn, 32.
7. Kahn, 32.
8. Jameson.
9. "Golf Talk Live," The Golf Channel, June 1998.
10. "Golf Talk Live."

Chapter 3
Patty Berg

1. Author's personal experience, 1983.
2. Rhonda Glenn, *The Illustrated History of Women's Golf* (Dallas, Texas: Taylor Publishing Company, 1991) 125.
3. Glenn, History 125.
4. Rhonda Glenn, "Interview: Patty Berg," *Golf Magazine* (Fairway, Special Advertising Section), Feb. 1989: 129.
5. Glenn, Interview, 131
6. Carol Mann, *The 19th Hole: Favorite Golf Stories* (Stanford, Conn.: Longmeadow Press, 1992) 11-16.
7. Mann 16.
8. Glenn, History 123.
9. Glenn, History 124.
10. Glenn, History 130.
11. Glenn, History 127.
12. Glenn, History 127.
13. Glenn, History 157.
14. Glenn, History 158.
15. Glenn, History 159.
16. Glenn.
17. Glenn, History 160.

Chapter 4
Louise Suggs

1. Rhonda Glen, *The Illustrated History of Women's Golf* (Dallas, Texas: Taylor Publishing Company, 1991)163.
2. Liz Kahn, *The LPGA: The Unauthorized Version* (Menlo Park, Ca.: Group Fore Productions, 1996) 89.
3. Glenn 172.
4. Kahn 86.
5. Louise Suggs, *Golf For Women* (New York: Doubleday & Co., 1960) 10.
6. "Johnny Suggs' Daughter," *Time* 6 Oct. 1947: 56.
7. Susan E. Cayleff, *Babe: The Life and Legend of Babe Didrikson Zaharias* (Chicago: University of Illinois Press, 1996) 195.
8. Kahn 89.
9. Glenn 172.
10. Kahn 89.
11. Suggs 9.
12. Suggs 10.
13. Author's personal experience, May 1998.

Chapter 5
Betsy Rawls

1. Joe Juliano, "Rawls to be honored with Jones Award for sportsmanship," Knight-Ridder/Tribune News Service (1996)118 (Infotrac SearchBank A17799967).
2. Liz Kahn, *The LPGA: The Unauthorized Version* (Menlo Park, Ca.: Group Fore Productions, 1996) 77
3. Kahn.
4. Kahn.
5. Kahn.
6. Kahn 78.
7. Kahn.
8. Rhonda Glenn, *The Illustrated History of Women's Golf* (Dallas, Texas: Taylor Publishing Company, 1991) 174.
9. Kahn 80.
10. Kahn.
11. Kahn 79.

12. Mickey Wright, personal interview, July 1995.
13. Betty Hicks, *Travels with a Golf Tour Gourmet* (Palo Alto, Ca.: Group Fore, 1986) 117.
14. Kahn 80.
15. Kahn.
16. Kahn 78.
17. Juliano 118.
18. Kahn 80.
19. Glenn 168.

Chapter 6
Mickey Wright

1. Mickey Wright, personal interview, 1994.
2. Mickey Wright, *Play Golf the Wright Way* (Dallas, Texas: Taylor Publishing Company, 1962) 19.
3. Wright 1994.
4. Mickey Wright, personal interview, 1997.
5. Wright 1997.
6. Wright 1997.
7. Wright 1997.
8. Wright 1997.
9. Wright 1994.
10. Wright 1994.
11. Wright 1994.
12. Wright 1994.
13. Author's personal experience, 1979.
14. Wright 1994.
15. Wright 1997.
16. Wright 1997.
17. Wright 1997.
18. Rhonda Glenn,
19. Glenn.
20. Wright, 1994.
21. Wright, 1994.

Chapter 7
Kathy Whitworth

1. Kathy Whitworth, *Golf for Women* (New York: St. Martin's Press, 1990) 143.
2. Whitworth.
3. Whitworth.
4. Barry McDermott, "Wrong image but right touch," *Sports Illustrated* 25 July 1983 (Infotrac SearchBank A2853878) : 38
5. Rhonda Glenn, *The Illustrated History of Women's Golf* (Dallas, Texas: Taylor Publishing Company, 1991) 255.
6. Whitworth 140.
7. Whitworth.
8. Whitworth.
9. Whitworth 138.
10. Whitworth.
11. Whitworth 142.
12. Whitworth 146-147.
13. Whitworth 149.
14. McDermott 38.
15. Glenn 259.
16. Rhonda Glenn, "It's a long way back," *Golf Magazine* Sept. 1983:56
17. Glenn History 261.
18. Glenn History 262.
19. "Golf Talk Live" The Golf Channel May, 1998.
20. Glenn Back 98.
21. Glenn Back 98.
22. Whitworth 137.
23. Whitworth 143.
24. Whitworth 144.
25. Liz Kahn, *The LPGA: The Unauthorized Version* (Menlo Park, Ca.: Group Fore Productions, 1996) 93.
26. Kahn.
27. Whitworth 158.
28. "Golf Talk Live," The Golf Channel, May 1998.

Chapter 8
Sandra Haynie

1. Liz Kahn, *The LPGA: The Unauthorized Version* (Menlo Park, Ca.: Group Fore Productions, 1991) 130.
2. Kahn 129.
3. Kahn 130.
4. Kahn.
5. Kahn.
6. Kahn.
7. Barry McDermott, "And then thing were putt in order," *Sports Illustrated* 29 July 1974: 18.
8. McDermott.
9. McDermott.
10. McDermott.
11. Kahn 131.
12. Kahn 130.
13. Martina Navratilova, Martina (New York: Alford A. Knopf, 1985) 140-158.
14. Navratilova 158.
15. Kahn 131.
16. Kahn.
17. Kahn 132.
18. Navratilova 158-159.
19. Kahn 132.
20. Navratilova 165.
21. Kahn 132.
22. Kahn 133.
23. Kahn.
24. Kahn 130.

Chapter 9
Carol Mann

1. Sarah Ballard, "History of the LPGA Tour," *Golf Magazine* Feb. 1986: 99.
2. Rhonda Glenn, *The Illustrated History of Women's Golf* (Dallas, Texas: Taylor Publishing Company, 1991) 280.
3. Sally Raque, "You've come a long way, ladies," *Women's Sport and Fitness* May-June 1990: 61
4. Raque.
5. Liz Kahn, *The LPGA: The Unauthorized Version* (Menlo Park, Ca.: Group Fore Productions, 1996) 140.
6. Kahn.
7. Kahn.
8. Carol Mann, *The 19th Hole: Favorite Golf Stories* (Stanford, Conn.: Longmeadow Press, 1992) x.
9. Mann xi.
10. Mann.
11. Mann.
12. Mann xii.
13. Mann.
14. Kahn 141.
15. Kahn.
16. Kahn.
17. Kahn.
18. Carol Mann, "The girl next door grows up," *Women's Sports* July 1981: 6
19. Kahn 141.
20. Kahn 142.
21. Jim Burnett, *Tee Times* (New York: Scribner, 1997) 117.
22. Kahn 142.
23. Kahn.
24. Mann "Grows up" 6.
25. Gwilym S. Brown, "Carol is the Ladies Mann," *Sports Illustrated* 12 July 1965: 24.
26. Kahn 143.
27. Kahn.
28. Kahn 145.
29. Ballard 99.
30. Ballard.
31. Ballard.
32. Kahn 143.
33. Kahn 144.
34. Kahn.
35. Kahn 145.
36. Kahn.
37. Kahn.
38. Mann "Grows Up" 6.
39. Mann "Grows Up" 6.
40. Kahn 146.
41. Kahn 145.

42. Tom Callahan, "Golf's Country-Club Dilemma," *U.S. News & World Report* 20 Aug. 1990: 60
43. Callahan.
44. "Happy Birthday Carol Mann," World Golf Village Website, http://www.wgv.com/library.nfs/news 3 Feb. 1999.

Chapter 10
JoAnne Carner

1. Author's personal experience, summer, 1979.
2. Barry McDermott, "No fish story: golf's top lady," *Sports Illustrated* 5 July 1982: 32.
3. Liz Kahn, *The LPGA: The Unauthorized Version* (Menlo Park, Ca.: Group Fore Productions, 1996) 199.
4. Kahn.
5. Kahn.
6. Kahn.
7. Rhonda Glenn, *The Illustrated History of Women's Golf* (Dallas, Texas: Taylor Publishing Company, 1991) 245-246.
8. Mike Bryan, "A conversation with JoAnne Carner," *Golf Magazine* Jan. 1989: 22.
9. Bryan.
10. Kahn 202.
11. Bryan 24.
12. Bryan.
13. McDermott 32.
14. James Dodson, "Slow walk to immortality," *Golf Magazine* Nov. 1994: 12
15. Kahn 202.
16. Kahn.
17. Kahn 198.
18. Author's personal experience, Jan. 1995.
19. Bryan 34.
20. Kahn 200.
21. Kahn 200 and Bryan 22.
22. Bryan 22.

23. Bryan 23.
24. Kahn 201.
25. Bryan 23.
26. Dodson 13.
27. Bryan 34.
28. McDermott 33.
29. Author's personal experience, summer, 1979.
30. Dodson 14.
31. Kahn 203.

Chapter 11
Nancy Lopez

1. Nancy Lopez, *Education of a Woman Golfer* (New York: Cornerstone Library, 1979) 17.
2. Lopez 9.
3. Lopez.
4. Lopez 10-11.
5. Lopez 45 and Sally Jenkins, "Dialogue on Golf: Nancy Lopez" http://golf.com/golfdigest/profiles/lopez08 97.htm.
6. Lopez 22-23.
7. Jenkins 2.
8. Lopez 22-23.
9. Lopez 16-17
10. Lopez 11.
11. Lopez 154.
12. Lopez 23-26 and Jenkins 6.
13. Lopez 23-24.
14. Lopez 24.
15. Lopez 26.
16. Jenkins 6.
17. Jenkins 5.
18. Lopez 18-19.
19. Lopez 19.
20. Lopez 152.
21. Lopez 141.
22. Jenkins 5.
23. Lopez 74.
24. Mike Purkey, "Nancy Lopez," *Golf Magazine* May 1990: 86.
25. Jenkins 8.
26. Jenkins.
27. Bruce Newman, "The very model of a

modern marriage," *Sports Illustrated* 4 Aug. 1986: 34.
28. Newman 35.
29. Newman 36.
30. Newman.
31. Richard Lemon, "On the Beach no more," *People Weekly* 25 April 1983 (Infotrac SearchBank A2730470) 85.
32. Jenkins 7.
33. Jenkins 6.

Chapter 12
Pat Bradley

1. David Barrett, "A major claim to fame," *Golf Magazine* Sept. 1986: 64.
2. Liz Kahn, *The LPGA: The Unauthorized Version* (Menlo Park, Ca.: Group Fore Productions, 1996) 194.
3. Kahn.
4. Kahn.
5. Barrett 72 and Kahn 194.
6. John Garrity, "Hitting the Hall," *Sports Illustrated* 3 Feb. 1992: 42.
7. Kahn 196.
8. Garrity 42.
9. Sandy Keenan, "Not yet at her peak," *Sports Illustrated* 25 Feb 1985: 42
10. Keenan.
11. Kahn 194.
12. Rhonda Glenn, *The Illustrated History of Women's Golf* (Dallas, Texas: Taylor Publishing Company, 1991) 295.
13. Kahn 194.
14. Keenan 42.
15. Barrett 72.
16. Garrity 42.
17. Keenan 42.
18. Keenan.
19. Barrett 64.
20. Kahn 194.
21. Barry McDermott, "Now they call her payday Pat," *Sports Illustrated* 29 Sept. 1986: 82

22. Barrett 64.
23. Barbara Matson, "The rise and fall of Pat Bradley," *Golf Magazine* Jan. 1989: 32.
24. Matson 33.
25. Andrew Abrahams, "Finished with life as an also-ran," *People Weekly* 25 May 1987: 80.
26. Abrahams 80.
27. Matson 34.
28. Matson 35.
29. Matson 34.
30. Abrahams 80.
31. Abrahams.
32. Abrahams.
33. Abrahams.
34. Garrity 42.
35. Kahn 195.
36. Kahn 196.

Chapter 13
Patty Sheehan

1. Patty Sheehan and Betty Hicks, *Patty Sheehan on Golf* (Dallas, Texas: Taylor Publishing Company, 1996) note: All quotations in this chapter are taken from *Patty Sheehan on Golf* unless otherwise noted.
2. Liz Kahn, *The LPGA: The Unauthorized Version* (Menlo Park, Ca.: Group Fore Productions, 1991) 268
3. Patty Sheehan, "Bringing Up Bryce," *Golf World* March 1998: 64.

Chapter 14
Betsy King

1. James Dodson, "The King nobody knows," *Golf Magazine* July 1991: 56.
2. Author's personal experience, fall, 1984.
3. Liz Kahn, *The LPGA: The Unauthorized Version* (Menlo Park, Ca.: Group Fore Productions, 1996) 228.
4. Kahn 230.

5. Kahn.
6. Kahn 228.
7. Dodson 57.
8. Kahn 228.
9. John Garrity, "In a world of her own," *Sports Illustrated* 12 Feb. 1990: 184.
10. Garrity.
11. Dodson 57.
12. Garrity 184.
13. Dodson 57.
14. Kahn 230.
15. Garrity 184.
16. Garrity.
17. Garrity.
18. Shelley Smith, "Betsy King," *Sports Illustrated* 27 Dec. 1993: 81.
19. Dodson 56.
20. Dodson 56-57.
21. Kahn 230.
22. Stoda, Greg, "King, the '89 U.S. Open champ," Knight-Ridder/Tribune News Service 20 July 1994 (Infotrac SearchBank A15602490) 1.
23. Kahn 231.
24. Joe Juliano, "Victory for King would put her into Hall of Fame," Knight-Ridder/Tribune News Service 23 June 1994 (Infotrac SearchBank A15503338) 1.
25. Dodson 58.
26. Kahn 229.

Chapter 15
Amy Alcott

1. Molly Tyson, "Going for the Green," *Women's Sports* May 1981: 26.
2. Frank Chinnock, "Superstar in a Dodgers Cap," *Golf Magazine* Oct. 1980: 63.
3. Chinnock.
4. Liz Kahn, *The LPGA: The Unauthorized Version* (Menlo Park, Ca.: Group Fore Productions, 1996) 181.
5. Tyson 27.
6. Tyson.

7. Chinnock 63.
8. Kahn 181 and Chinnock 64.
9. Kahn 181.
10. Pamela Wallace, "Keep your eye on Amy," *The Saturday Evening Post*, Nov. 1975: 27.
11. Chinnock 64 and Frederick C. Klein, "On Sports: Knocking on the Hall Door," *The Wall Street Journal*, 15 May 1992: A11.
12. Kahn 180.
13. Wallace 26-27.
14. Mark Donovan, "They knew I was a contender," *Sports Illustrated*, 7 July 1975: 22.
15. Jamie Diaz, "Confronting Two Big Tasks in One," *The New York Times* 7 July 1991: S9.
16. Tyson 29.
17. Tyson 28.
18. Kahn 183.
19. Diaz S9.
20. Wallace 27.
21. Barry McDermott, "Winning was her just dessert," *Sports Illustrated* 11 Apr. 1983: 52.
22. Kahn 184.
23. Chinnock 104.
24. Jamie Diaz, "Alcott, Shore enough," *Sports Illustrated* 11 Apr. 1988: 72.
25. Diaz "Alcott" 73.
26. Diaz "Alcott" 72.
27. Wallace 27.
28. Diaz "Confronting" S9.
29. Kahn 180.
30. Diaz "Confronting" S9.
31. Sonja Steptoe, "A sure thing at the Shore," *Sports Illustrated* 8 Apr. 1991: 30.
32. Diaz S9.
33. Diaz.
34. John Strege, "Alcott still shooting for LPGA Hall of Fame," Knight-Kidder/Tribune News Service Mar. 29 1996 (Infotrac SearchBank A18140113) 1.
35. Amy Alcott, "Shame on the Hall," *Sports Illustrated* Dec. 7, 1998: G20.

36. "Fresh Start," *Sports Illustrated* 25 Jan. 1999: G8.
37. "Fresh Start."
38. "Fresh Start."
39. Kahn 183.

Chapter 16
Beth Daniel

1. Sue Hoover, "One Shot at a Time," *Women's Sports* July 1980: 43.
2. Barry McDermott, "The game is her one and only love," *Sports Illustrated* 2 Feb. 1981: 39.
3. Ron Green, "Good, Better, Beth," *Golf Magazine* Apr. 1991: 66.
4. Green.
5. McDermott, 39.
6. Rhonda Glenn, "In the eye of the storm," *Golf Magazine* Sept. 1983 (Infotrac SearchBank A2898949): 1.
7. Glenn 2 and Green 67.
8. McDermott 37.
9. McDermott 36.
10. Sarah Wilcox, "Will Beth catch Nancy?" *Golf Magazine* Apr. 1980: 100.
11. Hoover 40.
12. Hoover.
13. Liz Kahn, *The LPGA: The Unauthorized Version* (Menlo Park, Ca.: Group Fore Productions, 1996) 206 and McDermott 34.
14. Hoover 43.
15. Kahn 204.
16. Glenn 1.
17. Hoover 41.
18. Hoover.
19. Hoover 42.
20. McDermott 39.
21. McDermott.
22. Sonja Steptoe, "Thirty-something and happy at last," *Sports Illustrated* 15 Oct. 1990 (infotrac SearchBank A8947214) 2.
23. Steptoe.
24. Green 67.

25. Jamie Diaz, "Daniel Fulfills Expectations," *The New York Times* 12 Nov. 1990: B10.
26. Glenn 2.
27. Glenn.
28. Diaz B10.
29. Kahn 206.
30. Diaz B10.
31. Kahn 207.
32. Steptoe 2.
33. Kahn 207.
34. Kahn 208.
35. "LPGA players approve revised Hall of Fame criteria," http://www.golfonline.com/news/1999/lpgahalloffame0209.html.
36. "Beth Daniel third-round interview," http://sports.excite.com/lpga/news/990522/sl-sports-lpga-1053112
37. "Beth Daniel third-round interview."
38. Kahn 208.

PART IV
Perspectives

1. Mary Beth Rogers, *Barbara Jordan: American Hero* (New York: Bantam Books, 1998) xi
2. Joe Juliano, "Rawls to be honored with Jones Award," Knight-Ridder News Service 18 Jan. 1996: 118.
3. Rhonda Glenn, *The Illustrated History of Women's Golf*, (Dallas, Texas: Taylor Publishing Company, 1991) 188.
4. Alan Shipmuck, "A Slam-Bam Finish," *Sports Illustrated*, 5 July 1999: C5
5. Ron Sirak, "Victory Completes Grand Slam," *The New York Times*, 28 June 1999: D2

Bibliography

Abrahams, Andrew. "Finished with life as an also-ran, go-got-it golfer Pat Bradley climbs the Stare way to victory." *People Weekly* 25 May 1987

Abrahams, Andrew. "After beating what seemed bad odds, a top pro is back up to par." *People Weekly* 18 Sept. 1989: 80

Axthelm, Pete. " The Million-Dollar Lady." *Newsweek* 10 Aug. 1981: 62

Axthelm, Pete. " The Priorities of Patty Sheehan." *Newsweek* 18 June 1984: 65.

"Babe is a Lady Now." *Life* 23 June 1947

Barrett, David. "A major claim to fame: Pat Bradley is the first woman to capture the LPGA grand slam." *Golf Magazine* Sept. 1986

Barrett, David. "Lopez" Clean Sweep." *Golf Magazine* Feb. 1986: 71

Barrett, David. "The way things were: a guided tour through life's past." *Golf Magazine* June 1997

Beckwith, Ruffin. "Player of the Year". *Golf Magazine* Yearbook. 1981

Bernardino, Mike. "LPGA Hall should lighten up." *The Augusta Chronicle Online* 11 Jan. 1998

"Beth Daniel third-round interview. Sports Channel Feedback. http://sports.excite.com/lpga/news. 22 May 1999

Boswell, Thomas. "Playing favorites." *Golf Magazine* Dec. 1992: 16

Brennan, Christine. "Brotherly Love." *Golf Magazine* (Fairway, Special Advertising Section) Mar. 1996: 164

Brown, Clifton. "L.P.G.A. Hall of Fame Adds Alcott and Daniel". *New York Times*. 10 Feb. 1999

Brown, Gwilym S. "Carol is the Ladies" Mann." *Sports Illustrated* 12 July 1965: 22-23

Bryan, Mike. "A Conversation with JoAnne Carner." *Golf Magazine* Jan. 1989: 22

Burnett, Jim. "Back in the chips." *Golf Magazine* March 1993: 132

Burnett, Jim. *Tee Times*. Scribner, New York, 1997.

Butler, Judith. *Gender Trouble*. Routledge, New York, 1990.

Cahn, Susan K. *Coming on Strong: Gender and Sexuality in Twentieth Century Women's Sports*. Havard University Press, Cambridge, Mass., 1994.

Callahan, Tom. "Golf's Country- Club Dilemma." *U.S. News & World Report* 20 Aug. 1990: 60

Cayleff, Susan E. *Babe: The Life and Legend of Babe Didrikson Zaharias*. University of Illinois Press, Urbana and Chicago, 1996.

Chambers, Marcia. *The Unplayable Lie: The Untold Story of Women and Discrimination in American Golf*. Golf Digest Pocket Books, New York, 1995.

Chinnock, Frank. "Superstar in a Dodgers Cap." *Golf Magazine* Oct. 1980:63

Crosset, Todd W. *Outsiders in the Clubhouse: The World of Women's Professional Golf*. State University of New York Press, Albany, N.Y., 1995.

Deford, Frank. "Hello again to a grand group." *Sports Illustrated*. 5 Aug. 1985: 58

Diaz, Jaime. " Time for the Pat and Nancy show." *Sports Illustrated* 9 Feb. 1987: 84

Diaz, Jaime. "Alcott Confronting Two Big Tasks in One." *New York Times* 7 July 1991.

Diaz, Jaime. "Alcott, Shore Enough." *Sports Illustrated* 11 Apr. 1988: 72

Diaz, Jaime. "Bringing lives up to par." *Sports Illustrated* 21 Dec. 1987: 28

Diaz, Jaime. "Daniel Fulfills Expectations.". *New York Times* 12 Nov. 1990: B10

Dodson, James. "Slow walk to immortality." *Golf Magazine* Nov. 1994 12

Dodson, James. "The King nobody knows." *Golf Magazine* July 1991: 54

Donovan, Mark. " 'They Knew I Was a Contender.' " *Sports Illustrated* 7 July 1975

"Fresh Start." *Sports Illustrated* 25 Jan. 1999: 8

Garrity, John. " Joyless Open: wet weather and Patty Sheehan's collapse marred a tournament won by defending champ Betsy King." *Sports Illustrated* 23 July 1990: 26

Garrity, John. "Hitting the Hall." *Sports Illustrated* 3 Feb. 1992: 42

Garrity, John. "In a world of her own." *Sports Illustrated* 12 Feb. 1990

Garrity, John. "Shoot-out at Soakmont." *Sports Illustrated* 3 Aug. 1992: 66

Glenn, Rhonda, *The Illustrated History of Women's Golf*. Taylor Publishing Company, Dallas, Texas, 1991.

Glenn, Rhonda. " The toughest ball of all." *Golf Magazine* (Fairway, Special Advertising Section) Feb. 1992: 106

Glenn, Rhonda. "In the Eye of the Storm". *Golf Magazine* Sept. 1983 p74

Glenn, Rhonda. "Interview: Patty Berg." *Golf Magazine* (Fairway, Special Advertising Section). Feb. 1989: 129

Glenn, Rhonda. "It's A Long Way Back." *Golf Magazine* Sept. 1983: 55

Glenn, Rhonda. "Mickey Wright." *Golf Magazine* Jan. 1988: 41.

Golferines: Sport Section. Time 4 Sept. 1939: 27

Green, Ron Jr. "The stages of Beth Daniel"s life finally have returned her to the top of the LPGA Tour". *Golf Magazine* Apr. 1991. p 65

"Happy Birthday, Carol Mann!!!." World Golf Village Website, http://www.wgv.com/wgv/library.nfs/news. 3 Feb. 1999

Heinemann, Sue. *Timelines of American Women's History*. The Berkely Publishing Group, New York, 1996.

Hicks, Betty, *Travels with a Golf Tour Gourmet*. Group Fore, Palo Alto, Ca., 1986.

Hoover, Sue. "Toski gets a sound dubbing." Edited by Greg Hoffman *Women's Sports* Sept. 1981:: 8

Hoover, Sue. "One Shot at a Time." *Women Sports*. July 1980. p38

Jenkins, Sally. Conversations "Nancy Lopez" Golf Digest http://golf.com/golf digest/profiles/lopez Aug. 1997

"Jocks '81: fast cars and strong women: for six young athletes, their best is very close to great." *People Weekly*." 29 Dec. 1980 p108

Juliano, Joe. "Rawls to be honored with Jones Award for sportsmanship" Knight-Ridder/Tribune News Service Jan 18, 1996: 118

Kahn, Liz. *The LPGA: The Unauthorized Version*. Group Fore Productions, Menlo Park, Ca. 1996.

Keenan, Sandy. "Not yet at her peak." *Sports Illustrated* 25 Feb. 1985: 42

Kern, Mike. "Lopez says she can identify with Woods." Knight-Ridder/Tribune News Service." 15 May 1997

Kirkpatrick, Curry. "Relax, Girls, It's a Man's World." *Sports Illustrated* 6 May 1968: 22

Klein, Frederick C. "Mixed Greens: Couples Golf Tourney." *Wall Street Journal*. 15 Dec. 1995

Klein, Frederick C. "On Sports: Knocking on the Hall Door." *Wall Street Journal* 15 May 1992

Klein, Frederick C. "Mixed Greens: Couples Golf Tourney." *Wall Street Journal* 15 Dec. 1995

Lenskyj, Helen. *Out of Bounds: Women, Sport & Sexuality*. The Women's Press, Toronto, Can., 1986.

Lopez, Nancy. *The Education of a Woman Golfer*. Cornerstone Library, New York, 1979.

Lopez, Nancy (with Don Wade). *Nancy Lopez's The Complete Golfer*. Contemporary Books., Inc. Chicago & New York, 1987

Lopez, Nancy (with Peter Schwed). *The Education of a Woman Golfer*. Cornerstone Library, New Yorl. 1979

"LPGA players approve revised Hall of Fame criteria." Times Mirror Interzines. http://www.golfonline.com/news/1999/lpgahalloffame

Mann, Carol. "The girl next door grows up." *Women Sports* July 1981: 6

Mann, Carol. *The 19th Hole: Favorite Golf Stories*. Longmeadow Press, Stanford, CT. 1992

Martin, Pete. "Babe Didrikson Takes Off Her Mask." *Saturday Evening Post* 20 Sept. 1947: 26

Matson, Barbara. "The Rise and Fall of Pat Bradley." *Golf Magazine* Jan. 1989: 32

McDermott, Barry. "And Then Things Were Putt in Order." *Sports Illustrated* 29 July 1974: 18-19

McDermott, Barry. "Here's to the good 'ol times." *Sports Illustrated* 6 May 1985: 62

McDermott, Barry. "No Fish Story: Golf's Top Lady." *Sports Illustrated* 5 July, 1982

McDermott, Barry. "Winning Was Her Just Dessert." *Sports Illustrated* 11 Apr. 1983: 34

McDermott, Barry. "Wrong image but the right touch." *Sports Illustrated* 25 July 1983: 38

McDermott, Barry. "Now they call her Payday Pat." *Sports Illustrated* 29 Sept. 1986: 82

McDermott, Harry M. "The Game is Her Life and Only Love." *Sports Illustrated* 2 Feb. 1981 p34

McGrath, Charles. "Babe Zaharias, Most Valuable Player." *New York Times* 24 Nov. 1992

Navratilova, Martina. *Martina*. Alford A. Knopf, New York, 1985.

Nelson, Mariah Burton. *The Stronger Women Get, The More Men Love Football: Sexism and the American Culture of Sports*. Harcourt Brace & Co., New York, 1994.

Newman, Bruce. " The very model of a modern marriage." *Sports Illustrated* 4 Aug. 1986: 3

Pat Bradley Current Biography Yearbook 1994 (publisher)

"Patty Sheehan: player of the year." *Golf Magazine* Feb. 1984: 84

Pucin, Diane. "Lopez the Tiger Wood of her era." Knight-Ridder/Tribune News Service 14 July 1997: 714

Purkey, Mike. "Nancy Lopez." *Golf Magazine* May 1990: 86

Raque, Sally. "You've come a long way, ladies: on the 40th birthday of the oldest women's professional sports organization, it's more apparent than ever that the LPGA has always been way ahead of its time." *Women's Sports and Fitness*, May-June 1990:61-66

Reddy, Del and Maureen McDonald.. "Patty Berg...Golf's Grand Dame...still swings at 75." Sports and Recreation *CONQUEST and Senior News Network* 1977

Reilly, Rick. "Filling the gap with a flourish." *Sports Illustrated* 24 Mar. 1986: 26

Roberts, David. "The Babe is here." *Women's Sports and Fitness* Nov.-Dec. 1990: 42

Rubenstein, Lorne. " Lopez's win a pleasant pain reliever." Golf Web Library http://www.golfweb.com/library 1 May 1997

Saylor, Jack. "Nancy Lopez will retire before becoming a ceremonial golfer." Knight-Ridder/Tribune News Service 19 July 1994

Schumacher, Craig. Nancy Lopez, *Creative Education*, Mankato, MN. 1979

"Shame on the Hall." *Sports Illustrated* 7 Dec. 1998: 20.

Sheehan, Patty and Betty Hicks. *Patty Sheehan on Golf*. Taylor Publishing Company, Dallas, TX 1996

Shipnuck, Alan. " Open and shut." *Sports Illustrated* 21 July 1997: 44

Smith, Shelley. "Betsy King." *Sports Illustrated* 27 Dec. 1993: 8

Steptoe, Sonja. " Patty Sheehan." *Sports Illustrated* 21 June 1993: 54

Steptoe, Sonja. "A Sure Thing at the Shore." *Sports Illustrated* 8 Apr. 1991: 30

Steptoe, Sonja. "Playing out of the rough." *Sports Illustrated* 30 Sept. 1991: 6

Steptoe, Sonja. "Thirtysomething...and happy at last: in her 12 the year on the tour, Beth Daniel is measuring   up to early expectations, even her own." *Sports Illustrated*. 15 Oct. 1990 p74

Striak, Ron. " Nancy Lopez: a smile that's lasted 20 years." http://golf.com/tour/opinion/sirak 6 May 1998

Strege, John. "Alcott still shooting for LPGA Hall of Fame." Knight-Ridder/Tribune News Service Mar. 29, 1996: 329.

Suggs, Louise. *Golf for Women*. A Rutledge book published by Doubleday & Co., New York. 1960.

Tarde, Jerry. " A telephone call from Nancy Lopez." http://golf.com/golfdigest/news/tarde Jan 1997

Taylor, Dick. "Les Grande Dames." *Golf Magazine* Feb. 1982

"Too small a Hall?." *Golf Magazine* Nov. 1990: 24

Tyson, Molly. "Going For the Green." *Women's Sports* May 1981: 26

Voepel, Mechelle. " Lopez's great run began 20 years ago." Knight-Ridder/Tribune News Service 13 May 1998

Wallace, Pamela. "Keep Your Eye on Amy." *The Saturday Evening Post* Nov. 1975: 26

White, Gordon S. Jr. "Alcott and Lopez Vie at Top." *New York Times* 19 May 1988: D23.

"Who's Hot: The Inductees." *Women's Sports* (year): 6

Wilcox, Sarah. "Will Beth Catch Nancy?" *Golf Magazine*. Apr. 1980 p 100.

Williams, Jackie. "The Right Person in the Right Place at the Right Time." *The Stuart News*, Stuart, Florida, 24 July 1994.

Williams, Jackie. "Wright had great impact on LPGA." *The Stuart News*, Stuart, Florida 25 July 1994.

Wright, Mickey. *Play Golf the Wright Way*. Taylor Publishing Company, Dallas, Texas, 1962.

Zaharias, Babe Didrikson. *This Life I've Led*. Dell Publishing Co., New York, 1975.